2002

FROM

Pearl

TO

Gawain

FROM

Pearl

TO **Gawain**

FORME TO FYNISMENT

ROBERT J. BLANCH AND
JULIAN N. WASSERMAN

UNIVERSITY PRESS OF FLORIDA • *Gainesville / Tallahassee*
Tampa / Boca Raton / Pensacola / Orlando / Miami / Jacksonville

00 99 98 97 96 95 6 5 4 3 2 1

Library of Congress Cataloging-in-Publication Data

Blanch, Robert J.
From Pearl to Gawain: forme to fynisment / Robert J.
Blanch, Julian N. Wasserman.
p.   cm.
Includes bibliographical references (p.   ) and index.
ISBN 0-8130-1348-8 (acid-free paper)
1. English poetry—Middle English, 1100–1500—History
and criticism.   2. English poetry—England—West Mid-
lands—History and criticism.   3. Manuscripts, English
(Middle)—England—West Midlands.   4. Gawain and the
Green Knight.   5. Pearl (Middle English poem)   6.
Rhetoric, Medieval.   7. Closure (Rhetoric)   I. Wasser-
man, Julian N.   II. Title.
PR1972.G353B57   1994
821'.109—dc20   94-40999

The University Press of Florida is the scholarly publishing
agency for the State University System of Florida, comprised
of Florida A & M University, Florida Atlantic University,
Florida International University, Florida State University,
University of Central Florida, University of Florida,
University of North Florida, University of South Florida,
and University of West Florida.

University Press of Florida
15 Northwest 15th Street
Gainesville, FL 32611

For the *Joly compaignye* at Kalamazoo,
good *felawes alle.*

CONTENTS

INTRODUCTION

Beginnings and endings have always been of special importance to students of the anonymous fourteenth-century *Gawain* manuscript.[1] No doubt part of our special fascination with starts and finishes is due to the repetition of material from the beginnings in the respective endings of three of its four poems, a stylistic signature that concretizes the poet's recurrent theme that "the first shall be last."[2] Indeed, *Patience* finds its genesis in the poet's observation that the first and the last of the eight Beatitudes offer the same reward, the vision of the Creator.[3] Yet if beginning and end are, in the poet's words, "fettled in on forme, þe forme and þe laste" (38) in *Patience*, this is the same poet who, in *Sir Gawain and the Green Knight*, interrupts his own narrative in order to warn his protagonist to "þenk wel" (487) because beginnings often fail to match endings: "Þe forme to þe fynisment folde3 ful selden" (499). Sometimes our lines meet where they begin; sometimes they do not.

To the reader's possible chagrin, this is a book with a premise to be extended and explored rather than a thesis to be proven. A collection of connected observations rather than an argument where beginning and end meet, the chapters here form a line rather than a circle. The observation that follows concerning the historical continuum that comprises the Cotton Nero A.x manuscript was a starting place from which the rest of this volume grew and upon which the following chapters might be said to be founded. If subsequent discussion extends rather than overtly supports this observation, such a pattern is rooted in the evolution of the study itself, which began with some observations about history and historical process in a *Gawain*-Poet session at the annual International Congress of Medieval Studies at Kalamazoo, Michigan. Those reflections led to some unanswerable but very interesting questions which provided matter for subsequent papers in succeeding years. For example, the notion of historical process (a divine plan) expanded into the question of what happens when that process or the natural order is "interrupted." The consideration of such interruptions then evolved into a paper on miracles. In turn, a paper on the counterbalancing

imagery of the hand of God and the hand of man, a study fueled by
a discussion of miracles, provoked Paul Reichardt to ask us about
the "hand of the poet." That query led us on to the topic of the intrusive narrator. And so the manuscript grew in such a fashion that
its parts have sprung from a premise or observation and have moved
linearly, each from the other. The final judgment of the link between our "forme" and its "fynisment," we will leave to our readers.

As to our "intratextual" methodology, a word or two also seems
in order since this book contains many theses or, at least, an extended premise. Even in an age as skeptical of the Platonic universal as our own, full-length studies of the *Gawain*-Poet tend to
demonstrate certain unchanging verities of "substance" as well as
of "accident." For example, even a casual observer might note that
Gawain books often have green covers while books on *Pearl* frequently have white ones. And if such practices attest to an underlying unity of thought on the part of publishers (or their depart-
ments of marketing and design), there are deeply ingrained habits of
mind that are equally evident in both the content and structure of
Gawain-Poet scholarship. Books that treat themes in the whole
manuscript invariably have four chapters, each devoted primarily to
a single work in the manuscript. Occasionally, such a study is even
preceded by an introduction that speaks eloquently of the need to
take the poems out of isolation.[4] A single thesis allows, perhaps inevitably leads to, such an ordering which, in essence, produces an
idea empirically verified four times, once in each poem. Despite the
fact that scholarship on the four poems almost universally pays lip
service to the proposition that the four works are the product of a
single authorial hand,[5] critics writing about the Cotton Nero poems
have remained cautious, keeping our readings of the individual poems relatively insulated, in case someone working in a dark corner
of the Bodleian might hit it lucky and establish separate authorship,
thereby forcing us to crack the spines, white or green, and separate
our chapters.

In the study that follows, we will assume not only that the works
share a common author but that they are connected and intersect in
fundamental ways that work against discussion in isolation. For example, Paul Reichardt's recent work with the affective faces which
adorn four of the manuscript's capitals transcends the parts for the

sake of recovering the larger whole.[6] The poems' various editors as well as critics have long struggled to account for the sometimes curious positioning of the manuscript's 133 capitals, inventing a number of ingenious rhetorical and thematic explanations for their placement, each based on the narrative divisions within the individual poems. The recent work of Donna Crawford in explicating the proportional, rather than the thematic, arrangement of the capitals in *Purity* clearly may be applied to the manuscript as a whole, rather than just to individual poems, and has great potential for unraveling the larger mystery.[7] We should, then, pay more heed to the juxtaposition of these four poems in the same manuscript, brought together in a deliberate act of association either by the poet or the compiler who acted as the poet's first literary critic.[8]

In a sense, the question that faces the reader of the *Gawain* manuscript is the same problem of unity facing the audience of Malory's *Morte D'Arthur* or of Joyce's *Dubliners*—whether, say, the tales of Lancelot or Tristram are separate books or chapters in one work; whether *Dubliners* is a novel or a collection of short stories. And, of course, the answers to these questions shape our readings of those works. As is apparent, although we have weighted our argument somewhat toward *Sir Gawain and the Green Knight* as the chosen "fynisment" of the manuscript, we presume an underlying unity that includes the temporal continuum in which the parts are microcosms of the whole. In doing so, we presume to lay claim to the unity that underlies medieval iconography,[9] or even the mutual reflexivity of events grouped together on any given page of a *Biblia Pauperum* or in Alanus de Insulis's famous lines from the *Rhythmus alter*:

Every creature in the world
is like a book, and a picture,
and a mirror for us
of our lives, of our death,
of our condition, of our kind,
a faithful reflection.[10]

All creation is not only a book or picture but a mirror. All creatures as microcosms reflect each other as well as the larger whole. The inability to read that book, to see the visual signs, or even to recognize one's own reflection is a recurrent warning of the cost of not recognizing such interconnectedness: Nebuchadnezzar fails to read the text on the wall; Gawain and the *Pearl*-Dreamer fail to decode the visual icons that fill their worlds; Jonah persists in condemning the repentant Ninevites, not recognizing within them the image of his own sin and repentance.

The same presumption of the essential interconnectedness that permits the parts of Creation—or even the events in the pageant of history—to gloss each other allows the animals in the hunt scenes of *Sir Gawain and the Green Knight* to be different from but at the same time tokens of Gawain and his behavior in the temptation scenes.[11] Thus we suggest that the different works forming the Cotton Nero A.x manuscript had for their author the same type of underlying unity as the disparate Bible stories that comprise *Purity*. In short, the similarity that causes one object, trope, or even poem to gloss another is privileged over the individualizing difference so important in modern thinking. So, with these principles in mind, we shall begin with our own beginning, a rather simple observation concerning the notion of history underlying the four poems of the manuscript.[12]

If any one element binds together the four works ascribed to the common authorship of the late fourteenth-century *Gawain*-Poet, it is most assuredly their shared view of a God who is anything but remote, a Creator who intervenes directly in the affairs of humans—whether in the destruction of Sodom or in the answered prayers of Gawain. In short, the presence of an active intervening God bespeaks a providential history, a purposely laid out plan for humankind where the course of events is the unfolding of the will of the divinity.[13] To appreciate the poet's overwhelming concern with this historical process, it is first necessary to realize that, taken as a whole, the four poems that comprise the Cotton Nero A.x manuscript delineate a temporal continuum that spans the entire course of history, reaching from the beginning of time in Creation to the end of time in the Apocalypse and its transcendence in the Heavenly Jerusalem. *Purity*, for instance, begins with the eternal world of the heavenly kingdom, as illustrated in the parable of the man in the dirty garment, and moves quickly into the biblical history traced in Genesis, progressing from the fall of the rebel angels, through the creation of Adam, the Flood, the destruction of Sodom, and concludes with the tale of Belshazzar's feast taken from the book of Daniel. *Patience* continues the historical narrative by depicting events of the book of Jonah, thereby extending the poet's historical account into the time of the later prophets. *Sir Gawain and the Green Knight*, by means of the rapidly expanding series of kingdoms and city states that form its opening stanza, further extends the temporal continuum. Beginning in the remote pagan past at the fall of Troy and skillfully guiding the reader westward through time and space through Rome, Tuscany, Lombardy, and eventually into the Christian age of the recent past as embodied by Arthurian Camelot, *Gawain* positions itself in the poet's own present with its reference to the contemporary "toun" in which he heard the tale. *Pearl* completes the historical progression by locating its narrator in the historical present and, in the course of the dream vision, by returning to the transtemporal, although decidedly apocalyptic, New Jerusalem.[14] Since this celestial city is presumably the site of the parabolic feast found at the outset of *Purity*, the continuum is thus brought full circle, like the "endless knot" of the pentangle, beginning where it ends.

Before proceeding further, it is, however, necessary to note that in presenting the poems as comprising the entire scope of history, we have already deviated from the order in which the poems appear in the manuscript, a pattern that seems purposeful because scholars have generally agreed that the manuscript order of the Cotton Nero poems fails to reflect the chronology of their composition.[15] *Pearl*, which should come last, according to the chronological sequence we have just outlined, comes first in the manuscript, with the other poems—*Purity, Patience*, and *Sir Gawain and the Green Knight*—following in their appropriate historical order. *Pearl*, the very capstone of the historical sequence the manuscript seems to embrace, appears at its outset rather than at its ending so that the poems chronologically form a circle, the geometric figure that dominates the manuscript both numerically in the 101 stanzas of *Pearl* and *Gawain* as well as in the repetition of its first lines as last lines in three of the manuscript's four poems. Interestingly enough, *Pearl, Gawain*, and *Patience*—which demonstrate such repetition—are, as we shall see, primarily about the completed cycle of error and redemption/salvation—the spiritual correction of the Dreamer, the moral correction of Gawain, the repentance and salvation of Nineveh (and Jonah). In contrast, *Purity*—which lacks the repetition and hence does not come full circle—is about the falls of men and the destruction of cities, about the failure to complete the circle initiated by the felix culpa.[16] Indeed, *Purity*'s "Exhortation to Purity"[17] presents the redemption after sin but, in fact, places greater emphasis on the special damnation for those who break the circle of redemption by returning to sin and by beginning an incomplete and unfinishable cycle that can no longer end where it begins.

If ends and beginnings do not always coincide, what links them is clear. Cycles, both natural and man-made, reflect the basic temporal unit in the poet's march through time.[18] Of the two poems that comprise the greatest part of that continuum, *Purity* presents a cyclical series of the rises and falls of biblical cities, and *Gawain*, as every reader of its famous opening and closing stanzas knows, presents the cyclical rises and falls of secular postbiblical towns as its settings.[19] *Pearl* and *Patience* present the microcosm, the personal stories of individual cities, Jerusalem and Nineveh, set like pearls "sengeley in synglure."[20]

Pearl, however, gives the figure of the circle an interesting twist. The first of the Cotton Nero poems reverses biological time through the premature death and the subsequent elevation of the *Pearl*-Maiden over her father. In its content, the poem confounds both the reader's and the Dreamer's chronologically based expectations concerning the two-year-old maiden and her father, since one would expect the father to die before the child and certainly to be wiser than the child. Perhaps the magnitude of the reversal is lost on the post-Romantic reader accustomed to such youthful philosophers as the "Little Black Boy," the chimney sweeps of Blake's *Songs of Innocence*, or even the precocious cottage child of Wordsworth's "We Are Seven." Such reversal, however, would surely have been a cause for surprise for the medieval reader of Hrothgar's speech on wisdom or the Wanderer's assertion that "no man may become wise until he has passed many a winter in the world" (For þon ne mæg wearþon wis wer, ær hē āge / Wintra dæl in woruldrice").[21] Much more typical of youth would be the ignorant babes in *Patience* or the pejorative cast given to youth, especially in the term "childgered" (86) in *Sir Gawain and the Green Knight*.[22] *Pearl* self-consciously raises the question of its positioning within the manuscript with its parable of the workers in the vineyard, its emphasis on the reversal of temporal expectations, and its explicitly stated theme of "the laste schal be the fyrst." The poem's placement in the manuscript, the temporally last being placed first, demonstrates the reversal that is not only evident in its content but in its physical manipulation of its stanza-linked words as well as in its "signature" repetition of material from its first stanza in its last.

The relationship between first and last, between *Pearl* and the rest of the manuscript, sheds much light on the poet's concept of history. Certainly, a Christian view of history is by definition a teleological one, and it is this *teleos* that imparts meaning to all that comes before.[23] Hence, the last comes first in order to introduce that which it illumines, thereby making the progression from *Pearl* to the remainder of the Cotton Nero manuscript a natural one. Moreover, of the poems that comprise the manuscript, *Pearl* is uniquely personal—so much so that it was at first taken as an elegy wrought as much of personal experience as of theological exposition.[24] Like Augustine's *Confessions*, *Pearl* moves from personal history to a revelation of the divine process of which the individual is both microcosm and part. In the *Confessions*, personal history is the prelude to a consideration of Genesis. In the Cotton Nero manuscript, moreover, this most personal of poems, *Pearl*, leads just as naturally to *Purity*'s recapitulation of Genesis wherein the historical process of individual salvation is placed and glossed by the history of mankind.

Finally, the presentation of the apocalyptic future (placed in a most personal and contemporary context in *Pearl*), followed by a lengthy exposition of the past (*Purity, Patience,* and *Sir Gawain and the Green Knight*), is not only the ordering of the individual poems of the manuscript but is also the homiletic structure of *Purity*. After its brief proem announcing its topic, that poem begins with an analogy taken from contemporary life (35–48) and quickly moves to a New Testament parable of the apocalyptic judgment (49–160).[25] The remainder of the poem consists of the history of humankind from Genesis to Daniel as a gloss or explanation as to how such judgments are affected. In both *Purity* and the manuscript as a whole, then, the apocalyptic future of the New Jerusalem is placed in the context of the present, while the past serves to explain or to gloss the relationship between the two. The manuscript itself thus might be thought of as a homily, moving like *Purity*—or, for that matter, the discourse of the *Pearl*-Maiden—from an announced abstract subject through progressively concrete exposition, from abstract to concrete, from the otherworldly spiritual *Pearl* to the overtly time-bound and "secular" *Gawain*. If the announced goal is a presentation of the Last Judgment or of the end of time, the means of getting there is history, which forms the subject matter of all that follows.

With the *Gawain*-Poet's conception of providential history in mind, it is now possible to examine the thematic focus of the remaining chapters of this study. Chapter 1, for example, explores the poet's concern with language and culture and their roles in the historical continuum which underlies and unifies all four poems in the manuscript. If "In the beginning there was the Word," history, as we shall see, was for this poet the unfolding of all that exists *in potentia* in the verbal act of Creation. The civilizations whose individual histories are both parts and microcosms of the larger whole will be seen to define themselves as linguistic communities built around the common bond of shared symbols, with the king acting as the verbal center, or defining fixed point, in the flux and evolution of society. Set against such wise keepers of the word as *Patience*'s king of Nineveh and *Purity*'s Daniel, Arthur of *Sir Gawain and the Green Knight* will be presented as an exemplum of improper stewardship of the word, sharing much in common with Belshazzar in their fundamental inability to read as well as to fix the language of the societies that they govern.[26] Throughout the chapter we shall explore the theme of the inability to read or comprehend—whether it be the "rurd" that rings in the ears of the reluctant prophet Jonah or the seemingly nonsensical wisdom of the *Pearl*-Maiden whose speech is illogical, if not incomprehensible, to the mind of the Dreamer. In the end, moral survival will be linked with linguistic survival. The court's inability to read Alanus de Insulis' "liber et pictura"—both the words and the iconographic visage of the Green Knight—is a failure that answers the question, "Why did Camelot—the greatest city of all, filled with the 'comlokest' and 'hendest'—fail to survive?" The simple answer is that the court failed because its linguistic center gave way. Such a response will be seen to shed considerable light on a poet whose works are so often about the survival and destruction of earthly cities and the transcendence of the heavenly one.

While chapter 1 has language as its focus, chapter 2 examines the covenants into which words are "knyt" and sets forth the "covenantal theology" underlying the poet's presentation of history by delineating the series of "couenaunteȝ" and "forwardeȝ" framed between God and humanity. The first part of the chapter employs illustrations from *Purity*, *Patience*, and *Pearl* in order to underscore the significance of free or good "wylle" as part of such covenants. More than a word of obvious theological import, *wylle*—along with the concepts of contract, covenant, surety, and tally in English common law and juridic procedure—will be presented as an essential element in any binding contract, whether the Old Testament covenants of *Purity* and *Patience* or the courtly/chivalric pledges of *Sir Gawain and the Green Knight*. In fact, the poet's courtly romance will be seen as a virtual mirror of the status of legal contracts framed between the occupants of the worldly city. *Purity* and *Patience* will chronicle the binding agreements between God and the human communities, both the virtuous and the sinful, while *Pearl* will explore the contractual bonds between God and the elect in the heavenly city. Focusing on Gawain, we will demonstrate that the protagonist's inability to live up to the covenant that binds him to his host is indicative of the failure of societal bonds in Camelot. Hearkening back to the first chapter, we will contend that if the linguistic center of the human city cannot hold, then the contracts knit of such stuff, likewise, cannot be anything but impermanent. In the end, the individual contract acts as a microcosm of the grand contract between the Creator and Creation as well as of the intermediate covenant between God and humanity, so that the poet's concept of history is an expressly covenantal one. As a result, the complex web of covenants woven in *Sir Gawain and the Green Knight* both informs and is informed by the covenantal history that takes humanity from the fall of Adam to the salvation of Nineveh in *Purity* and *Patience*.

In the third chapter, our focus is on the role of miracles—those peculiar moments that represent the confluence of divine will and human events and that trigger a suspension of natural law or of the contract of "kynde"—within the context of covenantal history. Of particular significance will be the ways in which miracles shape the history that underlies the manuscript's four works. While we trace the nature and importance of key miraculous events—the woodbine episode (*Patience*) or the puzzling conception of nature in the creation of the Dead Sea (*Purity*)—special attention will be paid to the motif of the confounding of reason, particularly in such instances as the mysterious writing at Belshazzar's feast (*Purity*), the beheading game of the Green Knight, and the inverted relationship between the Poet-Dreamer and the Maiden (*Pearl*). What emerges from these numerous illustrations from the works of the *Gawain*-Poet, then, is a sense of the "meruayle" as a deliberately transrational sign, the function of which represents paradoxically the beginning of true understanding. Finally, as presented in the poems of the *Gawain* manuscript, the central motif of miracles is intertwined with a problem at the heart of Augustine's *Confessions:* whether it is necessary first to know God in order to believe or whether one must first believe in order to know God.

Chapter 4 takes up the verbal and pictorial iconograph frequently associated with miracles, such as those appearing throughout the *Gawain* canon. The image of the hand, both divine and human, serves as a major unifying thread in the presentation of the miraculous in the *Gawain*-Poet's works. As we shall attempt to demonstrate, history, for the author of the four *Gawain* poems, represents a series of interruptions fashioned by the often conflicting hands of God and humanity. Ranging from the *Pearl*-Maiden's declaration that the saved are those who "Hondelynge3 harme þat dyt not ille" (681) to the Green Knight's challenge (the "ax þat is heué innogh, to hondele as hym lykes" [289]), there is within the Cotton Nero poems a concern with the way men "hondel" the world around themselves. Indeed, whether we focus upon *Purity*'s priests who "hondel þer [God's] aune body" (11) or upon *Patience*'s innocent who " 'no3t cunen' / What rule renes in roun bitwene þe ry3t hande / And his lyfte" (513–15), the uses to which men put their hands are identified with the exercise of will or with the formulation of moral choices. We shall observe the poet's employment of this traditional iconographic motif in his two "biblical" works (*Patience, Purity*) wherein the poems may be compared with their sources, noting that of the nineteen references to hands in *Purity* and *Patience*, all but three represent the poet's interpolations to his sources. In discussing the poet's use of these additions, we will explore the frequent juxtaposition of the hand of God and the hand of man—forces that often disrupt the normal course of nature. In general, the divine hand is associated with the work of God's presence or voice and with divinely accepted sacrifice, whereas the human hand is emblematic of sin.

The hand of man, likewise, is ordinarily linked with magicians or the devil, both of whom are credited with the power to create the appearance of miracles or of a violation of nature.

Our final chapter takes up the complementary question of the hand of the poet as we scrutinize the idea of the poet in his position as maker of a fictive world and the ways in which that role parallels that of the "Creator of mankynd." We will begin by noting that despite a general critical assessment that this narrator is unobtrusive, the narrators of *Purity, Patience,* and *Gawain* are active storytellers, frequently intruding into their respective creations much like the actively intervening God whose miracles are the subject matter of so much of his work. Indeed, these narrators will be shown to be active brokers of their tales, alternately turning their backs on their audiences to address their characters and abandoning their narratives to exhort their audiences. Keeping in mind God's warning to Jonah that the man who hastily rends his garment often has to mend it, we wish to explore how some of those narrative seams work in tailoring the reader's response to *Patience, Purity,* and *Sir Gawain.* In doing so, we will focus on the poet's manipulation of pronouns—the juxtaposition of "I" and "thou" and the mediation of "we" and "us"—in order to create the shifting axes of narrator-character and narrator-reader as we trace the development of the manuscript's successive narrators. In delineating this progression, we will trace the movement from the strongly centered narrative consciousness of *Purity* and *Patience* to the slightly decentered narrator of *Sir Gawain and the Green Knight* and conclude with the metamorphosis of the narrator into an active character in *Pearl.* Thus, we will, in circular fashion, close where we began by returning to the order of the poems in the manuscript with the *fynisment* reflecting the *forme,* if not meeting it directly.

One

AS GOOD AS YOUR WORD: LANGUAGE, CULTURE, AND BUILDING BLOCKS OF HISTORY

"In the beginning was the Word," and it is homage to that *forme* and a recognition of the complexities of that metonymy that mark so much of medieval art and thought—for Creation itself was to the medieval mind a linguistic act that began with the verbalization, "Let there be . . . ."[1] History in the strictest sense was the unfolding of all that lay in potentia within the creative word. If the *forme* were the linguistic act of Genesis 1:3–15 and if the *fynisment* were the Last Judgment, all that lay between was history, which serves as the means by which the beginning and the end are joined.

Such is the power of the intertwined concepts of history and language for the medieval mind, and it is difficult to pass much time with the poems of the Cotton Nero A.x manuscript without becoming aware of the medieval notion of the creative word as well as of the poet's preoccupation with history, or, more accurately, the process of history. As we have noted in our introduction, the four poems that comprise the Cotton Nero A.x manuscript survey the entire course of history—from Creation in *Purity* to the apocalyptic New Jerusalem in *Pearl*. History, it would seem, is at the center of this poet's thinking, an assertion that is supported by even a cursory examination of contemporary criticism focusing on these four poems. Yet, as post-Romantics wedded to the notion of the individual, those of us who have written about these poems in such contexts would do well to remind ourselves that for this poet, as well as for his medieval contemporaries, history is not the story of individuals—of Lot or Daniel or Jonah—nor even of collections of individuals, but rather of societies—that is, of cities and city-states: Sodom and Babylon in *Purity*, Nineveh in *Patience*, Camelot in *Sir Gawain*, Jerusalem in *Pearl*.[2] Whereas in *Pearl* the waking world with its seasons and mortality is quickly left behind so that the bulk of the poem takes place in the timelessness of the other world,[3] in *Sir Gawain and the Green Knight*, we are never allowed to forget the ongoing march of time so precisely captured in the passing of the seasons.[4] *Gawain* itself begins with a pluperfect past, a series of fallen civilizations and cities that precede the action of this tale of past events in Camelot—a tale, as we are told, learned by the poet in a city of the present.[5] Thus, in *Sir Gawain and the Green Knight*, the temporal human city is placed at center stage while in *Pearl* the great Augustinian symbol of historical process, the earthly city of Jerusalem, is but briefly invoked as an unseen counterpoint to the heavenly city, the subject of the Jeweler's visionary experience.[6] In *Sir Gawain and the Green Knight*, this view of history is announced at the outset of the first stanza and underscored in the last. Camelot, as it is presented to us, is set in its historical context: Before there was a Camelot, there was first Troy, then Rome, followed in succession by the rises—and, more significantly, the falls—of Tuscany and then of Lombardy.[7] Everywhere there are reminders of the means by which civilizations and their members mark time.[8] There are, of course, the references to the canonical hours and the feasts of the liturgical calendar,[9] but we are also aware of the season of the deer, the "fermysoun tyme" (1156),[10] as well as the season of the court which is, as the narrator notes, in its "first age" (54).[11] Camelot, we are reminded in this tale told in the preterit, is a fallen city—and as such it is heir to the succession of fallen kingdoms of the past and precursor of contemporary London, presumably the town in which the poet has heard the tale. The concern with the progression of time captured in the sequence of cities seems to permeate virtually every aspect of the poem, from the year and a day contract to the crowing of the cock, which, like the ticking of an anachronistic clock, punctuates most of the action at the court of Bercilak.[12]

Yet if Camelot—whose description is virtually awash with superlatives of the "louelokkest," "comlokest," and best—is a doomed city within the context of the poet's apocalyptic vision, one must ask why this is so.[13] To understand, in Yeatsian terms, why the "center cannot hold," it is first necessary to inquire what, in fact, constitutes that center, what it is that constitutes a society. Indeed, the poet seems preoccupied with what holds a society together, preoccupied with obligations—personal, social, knightly, spiritual—an emphasis manifested in the ubiquitous language of binding, both physical and contractual.[14]

What, then, are the ties that bind? What is the paste that holds any society together, whether it be the City of God or one of the many cities of man that appear in this poet's work? The answer, at least from this poet's perspective, is shared values or culture—symbolized by a shared system of signs.[15] To put the matter in the terminology of the contemporary linguist, a society is for the poet of the fourteenth century a "speech community"—a group whose discourse is mutually intelligible and, above all, whose success as a distinct and identifiable group is dependent on the status of its body of common knowledge as well as on the system by which the members of a society learn and transmit, that is, decode and encode, those shared values. The essence—the central, self-defining task—of society is communication, and when that communication begins to falter, what ensues is the privatization of language, a type of dangerous individualism that for the poet stands in juxtaposition to the common profit.[16]

The act of naming, the shared conventional association between an arbitrary signifier and a signified, is, of course, the most basic act in the creation of such a society. And indeed, the problem of naming, of using the true or conventional names for things is a theme that is foregrounded throughout the manuscript but especially in *Sir Gawain and the Green Knight*.[17] For example, the question of applicability of titles or names hinges on the link between the Green Knight's appearance and the "trwe tytel" of "wonder" ("Trwe tytel þerof to telle þe wonder" [480]); the proper "tytel" of the pentangle ("Hit is a syngne þat Salamon set sumquyle / In bytoknyng of trawþe, bi tytel þat hit habbeʒ, . . . and Englych hit callen / Oueral, as I here, þe endeles knot" [625–30]); the feast at Bercilak's court ("þe freke calde hit a fest" [894]); Lady Bercilak ("A mensk lady on molde mon may hir calle" [964]); the proper terms for the hunt ("þay neme for þe noumbles bi nome, as I trowe, / Bi kynde" [1347–48]); and, above all, the "tytelet token" as well as the "tyxt" of knighthood ("ʒisterday I taʒtte / Bi aldertuest token of talk þat I cowþe, / . . . For to telle of þis teuelyng of þis trwe knyʒteʒ, / Hit is þe tytelet token and tyxt of her werkkeʒ. . . . How ledes for her lele luf hor lyueʒ han auntered" [1485–1516]). One might note that there is in all of this naming a strong Realist undercurrent, as, for example, the "noum-

bles" are called such "bi kynde," and the signifiers of love are not
merely tokens but "aldertuest tokens." "Tytels" here are not merely
"tytels" but "trwe tytels."[18]

For "tytels"—that is, names—it is important to realize that for
this poet the discourse that defines a society is, above all, an authorized discourse, a system of communication handed down to those
who are under the rule of the king. God, upon whom all kingship is
modeled, is apotheosized by the poet as "He þat spedeȝ vche spech"
(1292), and it likewise becomes the duty of the secular king to
"spedeȝ spech," to set names and fix discourse.[19] In *Sir Gawain*, as
we follow the course of history mapped out in the poem's first
stanza, we note that the poet takes care to tell us that, in regard to
the city he founds, Romulus "neuenes hit his aune nome, as hit now
hat" (10), "gives it his own name, as it is now called." And in the
curious history that follows, in order to reach Britain, itself named
for Felix Brutus, we must travel through Tuscany, named for Ticius, and through Lumbardie, so-called after Langaberde.[20] Kings, it
would seem, are the Adams of their countries, receiving the right to
fix names—that is, the power to establish and, as we shall see, to uphold discourse—and as such are blessed with both the power and re-
sponsibilities of their stewardship of the word.

Two models for that stewardship become evident in the poems
Purity and *Patience*. One might first consider the fate of Belshazzar,
whose demise is linked with the breakdown of language, and, in particular, the inability to read signs. The idols that he worships "were
of stokkes and stones, stille euermore; / Neuer steuen hem astel, so
stoken is hor tonge" (1523–24).[21] Their muteness is set against God
who "Expouned his speche . . . to special prophetes" (1492), a God
whose apocalyptic judgment assumes linguistic form in the "purtrayed lettres" on the wall (1536). Moreover, once Daniel deciphers
those mysterious letters, it is clear that Belshazzar still fails either
to comprehend their true meaning or to make Daniel's explication
"malt my mynde wythinne" (1566), even though the fate of the community literally depends on his ability to do so. In this episode,
linguistic failure and moral failure are inextricably linked.[22] In
contrast, *Patience*'s king of Nineveh practices an entirely different stewardship of the word. Faced with Jonah's prophecy—words
placed in the prophet's heart by God—the Ninevite king not only
understands it but, acting in his role of king, incorporates it into his

own speech, the "decré demed of [hym]seluen," thereby making a proclamation concerning the repentance of the city as he tells people to

> ... dryue out a decré, demed of myseluen,
> Boþe burnes and bestes, burdeȝ and childer,
> Vch prynce, vche prest, and prelates alle,
> Alle faste frely for her falce werkes ...
> Al schal crye, forclemmed, wyth alle oure clere strenþe.
> Þe rurd schal ryse to hym þat rawþe schal haue.
>
> (386–96)[23]

Speech thus begets speech: God speaks to Jonah in a "rurd," Jonah preaches to the city whose king's decree, in turn, makes all cry out with "clere strenþe," creating a "rurd" that returns to God as the message comes full circle.

From the stories of these two kings, we gradually come to understand the nature of the proper stewardship of the word, a stewardship that is founded on a recognition, both medieval and modern, of the two essential dynamic properties of language. Language is both fixed and fluid, conventional as well as arbitrary. As the "keeper of names," the king has the right as well as the responsibility to fix language, to preserve its conventions, to protect discourse from the potential chaos of the arbitrariness of signs. At the same time, it becomes the duty of the king as keeper of the language to preside over linguistic renewal by recognizing the creative nature of the word, to foster what might in Bakhtinian terms be called a purposeful heteroglossia, and to restore order by incorporating that creativity into the remaking of conventions.[24] The inability, or the repressive refusal, to participate in such dialogue is the fatal flaw of Belshazzar.

Interestingly enough, an extremely effective model for proper stewardship might also be found in the particularly intrusive narrator of *Sir Gawain* who, as both master of revels and arbiter of the word within his own work, not only narrates a tale but has occasion to address himself directly both to his audience and to his characters. As we shall note in chapter 5, with his frequent destabilizing and undermining of the word through his deliberate ambiguities, his recursive forms, and his purposeful ironies, the narrator shapes the poem into a factotem image of the Bakhtinian concept of carnival, with the word constantly reinvolved with itself in a renewing dialogue, which "by virtue of its challenge to authoritarian discourse results in the unmasking, disclosing of the unvarnished truth under the veil of false claims and arbitrary ranks."[25]

If *Sir Gawain and the Green Knight* reminds one of the give-and-take of Bakhtinian linguistic carnival, the resemblance results less from the laughter that pervades the poem than from the central conflict between conflicting systems of communication.[26] Like the courts of Belshazzar and the king of Nineveh, Arthur's Round Table is confronted by an external messenger and, more importantly, by a message that tests the ability of the authorized sign system to comprehend and incorporate that message into its own linguistic economy. Because the transmission/reception of signs, both aural and visual, is the ultimate vehicle of culture, such challenges are direct measures of their respective courts' potential for renewal and, hence, survival. As in the case of Belshazzar and the writing on the wall, that message is unintelligible to those within the court. Indeed, that this is a competition between disparate sign systems is quickly revealed as the Green Knight defies the court by demanding, "Where is now your . . . grete wordes? / Now is þe reuel and þe renoun of þe Rounde Table / Ouerwalt wyth a worde of on wyȝes speche" (311–14). For his own part, Arthur responds in kind: "I know no gome þat is gast of þy grete wordes" (325). In short, words are the real weapons in the Green Knight's verbal game or riddle, and as such come into play long before *gisarmes.* The linguistic nature of the conflict is then underscored by Gawain's own admission to Bercilak that the Green Knight, "Þer watȝ stabled bi statut a steuen vus bytwene" (1060), as well as by his host's response: "I schal teche yow to þa terme bi þe tymeȝ ende" (1069). While the terms of the obligation "steuen" and "terme" are frequently glossed as "appointment" and "appointed place," respectively,[27] both more commonly have linguistic associations, signifying as they do "voice" and "word." Gawain's quest is, in fact, a journey to find a voice, a word, a new "token" or "tytel," although he is ignorant of the fact. And, of course, the meeting place, the "terme," is significantly enough an "oratorie."

That the conflict at the core of the poem is between mutually unintelligible sign systems may be demonstrated by the Green Knight's introduction to the court. Since Arthur's Camelot is characterized by noise,[28] early in the poem we are told of the Babel-like "dyn" (47) and "glaum" (46) of the Yuletide celebration.[29] This effect is underscored by the poet's onomatopoeia in the description of the kettledrums, the cracking of trumpets, and finally the "Nwe nakryn noyse" of the pipes (118). Then switching from his depiction of "hor seruise" (130), the poet devotes his first words to the Green Knight who, here and at the Green Chapel, is heard before he is seen: "Anoþer noyse, ful newe, neȝed biliue, / Þat þe lude myȝt haf leue liflode to cach" (132–33).

Note that a noise, not a *gome* or man, will allow Arthur to fulfill his pledge. And as if to emphasize that these are two competing systems of *noyse*, the poet immediately follows these lines by observing the cessation of noise at Arthur's court: "For vneþe watȝ þe noyce not awhyle sesed, / And þe fyrst cource in þe court kyndely serued, / Þer hales in at þe halle-dor an aghlich mayster, . . ." (134–36). Although the exact referent of "noyce" is, like many other elements in the poem, ambiguous, its parallel placement with the serving of the first course would logically make its referent the noise of Arthur's court, noise stifled if not supplanted by "anoþer noyse" of the Green Knight.

At this point in the narrative, the reader might well ask why the Green Knight is characterized by *noyse*—that is, signs incomprehensible to Arthur's court—and, more importantly, why Arthur's court is characterized by a jarring mixture of "dyn," "glaum," and "noyse." Is it to suggest that they are, in counterpoint to a pre-Babel society, a group whose members' discourse is mutually incomprehensible?[30] In order to answer these questions, one must realize that Arthur's own failure at speech is pinpointed in the narrative, first, in his poor stewardship of the word through a rash oath, a linguistic blunder fulfilled by the "oþer noyse" of the intruder, and second, in his egregious misreading of signs, both visual and verbal.

In his description of the Green Knight, the narrator emphasizes that knight's lack of battle gear: "Wheþer hade he no helme ne hawbergh nauþer, / Ne no pysan ne no plate þat pented to armes, / Ne no schafte ne no schelde to schwue ne to smyte . . ." (203–5). As if to underscore that very point, the Green Knight prefaces his announcement of his "errand" by stating:

> ȝe may be seker bi þis braunch þat I bere here
> Þat I passe as in pes and no plyȝt seche,
> For had I founded in fere in feȝtyng wyse,
> I haue a hauberghe at home, and a helme boþe,

A schelde and a scharp spere, schinande bryʒt,
Ande oþer wappenes to welde, I wene wel als;
Bot for I wolde no were, my wedeʒ ar softer.

(265–71)

Arthur's immediate response to these words, however, demonstrates a linguistic inattentiveness more fitting a somnambulant
student than a king: "Sir cortays knyʒt, / If þou craue batayl bare, /
Here fayleʒ þou not to fyʒt" (276–78).

With the possible exceptions of the dreamer Geoffrey in the *Book
of the Duchess* and the obtuse clerks of Belshazzar's court, one is
hard-pressed to come up with a parallel to such verbal obtuseness.
And like the world-weary teacher that he probably is at this point,
the Green Knight begins his speech anew by repeating, "Nay, frayst
I no fyʒt . . ." (279).[31] Yet this teacher, like many an instructor whose
class is not really paying attention, resorts to an assay, a quiz. In
fact, as we shall see in chapter 4, the "game" or riddle that makes
up the Green Knight's challenge is seriously misread by Arthur and
the court, who mistakenly understand the ax as the instrument for
the execution of their contract, rather than the "hondeselle" or gift
that it is.

If we recall the lines from the *Rhythmus alter* of Alanus de Insulis,
it appears as though Arthur has failed to read the "pictura" or visual
clues of the Green Knight's visage, to understand the "liber" of the
Green Knight's words, or to recognize a reflection of his own request
for a "wonder" in the Green Knight's appearance. Yet Arthur and his
court's inability to decode the Green Knight's message stems from
far more than the Green Knight's *straungenesse*, his verbal indirection, or even his status as an outsider. Arthur's court is characterized by an unwillingness to speak, whether out of fear or arrogance
or inability. To be sure, the narrator emphasizes this aspect of the
Arthurian entourage, a group of men who are as mute as Belshazzar's
stone idols. There is, for instance, the narrator's delightfully obvious sarcasm in assuring us that

In a swoghe sylence þurʒ þe sale riche,
As al were slypped vpon slepe, so slaked hor loteʒ
    in hyʒe,
I deme hit not al for doute,
Bot sum for cortaysye.

(243–47)

The poet next has the Green Knight ask if "Dar any herinne oȝt say" (300) and then has him coughing mockingly at the silence. The whole point of Gawain's unnecessarily lethal blow is to silence the Green Knight, to cut off discourse, a motive the latter acknowledges himself when he says "If I spende no speche, þenne spedeȝ þou þe better" (410). Significantly enough, Arthur promotes the same notion as he tells Gawain, "Kepe þe cosyn . . . þat þou on kyrf sette, / And if þou redeȝ hym ryȝt, redly I trowe / Þat þou schal byden þe bur þat he schal bede after" (372–74). The king's weak control as linguistic head of his own community is evident in his own unconscious irony, his lack of understanding of the true meaning of his own words, "redeȝ hym ryȝt." And of course, given the linguistic habits of the court, there is no chance that Gawain will "rede" this or any other token in "ryȝt" manner. Arthur's inability to act as the linguistic center of his own society, in direct contrast to the name-giving founders of Rome, Tuscany, Lombardy, and Britain, is as serious and as obvious a breach as his failure to remain in the proper place at the feast table, an unkingly act underscored subtly by Morgan's retention of the highest place at her own table.[32] Significantly, because Gawain cannot perceive the "auncian's" own place as highest on the dais at Bercilak's court, he also fails to realize that the central figure in the court is the crone, not the younger woman who is the center of his courtly attentions. Of course, in failing to recognize the importance of the crone's position at the banquet, Gawain is acting as the perfect mirror of the values of his own court whose leader is absent from the place of honor at Camelot. Such a lapse then allows the Green Knight to ask the scathing and double-edged question, "Wher is . . . Þe gouernour of þis gyng" (224–25), for part of governing is presiding over the conventions of communication.

More serious than the failure to speak or to perceive the meaning of one's own discourse is the deliberate abuse of speech occurring within the court. According to Augustine, speech is a divine gift, the purpose or correct use of which is disclosure.[33] Using speech to hide truth, however, constitutes an abuse of that gift, a "true marvel." Indeed, as Gawain says, the green girdle should be employed as an outward "token of vntrawþe þat I am tan inne" since none "may hyden his harme bot vnhap ne may hit" (2509–11). Yet Arthur and his court are noted for just such attempts to veil truths, to disguise their true feelings. The chief business of Arthur and his courtiers at the outset of the poem is the masking of their feelings, the concealment of any

trace of their true reactions to the events surrounding the Green
Knight, so that these chivalric representatives are, in a sense, no less
disguised than the green intruder. At the poem's conclusion, their
universal adoption of the green baldric, whose meaning they clearly
do not understand, is merely an attempt to rob the "trwe token" of
its semanticity, to hide its meaning or the *differance*, in the Derrid-
ian sense, that it denotes for Gawain. Certainly the universal adoption of the green baldric as a fashion robs Gawain of his uniqueness,
his difference. In essence, the court deals with the threat of Gawain's newfound knowledge by co-opting its "sygne" and thereby
robbing it of its semanticity by destroying its difference. Again in
Bakhtinian terms, permitting rather than repressing such a challenge to the status quo has as its goal—in poetry as well as in kingship—growth rather than chaos, renewal rather than annihilation.

In terms of such verbal masking, Gawain is once again a true exemplar of the values of the Arthurian court. His first words, though
courtly, represent insincere hyperbole concerning his own lack of
worth, an opinion given the lie by almost every succeeding word and
deed. In fact, the basis of the knight's renown is his ability at
"derne" or secret "luf-talkyng" (927),[34] a courtly skill whose hall-
marks are indirection, innuendo, and double entendre. Upon learning the name of their guest at Hautdesert, the courtiers thus link
Gawain with such double speech:

> Now schal we semlych se sle3te3 of þewe3,
> And þe teccheles termes of talkyng noble,
> Wich spede is in speche, vnspurd may we lerne,
> Syn we haf fonged þat fyne fader of nurture.
> God hat3 geuen vus his grace godly forsoþe,
> Þat such a gest as Gawan graunte3 vus to haue,
> When burne3 blyþe of his burþe schal sitte
>   and synge.
>   In menyng of manere3 mere
>   Þis burne now schal vus bryng.
>   I hope þat may hym here
>   Schal lerne of luf-talkyng.
>
>   (916–27)

After overhearing such "praise" of his singular linguistic skills,
Gawain attempts to live up to this reputation, thereby allowing
himself to be seduced by the lady. Moreover, such acclaim is, at the

least, of dubious distinction, for it echoes the use of the term "sleȝe"—used only twenty lines earlier—to describe the sauces masking the penitential fare of fish in order to give it the appearance of a feast.[35] Much excellent work has already been done on the wealth of decoration permeating the work, often as deceptive as the Green Knight's disguise. Moreover, in *Sir Gawain and the Green Knight,* words themselves form another sly means of veiling or masking rather than of disclosing. Such "sleȝteȝ of þeweȝ" thus look forward to the green girdle with its peculiar lifesaving property— "For he myȝt not be slayn for slyȝt vpon erþe" (1854). As if in response to this claim, the narrator, entering into the mind of Gawain, declares, "Þen kest þe knyȝt, and hit come to his hert, / Hit were a juel for þe jopardé þat hym jugged were, / When he acheued to þe chapel, his chek for to fech; / Niyȝ he haf slypped to be vnslayn, þe sleȝt were noble" (1855–58).

The green girdle is a "juel" for Gawain's "joparde," but it possesses this property because it is explicitly transformed from object to sign. That is, as a result of the very exchange of words between Gawain and the grene gome, the girdle is endowed with semanticity. This act of decoding and subsequent encoding is deftly symbolized by Gawain's untying and then retying the green baldric as he unravels the game or riddle of the Green Knight and reintegrates his new perception into his own self-knowledge. No longer hidden or privatized, or for that matter the product of "sleȝteȝ"—the green girdle is visibly displayed and is openly explained as Gawain asks to "welde" the "token," explicitly juxtaposing its physical properties with its nature as "sign": ". . . not for þe wynne golde, / Ne þe saynt, ne þe sylk, ne þe syde pendaundes, / For wele ne for worchyp, ne for þe wlonk werkkeȝ, / Bot *in syngne* of my surfet" (2430–33), and as if to emphasize the semantic function of the girdle, the narrator informs us, ". . . þe blykkande belt he bere þeraboute, / Abelef, as a bauderyk, bounden bi his syde, / Loken vnder his lyfte arme, þe lace, wyth a knot, / In tokenyng he watȝ tane in tech of a faute" (2485–88).

Finally, in recounting his adventures to the court, Gawain emphasizes the girdle as "token," publicly explaining its meaning: "Þis is þe bende of þis blame I bere my nek; / Þis is þe laþe and þe losse þat I laȝt haue / Of couardise and couetyse þat I haf caȝt þare. / Þis is þe token of vntrawþe þat I am tan inne . . ." (2506–9).

In each case, the girdle is presented explicitly as "token" or "sign"—as a semanticized object whose linguistic transformation or revaluation functions as a symbol of Gawain's new understanding. Another model for such formulation of a new linguistic order has been demonstrated by Allan A. Metcalf in his essay "*Sir Gawain* and *You*."[36] Metcalf underscores the poet's skillful use of the second person so that Gawain evolves from the informal and slightly disrespectful "Thou" to the more formal "You" by the end of the poem. The word *You* is no longer appropriate as a signifier for the signified. New knowledge creates new forms and habits of discourse. As perception changes, so too does language, the undoing and revaluation of which are signified by the untying and retying of the girdle, the "trwe token" of "vntrawþe" at the end of the poem.

While Gawain succeeds in linguistic integration, in the revaluation of parts of his own discourse, Arthur fails in his stewardship of the word, thereby providing the answer to the question "why then did Camelot fall?" Arthur cannot articulate any meaningful response to Gawain's tale of shame as embodied in the knight's public attempt to decode the meaning of that "trwe" token. Offering moral noncommunication—empty consolation and very un-Bakhtinian laughter—Arthur, together with his court, experiences a type of verbal obtuseness, a paralysis in which misunderstood signs—notably the radically privatized green baldric as an emblem of the Round Table's honorable reputation—are substituted uneasily for true leadership and communication of Christian values. Camelot, it would seem, fell because it was no longer a society; it was no longer a collection of people capable of communicating either by sending or by receiving mutually understood messages. Camelot has become a type of Babel with each member using his own unique language to encode, to hide, rather than to disclose meaning. As a society in which language has become dangerously privatized, Camelot is no longer able to absorb or reintegrate what Gawain has learned into its own sign system, into its own body of knowledge. In effect, Arthur's court is unable to retie the knot—for while the court adopts the sign of Gawain's "vntrawþe," they have converted a "trwe token" into little more than a fashion statement.[37]

The poem concludes not with the court but, rather, ends by coming full circle, repeating its first stanza as its one-hundred-first. As a result of this narrative "signature," the audience is again presented with the image of a fallen Troy, this time revalorized by its reading of the intervening hundred stanzas. As the last stanza returns us to the first, the repetition redirects us back into the poem, albeit a very different one in which many of the ironies are laid bare, self-reflexively glossed by our previous experience of the poem. In returning us to lines for which we have already found meaning in an earlier context, the poem demonstrates for its readers not only how signs are made but how societies survive and in particular why this one did not. Indeed, the narrator's deliberate avowal that he heard his tale "in toun" points in two directions. His aside serves to remind us of his contemporary present and, hence, to confirm the notion that Camelot is a lost "toun" of the vanished past. But if the reference to the contemporary town serves to define Camelot as a fallen city, the cycle of fallen cities, of which Camelot is a member, reaches outward to include the "toun" of the poet's present. In an apocalyptic warning appropriate for Jonah preaching at Nineveh, the poet seems to be saying that, without repentance, the "toun" of today will share the fate of Camelot, which did not listen, rather than that of Nineveh, which did heed the danger.

As its opening and closing stanzas make clear, *Sir Gawain and the Green Knight* is a tale about history. As such, this romance becomes a story about a moment in the life of an individual—a moment that, in turn, illuminates the chronicle of a city which itself is but a chapter in the unfolding course of the history of humankind, notably the rises and falls of civilizations or cultures which are dependent on communication, on the free and direct use of language. In this vision of the past, the poet has not moved very far from the underlying presumptions of Augustine's *Confessions*, which, as we noted in the introduction, moves deftly from the personal history of its author to an explication of Genesis, from the infant acquisition of language to an understanding of Creation through the speech acts of the Creator.

In the end, however, we are left with two counterbalancing images. On the one hand, there is the city of Nineveh where, as a result of the king's decree, "alle crye"—the "burnes and bestes, burdeȝ and childer, / Vch prynce, vche prest, and prelates alle" (388–89). Presumably beasts, children, prelates and the rest do not all speak alike, and yet, despite such insurmountable heteroglossia, all say the same thing as they implore God, "hym þat rawþe schal haue" (396), to spare the city. In sharp contrast to the linguistic network of Nineveh stands the splendor of Camelot. While the members of

Arthur's court outwardly seem to speak the same tongue, their words are so privatized that though the signs are the same, the meanings are different. Even the king, as in his advice to "rede3 . . . ry3t" (373), does not understand the meaning of his own counsel.

The historical moment, whether at Camelot or in Nineveh, is the microcosm of the process by which cities are saved or lost. And as we shall see in the succeeding chapter, the verbal contract, a very special form of linguistic endeavor, is the fundamental act or binding tie in both the history of the individual and the history of a nation. The history of nations is the process whereby all that is implicit or exists in potentia within the words of Creation becomes manifest.

As we noted earlier, *Gawain* concludes with a return visit to the fallen realms traced at the beginning of the poem. In this circular movement, the poet forces us to turn our attention from the Arthurian court to the all-embracing pageant of history, which shapes and is shaped by the Camelot myth. *Sir Gawain and the Green Knight* is thus a recursive work, a romance that constantly rewrites itself, thereby providing new meaning for the audience which savors and reflects upon the fallen cities of the poem's opening.

Two

AS GOOD AS A HANDSHAKE:
COVENANTAL HISTORY AND
THE FATE OF *MONKYNDE*

Perhaps the most frequent question asked by the first-time undergraduate reader of *Sir Gawain and the Green Knight* is a rather commonsense one, at least to modern sensibilities: Why does Gawain seek out the Green Knight in order to keep an appointment that, as far as everyone in the poem is concerned, can only lead to his death? In fact, the same question arises in regard to the far less sympathetic knight of the *Wife of Bath's Tale*, where the central character is given a similar period of a year and a day to find the correct response to the riddle, "What is it that all women desire."[1] Failure to find the answer means death, and, yet, we are told: "Whan that he saugh he myghte nat come thereby— / This is to seye, what wommen love moost— / Withinne his brest ful sorweful was the goost. / But hoom he gooth; he myghte nat sojourne; / The day was come that homeward *moste* he tourne" (3.984–87; emphasis added).

"Hoom he gooth" and "homeward moste he tourne"—here an almost unthinkable action, at least in modern terms, is reduced to two remarkably brief clauses whose compactness is all the more pronounced given the psychological depth that informs the prologue and the tale's denouement. The knight simply "must" return as if the logical force of the situation makes further explanation completely unnecessary. As with Gawain's decision to seek out the Green Knight, the modern reader asks why neither character considers, in the one case, not going, and, in the other, not coming back. The fact that such options are actively resisted by Gawain and, more remarkably, not even considered by the wife's young knight, who is already guilty of rape and *surquidré*, attests to an assumption of a principle not at work in our own ethos.

Asked how Gawain would respond if the tale's setting were a modern corporate boardroom and if the "game" were converted into a difficult but seemingly lucrative merger/takeover whose dangers were not apparent until *after* the contract had been signed, modern students invariably reply that they would simply break the contract, usually with the aid of a lawyer, often suggesting that some sort of deception makes the contract invalid. As to the divergence between the "medieval" response and our own to such contractual bonds, students tend to focus on what they perceive to be our sophistication as opposed to medieval naiveté, especially in the medieval regard for abstract honor and a powerfully totemistic reverence for the pledged word, qualities that we can admire condescendingly from afar. To be sure, there is a strong tradition of adhering to even the rashest of promises in Arthurian literature. Arthur, for example, is often victimized by his own rash vows, honoring them at his own expense because a king may not be forsworn and remain a king. But the force that holds Gawain and the wife's knight—two characters of different temperaments and outlooks—to their appointed rounds is far more specific than a general predilection for keeping one's word. Rather, it is the power of covenant, the express power of law.[2]

The power of law is evident in the virtual air of obligation that permeates *Sir Gawain*. The poem presents a world characterized by increasingly complex webs of words and obligations, a world in which words are expressly "knyt" into "couenaunts," where riddles and love talk are transformed into formalized legal contracts.[3] History, as we have seen in chapter 1, is inseparable from language. As such, it is equally important to note that words are the *matière* out of which contracts are created, and that the history that underlies all of this poet's works is an expressly covenantal one.

One of the most striking aspects of *Sir Gawain and the Green Knight* is the poet's careful delineation of the contracts or "couenaunts" that occur throughout the poem—for, in the course of his adventure, Gawain is bound to the Green Knight, Bercilak, and Bercilak's wife by a series of contractual agreements that mirror in form and in content the juridical procedures outlined in English common law.[4] To be sure, Gawain's failure to fulfill his voluntary pledges because of a self-created web of mutually contradictory promises lies at the heart of most interpretations of the poem.[5] Central to this understanding, as in the historical/personal analysis of Augustine, is the concept of free will ("goud wylle"), which represents in medieval legal theory and practice an essential element in the shaping of binding contractual agreements.[6] Through an examination of the legal role of "wylle" in the medieval contractual tradition, then, we will illuminate the significance of this concept in the creation of Gawain's contracts and to highlight the thematic and structural employment of will in *Gawain*—the particular quality that is weighed, tested, and repeatedly shaped throughout this romance.

In medieval legal practice, contracts are, first of all, divided conventionally into two distinct parts. A set of stipulations, the quid pro quo and terms of enforcement, constitutes the first part, whereas a formally sworn oath represents the second.[7] Significantly, this traditional legal distinction between the "couenaunt" (quid pro quo) and the "forwarde" (oath) is strictly maintained in each of the sworn contracts within *Gawain*.[8] Furthermore, according to medieval contractual practice, any breach of formal contract is defined as a breach of oath or "forwarde" rather than as a failure to act or to deliver the quid pro quo.[9] While the oath constitutes the legally forcible element of the contract, the validity of the oath springs from the oath taker's "goud wylle," a quality including both conscious, free assent to the declaration and the ability to make such a promise.[10] For example, one cannot swear with good will to sell as one's own possessions the goods belonging to another individual. In a similar vein, a married man's bigamous promise to wed someone else cannot be offered with "goud wylle," for the promised action is unperformable.

Like most elements of medieval culture, this legal concept of will is rooted in matters secular and spiritual, with the practical lessons of experience standing inseparable from the theoretical speculations of "auctoritee." Curiously enough, the Roman legal code fails to include any provision for a proxy, a concept vital to modern jurisprudence.[11] As multinational trade and banking became increasingly complex and extensive, however, the formulation of the proxy concept by medieval mercantile circles called for more lucid legal definitions of what could and could not be promised legally by oath. Along with this secular interest in the nature and limitations of oaths, the centrality of will in the construction of oaths gradually played an important, evolving role in medieval religious thought. By the eleventh century, at least, numerous patristic writings focusing upon the status and effectiveness of oaths for initiates into religious orders had been amassed.[12] Of particular significance to the devel-

opment of thought on the proper employment of oaths was the on-
set of the Crusades along with the Christian knights' sacred vows to
recapture the Holy Land. Each of the Crusades generated both a
flurry of vows by potential defenders of the Christian faith and a cor-
responding spate of legal/ethical theorizing upon the efficacy of
those vows once, as was often the case, the object of the binding
obligations proved unattainable.[13]

Another important step in the refinement of medieval contractual
theory is the concept of the vow as a self-limiting action for a
promisor.[14] Since vows in the Middle Ages reflect God's conduct as
covenantal partner in Old Testament agreements, a vow represents
a pledge whereby the will chooses to place limits upon its freedom
of action. For example, an individual's vow to be ordained as a priest
creates a self-limiting prohibition against marriage. In contrast, for
a person whose activities are not circumscribed by the taking of holy
orders, the bonds of matrimony may still be knotted with "goud
wylle." The scriptural basis for both the civil and canon law principles of the self-limiting function of the will is illustrated by the
Gawain-Poet's portrayal of the covenants made between God and
Noah in *Purity*. That God's role in the covenantal/contractual
process hinges on "wylle" is traced clearly in the announcement of
his intention to destroy mankind:

> Now God in nwy to Noe con speke.
> Wylde wrakful worde3 in his wylle greued . . .
> I schal strenkle my distresse, and strye al togeder,
> Boþe lede3 and londe and alle þat lyf habbe3.
> Bot, make to þe a mancioun, and þat is my wylle.
>
> (301–2, 307–9)

Somewhat later, moreover, God pledges not to repeat at any future
time this annihilation of the world:[15] "For quen þe swemande sor3e
so3t to his hert, / He knyt a couenaunde cortaysly wyth monkynde
þere, / In þe mesure of his mode and meþe of his wylle, / Þat he
schulde neuer, for no syt, smyte al at one3" (563–66).

In shaping a covenant with Noah (and, hence, "monkynde"), God
thus limits divine omnipotence by freely promising never "to quelle
alle quyke3 for qued þat my3t falle, / Whyl of þe lenþe of þe londe
laste3 þe terme. / Þat ilke skyl, for no scaþe, ascaped hym neuer"
(567–69). Likewise, in bargaining with Abraham concerning the de-

struction of Sodom (*Purity:* 713–65), God enters into another formal "covenant" whereby divine freedom of action is restricted through the self-containment of will. In both of these contractual arrangements, the presence of divine will triggers the theological dilemma of limited actions for an omnipotent God; yet if limits are not placed on God's will, man's covenants with God—both the salvation of Noah (327–30) and of ten honorable men in Sodom (763–65)—are transformed into specious gestures. In attempting to resolve this knotty theological problem, then, late medieval nominalist thinkers perceive God as a covenantal partner, a deity who voluntarily limits his own will and actions. While God's omnipotence clearly includes the ability to abrogate any contract, God freely chooses to curb his will in order to fulfill contractual obligations. In the flood episode of *Purity,* for example, the active will seeking the destruction of the world (326) is thus limited by a voluntary covenant with mankind (564–65). Since God freely pledges his faith, any deviation from this formal agreement—any wholesale slaughter of human beings—would represent an action outside the bounds of prescribed contractual behavior.

Occasionally, however, individuals may implore God to prevent the terms of a duly executed agreement. In the New Testament parable of the vineyard (Matt. 20: 1–16), a story recounted in *Pearl* (497–588), the lord (God) hires workmen for his vineyard at various times of the day. Although those employed first by the lord "Into accorde . . . con declyne / For a pené on a day" (509–10), the penny of eternal beatitude granted equally to the saved, such laborers complain that they deserve more than the idle men engaged by their employer near sunset (549–56). After reminding the workers of the contractual obligation of a penny, "Wat3 not a pené þe couenaunt þore? / Fyrre þen couenaunde is no3t to plete" (562–63), the lord asserts his prerogative as employer to extend the penny of eternal life to all laborers, both early and late, in the vineyard. Through the free gift of divine grace and through heavenly "cortaysye," the manifestation of divine charity, those who performed little work in the vineyard may still receive everlasting bliss.[16]

As the parable of the vineyard illustrates clearly, God voluntarily restricts his unlimited freedom—an action representing an integral part of divine "cortaysye"—in order to enter into covenants with humanity (the laborers). At the same time, however, God may offer

freely the contractual reward of heaven to "latecomers," for God is
the true fount of grace and love. If the limitation of will represents
the hallmark of God, then the undisciplined reign of the will is frequently linked with Satan, who rebels against his lord and who
seeks to destroy natural order by establishing a throne in the North.
The inversion proposed by Satan in *Purity* (211–34) strikes at the
very heart of the lord/vassal relationship, the bond that knits together the fabric of heavenly and earthly courts.

Similarly, in *Patience*, the story of the recalcitrant Jonah begins
with the narrator's examination of true submission to the will of
one's lord:

> . . . ȝif my lege lorde lyst, on lyue, me to bidde
> Oþer to ryde oþer to renne to Rome in his ernde,
> What grayþed me þe grychchyng, bot grame more seche
> Much, ȝif he me ne made, maugref my chekes,
> And þenne þrat moste I þole, and vnþonk to mede,
> Þe had bowed to his bode, bongre my hyure.
>
> (51–56)

While Jonah's vassalage serves as a major theme in *Patience*, the
poet cogently suggests that the prophet's servitude cannot be perceived as license for the lord's exercise of unrestricted will. Just as
Patience opens with a statement outlining the servant's obligations,
so the poem concludes with the voice from the whirlwind, wherein
God articulates the divine "duty" (495–527) to the innocent and un-
knowing servants in Nineveh, a town Jonah wishes to be destroyed.
Indeed, Jonah is angry because God will not live by the letter of the
law:

> What! Wote oþer wyte may ȝif þe Wyȝe lykes,
> Þat is hende in þe hyȝt of his gentryse.
> I wot his myȝt is so much, þaȝ he be myssepayed,
> Þat in his mylde amesyng, he mercy may fynde;
> And if we leuen þe layk of oure layth synnes,
> And stylle steppen in þe styȝe he styȝtleȝ hymseluen,
> He wyl wende of his wodschip and his wrath leue,
> And forgif vus þis gult, ȝif we hym God leuen.
>
> (397–404)

"Gentryse" is such that "þaȝ he be myssepayed;" it demands the
granting of mercy if amends are made. The covenantal relationship

between vassal and lord is thus framed so that the obedience of the servant implies a responsibility for the master. This custodial obligation of a ruler to his subjects is illustrated, likewise, by the Ninevite king's tearful response to Jonah's cries for repentance:

> And he radly vp ros and ran fro his chayer.
> His ryche robe he torof of his rigge naked,
> And of a hep of askes he hitte in þe myddeʒ.
> He askeʒ heterly a hayre and hasped hym vmbe,
> Sewed a sekke þerabof and syked ful colde.
> Þer he dased in þat duste, wyth droppande teres,
> Wepande ful wonderly alle his wrange dedes.
>
> (378–84)

After acting as a penitential role model for his people, he orders them to fast and to abandon their sinful behavior (385–404), thereby increasing the chances for God's forgiveness.

Finally, in order to comprehend the significance of will in medieval contractual procedure, it may prove helpful to outline the contract framed between a mortal and another "grene gome." In Chaucer's *Friar's Tale*, a wily summoner agrees to exchange winnings with a fiend garbed in green. When an angry carter subsequently consigns his cart and horses to the devil and when the greedy summoner questions the demon's failure to claim this windfall, the fiend responds by noting the importance of "entente" ("goud wylle") in the offering of gifts: "'Nay,' quod the devel, 'God woot, never a deel! / It is nat his entente, trust me weel'" (3.1555–56).[17] That "entente" represents an important factor in determining full comprehension of the nature of an action is illustrated, likewise, in the concluding scene of the *Friar's Tale*. Once an elderly widow consigns the summoner to the devil, the fiend inquires, "Now, Mabely, myn owne mooder deere, / Is this youre wyl in ernest that ye seye?" (III, 1626–27). Without that genuine exercise of "wyl," then, the old woman's oath is as meaningless as that of the carter; yet the widow cannot willfully deliver the summoner's soul to the devil unless she gains the summoner's consent. However, after the summoner places himself within her power during a volley of angry words, all parties—the devil, the widow, and the summoner—freely execute an agreement so that the fiend may carry off the spoils of the hunt, the summoner, to hell.

Inasmuch as the summoner's exchange of "purchas" (III, 1530) with the yeoman-devil in the *Friar's Tale* constitutes a binding transaction, an agreement resembling the exchange of "cheui-saunce"[18] in Gawain's covenants, the same question of "wylle" plays a pivotal role in Gawain's contractual arrangements. Ironically, Gawain is the one who introduces the concept of will as the standard for judging human actions when he attempts to parry Lady Bercilak's hard-pressed suit for a kiss: "ȝe, be God . . . good is your speche, / Bot þrete is vnþryuande in þede þer I lende, / And vche gift þat is geuen not wyth goud wylle" (1498–1500).

Yet the good will to which Gawain alludes suggests more than the proper way of offering gifts or hearts. As even the casual reader of medieval literature may note, gift giving represents an important social and legal convention, for such an act creates an implicit contractual bond between giver and recipient,[19] as well as a debt liability in a unilateral contract,[20] the most common type of medieval legal agreement. In short, if one party contracts with a second party for the exchange of goods, the contract binds only when the first party delivers the promised merchandise, thereby creating a unilateral debt for the receiver. In a similar vein, then, the agreement for the exchange of blows framed between Gawain and the Green Knight constitutes a contractual obligation only when the "grene gome" offers his neck to Gawain, resulting in a unilateral debt for Gawain. Such a contractual debt imposed upon Gawain may serve to explain why he initially rejects the various gifts presented by Lady Bercilak during the third temptation. Since Gawain cannot offer suitable gifts in return, he would be indebted to Bercilak's wife; without a means of satisfying that debt, then, Gawain may not accept such gifts with proper good will. In fact, the legalities of obligation and the express indebtedness they create and then discharge provide the very rationale for the rather peculiar exchange instituted at Bercilak's court. To accept a gift is to accept indebtedness. To do so without hope of being able to discharge that debt, as Gawain tells Lady Bercilak, is a breach of the very high manners of which Gawain is supposed to be the exemplar.

What holds true for the exchange of bedroom trifles is also true of the hospitality of the household in general. Gawain, in accepting Bercilak's hospitality, has placed himself within the host's debt, creating an obligation that he cannot repay, for the knight-errant has nothing with which to quite the fare at Bercilak's table. Once the spoils of the hunt—the venison and the boar—are in Gawain's possession, the knight is allowed technically to provide the night's repast, to repay his host's hospitality and thereby cancel the obligation that the seemingly doomed knight cannot afford. But for Gawain to use the game in this fashion, the fare must be completely his, thus triggering the elaborate exchange of Bercilak's winnings for Gawain's winnings, an exchange contract that affords Gawain the means of discharging debt for the sake of honor. Such elaborate and circuitous exchanges make Gawain's breach of etiquette in proffering the three kisses before first receiving Bercilak's winnings all the more glaring, since Gawain's action creates presumptory debt without express permission and in violation of their stated agreement. Yet such a breach is already prefigured in the knight's previous exchange with Lady Bercilak. Although Gawain ultimately takes the lady's alluring green and gold girdle, his promise of concealment/silence (1863–65 and 1874–75) exchanged for the gift clearly violates the conditions of his previous agreement with Bercilak, the "exchange of winnings" (1106–7). Thus, from Gawain's acceptance of the girdle to the sudden offer of three kisses to Bercilak, the absence of "goud wylle" invalidates Gawain's promises and actions.

While Gawain, in the third temptation scene, lacks the good will with which valid contracts are constructed, the Gawain who returns chastened to Arthur's court is a strikingly different man from the proud knight who left Camelot in quest of the Green Chapel. The good will so deficient in Gawain's character at the beginning of the narrative finally takes shape when Gawain promises to wear the girdle, a memento of "þe faut and þe fayntyse of þe flesche crabbed" (2435), with proper "goud wylle" (2430). In order to present this development of will, an essential element in man's spiritual and social transactions, the poet creates a direct contrast between the courts of Arthur and Bercilak. Although balanced in many ways, the two courts are set apart in their disparate portrayals of the faculty of will.[21] From the very outset, moreover, Arthur's court is depicted as springing from the unrestricted will of its ruler,[22] for the narrator describes Arthur as "Kyng, hy3est mon of wylle" (57). Far from representing a sign of high spirits, such an arrogant use of uncurbed will is a reminder of what separates the sinner from God, as revealed in the delineation of the fallen Satan in *Purity*: "And 3et wrathed not þe wy3, ne þe wrech sa3tled, / Ne neuer wolde for wylnesful his worþy God knawe, / Ne þray hym for no pité, so proud watȝ his wylle" (230–32).

While the noble company of Camelot knights and ladies may be "in her first age" (54), the springtime of life, their youthful vigor may suggest a type of childishness, for reason has not yet regulated their immature desires. As the Green Knight seeks "raysoun," Arthur, who is associated with "sourquydrye" (311), "wex[ez] as wroth as wynde" (319). Furthermore, Arthur's unrestrained employment of will is signalized both by his "boyish" behavior and by his rash public oath not to eat until he witnesses or hears about a "meruayle" (94), a wonder specifically associated with Fortune. Even Gawain alludes to Camelot's lack of restraint by noting to Arthur: "Whil mony so bolde yow aboute vpon bench sytten, / Þat vnder heuen I hope non haȝerer of wylle" (351–52).

Although Arthur's court is presented in terms of unrestricted will, Bercilak's court at Castle Hautdesert is founded upon good will, a principle of limited volition or will harnessed by reason and moderation.[23] When Gawain is assured that a guide will be provided who can point the way to the Green Chapel, Bercilak tells Gawain, "In god fayþe . . . wyth a goud wylle / Al þat euer I yow hyȝt, halde schal I redé" (1969–70). As we noted earlier, limitations placed upon the will ("goud wylle") represent an integral part of contractual procedure, including contracts framed between persons or between humanity and God. Furthermore, this important concept of limitation constitutes the foundation for the legal principle of prior claim,[24] a rule pointedly espoused throughout the poem. Thus Gawain attempts to thwart Lady Bercilak's advances by reminding her that she is bound to a better man through a prior commitment (1276). In a similar vein, after the second exchange of winnings, Gawain begs leave to depart from Hautdesert, for his prior covenant with the Green Knight takes precedence over his agreement to stay at the castle. Only when he is satisfied that an extra day's lodging presents no conflict with his initial contractual duties, does Gawain consent to remain an additional night at Hautdesert (1670–83). In each of these instances, the self-regulation aspect of the will is invoked because the strictures of a prior agreement invalidate any further contractual activities.

That the power of will becomes the focus of the testing in *Gawain* is elucidated, likewise, in the poem's structure. The construction

and the execution of the covenant between Gawain and the Green
Knight are interrupted by the account of the events at Castle Hautdesert. Similarly, the framing and the completion of the covenants
at Bercilak's castle are interrupted by the hunting tableaux, at the
very center of which appear the temptation episodes.[25] Finally, at
the heart of the three indoor temptations lies the question of "goud
wylle" (1500). In each of these temptations, Lady Bercilak sets the
stage for the free exercise of Gawain's will by offering him those
things that may violate the stipulated terms of the "exchange of
winnings."[26] Seeking Gawain's affection as if it represents the payment of a debt, the lady then claims in legal fashion a kiss owed
through "cortaysy": "ȝet, I kende yow of kyssyng . . . / Quereso
countenaunce is couþe quikly to clayme; / Þat bicumes vche a knyȝt
þat cortaysy vses" (1489–91).

Constituting an important part of Lady Bercilak's argument,
"courtesy" is often viewed as a legal term denoting the right of possessions or inheritance.[27] Furthermore, the lady repeatedly invokes
courtesy, her version of the contractual quid pro quo, as an obligation that entitles her to Gawain's attentions. The narrator of *Gawain* quickly traces the dilemma of the knight entangled by
conflicting obligations to both Lady Bercilak and her husband,
Gawain's host: "He cared for his cortaysye, lest craþayn he were, /
And more for his meschef ȝif he schulde make synne, / And be tray-
tor to þat tolke þat þat telde aȝt" (1773–75).

While the lady places such contractual demands upon Gawain,
she also attempts to entice him into assuming new contractual
obligations, particularly the acceptance of her green girdle and a
promise not to show the gift to Bercilak. According to medieval legal theory and practice, however, Gawain's covenant with his
host—the "exchange of winnings"—takes precedence and nullifies
his subsequent promise to Lady Bercilak. In both her claim on
Gawain's courtesy and her demand for his concealment of the girdle, the lady thus is urging him to overturn the legal process by honoring an agreement that violates a prior covenant. Moreover, the
lady actually highlights the legal dilemma by inquiring whether a
previous pledge to another woman prevents Gawain from accepting
her love (1782–86). Gawain, however, misses the point underlying
the lady's question, for in his haste to deny the prior claims of another woman, he fails to be reminded of his covenant with Bercilak.

Accompanying these attempts by the lady to ensnare Gawain in a
legal noose is the consistent employment of the image of binding in
her speech: "... Bot true vus may schape, / I schal bynde yow in your
bedde, þat be ȝe trayst" (1210–11). Although "bynde" has many non-
legal referents, the concept represents a legal term appropriate to individuals participating in a contractual obligation. This theme of
binding is concretized, likewise, by the imagery of knots, emblems
of contracts, that permeate *Gawain*, especially since the poet refers
to covenants as objects to be "knyt."[28] Just as Lady Bercilak clearly
intends to bind Gawain, the knight's immediate response to her desire suggests a cheerful acceptance of bondage: " 'Goud moroun, gay'
... / 'Me schal worþe at your wille, and þat me wel lykeȝ, / For I
ȝelde me ȝederly, and ȝeȝe after grace, / And þat is þe best, by my
dome, for me byhoueȝ nede' " (1213–16).

In yielding himself contentedly to the lady's will, Gawain creates
a network of conflicting obligations; while both he and Lady Bercilak
are bound as guest and as wife, respectively, to Bercilak, Gawain has
already pledged himself through a formal, publicly sworn ceremony
to the will of the host.

Shortly after arriving at Castle Hautdesert, for instance, Gawain
surrenders to his host's will at least three times in the space of forty-
two lines. Once he accepts Bercilak's hospitality, Gawain informs
his host,

'Grant merci, sir,' ... 'in god fayth hit is yowreȝ,
Al þe honour is your awen. ȝe heȝe kyng yow ȝelde!
And I am, wyȝe, at your wylle, to worch youre hest,
As I am halden þerto, in hyȝe and in loȝe,
                bi riȝt'
                                                    (1037–41)

Gawain then claims that a prior obligation—his meeting with the
Green Knight at the Green Chapel—triggers his imminent departure
from Hautdesert. Inasmuch as Gawain has placed himself at the disposal of his host's will, the knight requests Bercilak's permission to
take his leave: "Forþi, iwysse, bi ȝowre wylle, wende me bihoues, /
Naf I now to busy bot bare þre dayeȝ, / And me als fayn to falle feye
as fayly of myyn ernde" (1065–67). Once he realizes that he may remain at Hautdesert and still fulfill his covenant with the Green
Knight, Gawain accedes to Bercilak's wishes: "Now I þonk yow

þryuandely þur3 alle oþer þynge, / Now acheued is my chaunce, I schal, at your wylle / Dowelle, and elle3 do quat 3e demen" (1080–82).

Thus having placed himself at Bercilak's disposal, Gawain may not satisfy the contradictory impulses of the lady. Furthermore, the covenant framed between Gawain and the knight at Camelot precludes any promise to remain at Hautdesert until Gawain is assured that his stay at Bercilak's castle will not violate his pledged appearance at the Green Chapel. In general, then, the temptations at Hautdesert are designed to test Gawain's mettle, especially the strength of his self-limited will, for he is offered the opportunity there to avoid prior contractual obligations by embracing more comfortable bonds to earthly pleasure.

This battle of conflicting demands imposed upon Gawain, however, is not unexpected, especially since Castle Hautdesert is depicted initially as a testing ground for the self-limiting powers of Gawain. Once Bercilak tells Gawain, ". . . al is yowre awen, to haue at yowre wylle / And welde" (836–37), Gawain is invited to frolic in a kind of opulent playground, wherein seemingly everything—sumptuous meals, costly robes, and Bercilak's wife—is offered freely. Within this setting of worldly splendor, the will quickly becomes the hallmark of action as well as the boundary of appetite. Thus, when Gawain and Bercilak meet for the first exchange of winnings, the reader is told that "þer wat3 bot wele at wylle" (1371); following the second and third exchanges, the members of Bercilak's court sport "in halle / As longe as hor wylle hom last" (1664–65) and celebrate "With merþe and mynstralsye, wyth mete3 at hor wylle" (1952), respectively.

Although the faculty of will represents an important element in the festivities at Hautdesert, Gawain's actions—unlike those of the other major participants in the hunting/wooing tableaux—are not depicted as being performed with "good will." When Bercilak, for example, provides Gawain with a guide to the Green Chapel, the lord alludes specifically to the fulfillment of his promises "wyth a goud wylle" (1969). Similarly, when Lady Bercilak offers her green girdle to Gawain, the narrator notes that the *luf-lace* is presented "with a goud wylle" (1861), especially since the temptation episodes are designed to test Gawain's moral character.[29] Ironically, however, Gawain claims that gifts should be offered with good will (1500) and then contends: "I am at your comaundement, to kysse quen yow lyke3, / 3e may lach quen yow lyst, and leue quen yow þynkke3, / in space" (1501–3).

Although Gawain undercuts his own assertion about the necessity of "goud wylle" in presenting gifts, good will is, likewise, a significant, albeit dimly perceived, standard for judging his confession to the priest at Hautdesert. Since confession represents a contractual exchange between unequal partners, God and humanity, the efficacy of this sacrament—like all contractual arrangements—stems from the "goud wylle" of its participants. As we have noted already, the *Gawain*-Poet's portrayal of God as a covenantal partner consistently emphasizes the function of divine will as a part of the covenantal union of God and humankind. Reflexive of the covenantal theology that underlies the other poems, the confessee, for his part of the exchange, must likewise curb his will in order to assume the role of a proper partner in such contracts. The importance of curbing one's will, moreover, does represent a vital thematic concern in *Purity*, for Satan's unbridled "wylfulnes" (231) prevents him from seeking absolution.

Perhaps the *Gawain*-Poet's most explicit view of confession as a contract may be found in his "Exhortation to Purity":

How schulde we se þen, may we say, þat Syre vpon throne?
3is, þat Mayster is mercyable, þa3 þou be man fenny
And al tomarred in myre, whyl þou on molde lyuyes;
Þou may schyne þur3 schryfte, þa3 þou haf schome serued,
And pure þe with penaunce tyl þou a perle worþe . . .
Bot war þe wel, if þou be waschen wyth water of schryfte,
And polysed als playn as parchmen schauen,
Sulp no more þenne in synne þy saule þerafter,
For þenne þou Dry3tyn dyspleses wyth dedes ful sore,
And entyses hym to tene more trayþly þen euer,
And wel hatter to hate þen hade þou not waschen.
For when a sawele is sa3tled and sakred to Dry3tyn,
He holly haldes hit his, and haue hit he wolde"
(1112–16, 1133–40)

In this passage, as God's right of possession indicates, confession includes a specific quid pro quo, wherein man fulfills his contractual obligations by offering true repentance in exchange for a purified soul. In *Sir Gawain and the Green Knight,* on the other hand, Gawain's role in the sacramental exchange is not performed, for he apparently intends both to receive confessional absolution and to violate his covenant with Bercilak by subsequently withholding the lady's *luf-lace.* While an individual's failure to observe contractual obligations is construed by English courts as the breaking of a legally binding pledge, Gawain's formally sworn oath in the "exchange of winnings" invokes God (1110), the surety or guarantor of Gawain's fulfillment of the covenant with Bercilak.[30] Thus Gawain's concealment of the green girdle—the manifestation of *vntrawpe*—may be viewed as a serious offense against God, not merely a misdemeanor or a chivalric lapse. Entering the confessional with the intention to commit spiritual fraud would, of course, invalidate Gawain's petition for absolution.[31] Because Gawain neglects to render his part of the quid pro quo, the contractual exchange in confession is not created, thereby necessitating his subsequent confession to the knight at the Green Chapel.

Once Gawain leaves Castle Hautdesert, he gradually learns how to limit his will. Springing from the humbling experience essential to the enforcement of Gawain's covenant with the Green Knight, "goud wylle" initially takes shape when Gawain resists his guide's advice to flee. Although the guide offers to swear a false oath, an act of defective will, "bi God and alle his gode halȝeȝ" (2122), Gawain finally resigns himself to God's will: " 'Bi Goddeȝ self' . . . / 'I wyl nauþer grete ne grone; / To Goddeȝ wylle I am ful bayn, / And to hym I haf me tone' " (2156–59). Thus deciding to fulfill his compact with the Green Knight, Gawain presses on toward the Green Chapel, and shortly after Gawain receives a nick from the third stroke of the knight's ax, the next stage in the development of "goud wylle" is traced. Employing the language of medieval mercantile exchange contracts, the Green Knight initially taunts and then instructs Gawain concerning the actions of a "Trwe mon" (2354) in the payment of debts. Behaving somewhat like the divine partner in Old Testament contracts, the Green Knight thus quitclaims what is owed him by the less important participant (Gawain) in their vertical contract, thereby demonstrating the same type of covenantal largesse as the owner of the vineyard in the biblical parable narrated by the *Pearl*-Maiden (*Pearl,* 501–72).[32]

Informed of his duplicity at Castle Hautdesert, Gawain admits his faults:

> 'Now am I fawty and falce, and ferride haf ben euer
> Of trecherye and vntrawþe: boþe bityde sorȝe
>   and care!
> I biknowe yow, knyȝt, here stylle,
> Al fawty is my fare;
> Leteȝ me ouertake your wylle
> And efte I schal be ware.'
>   (2382–88)

Playing the role of a lay confessor, the Green Knight then recognizes Gawain's contrition and offers absolution:

> 'I halde hit hardilyly hole, þe harme þat I hade.
> Þou art confessed so clene, beknowen of þy mysses,
> And hatȝ þe penaunce apert of þe poynt of myn egge,
> I halde þe polysed of þat plyȝt, and pured as clene
> As þou hadeȝ neuer forfeted syþen þou watȝ fyrst borne.'
>   (2390–94)

Through his penitential acknowledgment of his faults, particularly his treacherous violation of the "exchange of winnings" covenant with Bercilak, Gawain reshapes his will and receives the confessional forgiveness he could not obtain at Castle Hautdesert. Having gained self-awareness and impelled his will to conform to the "goud wylle" of the Green Knight, Gawain accepts the knight's offer (2395–99) of the green girdle:

> 'Bot, your gordel' . . . 'God yow forȝelde!
> Þat wyl I welde wyth guod wylle, not for þe wynne golde,
> Ne þe saynt, ne þe sylk, ne þe syde pendaundes,
> For wele ne for worchyp, ne for þe wlonk werkkeȝ,
> Bot in syngne of my surfet. I schal se hit ofte,
> When I ride in renoun, remorde to myseluen
> Þe faut and þe fayntyse of þe flesche crabbed,
> How tender hit is to entyse teches of fylþe;
> And þus, quen pryde schal me pryk for prowes of armes,
> Þe loke to þis luf-lace schal leþe my hert.'
>   (2429–38)

Finally, it is with Gawain's positive acceptance and attainment of the quality of good will that the ethical and legal themes of the narrative are entwined in the form of a knot (2487–88), a reminder of Gawain's fault and an emblem of his new contractual obligation to God. The carefully wrought covenant contracts that shape so much of the poem's form and content thus not only reflect the poet's familiarity with contemporary forms of assumpsit but also represent a continuation of the covenantal theology upon which are founded the Old Testament stories of *Purity* and the New Testament parable of the workers in the vineyard in *Pearl*. Just as the similarities of covenants made in the courts of Arthur and Bercilak serve to join the seemingly disparate beheading game and temptation scenes, so the quality of "wylle" that underlies those contracts serves as a measure by which those courts may be judged and, in the end, contrasted. Appearing at every juncture within the poem, the voluntary faculty of "wylle" becomes both the source of and the solution to the contradictory web of contractual obligations that comprise the ethical dilemma at the heart of the poem.

Three

PARDON THE INTERRUPTION: THE MIRACLES OF GOD AND THE COVENANT OF *KYNDE*

"And þus ȝirneȝ þe ȝere in ȝisterdayeȝ mony" (529) says the poet as he concludes his famous description of the passing of the year in the second fitt of *Sir Gawain and the Green Knight*. And, indeed, few works seem as relentlessly self-conscious concerning the process whereby the present "ȝirneȝ" or glides into the past, a process that becomes a major theme within the poem. While the unfolding course of history encompassed in the four Cotton Nero poems provides the poet with the bulk of his subject matter, the poet's ultimate focus rests in those moments in the process when the ongoing development of civilization is altered—when the historical narrative is seemingly interrupted and where the workings of natural law appear to be suspended. To be sure, the poet begins that same passage by observing "A ȝere ȝernes ful ȝerne, and ȝeldeȝ neuer lyke; / Þe forme to þe fynisment foldeȝ ful selden" (498–99). And indeed the *forme* demonstrates a narrative focus that the *fynisment* does not, for the narrative emphasis in these lines is not so much on the process, the "ȝerning" or the universal passage of time that makes one calendar cycle like the next, but on the discontinuities, the "neuer lyke" and the unexpected, the gap between beginning and end.[1] In short, the poet's narrative interest here as well as in the rest of the canon lies in moments of miracles—those multitudes of "ferlyes," "sellyeȝ," "selcouths," "meruayles," and "wonders" that pervade the poems.[2] As we noted in the last chapter, the poet's view of history is a covenantal one—a series of formally structured agreements, "forwardes," and "couenauntes" that humans make between themselves and with which they bind themselves to God. Yet the emphasis here is on those instances when the contract is broken, abrogated, or suspended, when the Green Knight quitclaims what is owed or when God—through grace—insists not on the letter of the contract from human covenantal partners. As we noted in chapter 2, Jonah's anger in *Patience* is a reaction to God's merciful suspension of the strict "laws" of literal justice, "þaʒ [God] be myssepayed" (399), so long as there is true repentance on the part of the sinner. As we shall see, within the Cotton Nero poems, *kynde*—nature or the natural cycle, the unfolding of God's law such as the process in which all years "ʒerne"[3]—becomes the covenant or contract. What interests the poet are such moments where God, the creator of "Kynde," and Christ, who is "kyng of nature," disrupt the unfolding of the historical process, which has its first cause in the Creator himself.

For the *Gawain*-Poet, such watersheds in the historical process spring from two sources. *Kynde* is, in essence, the covenant of Creation along with its laws and parameters; when the laws of *kynde* or nature are violated or suspended by God, the result is termed a "meruayl" or miracle. Furthermore, when *kynde* is disrupted by "monkynde," as in the case of the Sodomites in *Purity*, the result is sin.[4] History, as the poet presents it, thus represents a series of such interruptions wrought, as we shall see in chapter 4, by the often conflicting hands of God and humanity.[5] As we survey the four poems, we will note that *Pearl* presents the reader with an explanation of *kynde* and divine process. *Purity* introduces the metaphor of the earthly miracle as the workings of God's "honde." *Patience* serves to define God's "hondewerk," and *Sir Gawain and the Green Knight* presents a tropologic argument on the use of hands and sin.

Inasmuch as Augustine and Aquinas shape so much of medieval theological and philosophical thought, these two writers provide the starting point for almost every serious discussion of miracles in an age devoted to the miraculous.[6] Augustine, for instance, defines a miracle as "Something difficult, which seldom occurs, surpassing the faculty of nature and going so far beyond our hopes as to compel our astonishment" (*De utilitate credendi*, 6.34).[7] Aquinas, who cites Augustine's definition of the miraculous, argues, "Now a miracle is so called as being full of wonder; as having a cause absolutely hidden from all: and this cause is God. Wherefore, those things which God does outside those causes which we know, are called miracles" (*Summa theologicae*, prima pars, Qu. 105, art 7).[8] Generally speaking, then, a miracle represents an incident, either *praeter* or *supra naturam*, wherein the laws of nature and principles of reason are

seemingly violated or held in suspension in order to generate wonder; the breaking and eventual transcendence of reason are the first
steps on the journey to faith.

Both Augustine and Aquinas, it should be noted, seem to divide
miracles into two parts. There is the direct intervention in the normal course of worldly affairs—Augustine's "something difficult" or
Aquinas's event "outside the causes which we know." Such events
find their source in God. A miracle, however, includes a second
component—the "astonishment" or "wonder" which the observation of that "something difficult" generates within those who observe it. Augustine, for whom miracles are primarily signs, goes so
far as to find that this wonder, rather than the altering of the laws of
nature, is the ultimate "purpose" behind a miracle:[9]

> The miracles performed by our Lord Jesus Christ are indeed di-
> vine works, and incite the human mind to the apprehension of
> God from things that are seen. . . . He has, agreeably, to His
> mercy reserved certain works, beyond the usual course and order
> of nature, which He should perform on fit occasion, that they,
> by whom His daily works are lightly esteemed, might be struck
> with astonishment at beholding, not indeed greater, but uncom-
> mon works . . . [so] that we might admire the invisible God
> through His visible works; and being raised to faith and purged
> by faith, we might desire to behold Him even invisibly, whom
> invisible we come to know by things visible. (*De utilitate cre-
> dendi*, xvi: 34)[10]

Such a sense of wonder or astonishment is precisely what is so
keenly felt in the Cotton Nero manuscript. When the contract of
kynde is broken, words, the substance of all such contracts, fail.
Miracles repeatedly cause the cessation of human speech, for *Pearl*'s
place "þer meruaylez meuen" (64) is the realm of the ineffable.
Whether in the well-known Old Testament miracles of *Purity* and
Patience or in Arthur's demand for "sum mayn meruayle" (94) and
the subsequent appearance of the Green Knight, all four poems are
filled with the miraculous. Not surprisingly, however, the most ostensibly "personal" of the poems, *Pearl*, with its unique first-person
narration, is the work in which that wonder is most intensely felt.
Pearl is also the poem in which the ineffability topos comes most
into play.[11] Few works, in fact, seem to capture that sense of won-

der as well as the dream vision of the self-styled Jeweler whose every
expectation is turned *vp-so-doun* in his encounter with his lost
"perle."[12] The poem itself takes its shape from the poet's skilled use
of that overwhelming wonder. The dialogue in which the Dreamer's
expectations are inverted is framed by two "progressions" of "meruayles" and "wonders." First, as the Dreamer awakens in the fantastic landscape of the dreamworld, he tells us that his spirit has gone
"In auenture þer meruayleȝ meuen" (64). When he describes the
dazzling landscape, "more meruayle con my dom adaunt" (157) after his attention is captured by the *Pearl*-Maiden, his lost daughter,
across the river. As his excitement reaches its apex, his attention is
drawn to the pendant, the "wonder perle wythouten wemme" (221)
which "A manneȝ dom moȝt dryȝly demme / Er mynde moȝt malte
in hit mesure" (223–24). Again "dom"—judgment or reason—is
overcome by wonder. Thus, on his spiritual journey,[13] the Dreamer
moves from a type of superficial wonder at the beauty of the landscape to a more personal and more keenly felt astonishment at the
sight of his daughter, until his attention is ultimately captured by
the pearl, a symbol of the salvation and personal apotheosis of the
Pearl-Maiden. The progression from simple wonder to the more
complex emotions felt by the Dreamer is delineated by Augustine
who states that miracles

> . . . are divided into two classes: there are certain ones that only
> evoke wonder, and there are certain others which win great fa-
> vor and good will. . . . For, if anyone should see a man flying, in
> that act would yield no advantage to the spectator beyond the
> sight itself, he would only marvel. But if anyone, afflicted by a
> serious or hopeless disease, should, at a command, at once re-
> gain his health, love for the one who healed him will transcend
> his wonder at the cure. (*De utilitate credendi*, xvi: 34)[14]

The progressive intensity of the wonder felt by the poem's narrator is reflected, moreover, in the increasing importance of the pearls
in the poem.[15] As gravel trod underfoot (81–82), those pearls are simply a part of an overwhelming scene. Like the everyday wonders of
Creation to which, according to Augustine, people have become in-
ured through constant exposure, the "perleȝ" simply go unnoticed,
having no more iconographical significance than the leaves of silver
or the gems of the riverbed. In the person of the narrator's lost daughter, the pearl is imbued with an emotional intensity previously lack-

ing in its use as a mere descriptive detail. Finally, seen as the "pearl of great price," the gem becomes the focus of the Dreamer's emotional climax and serves as a token of salvation, the subject of the theological debate that comprises the bulk of the poem.[16] As that debate ends, the poem concludes with a vision culminating in a second tripartite progression of wonders. After viewing the Heavenly Jerusalem, the Dreamer informs us that he felt "Anvnder mone so great merwayle / No fleschly hert ne my3t endeure" (1081–82). Despite his absorption in that marvel, his attention soon shifts to an even greater wonder: "So sodanly on a wonder wyse / I wat3 war of a prosessyoun" (1095–96). Finally, the progressive sharpening of the Dreamer's narrative focus is demonstrated in the approach of the Lamb of God: "Delit þe Lombe for to deuise / Wyth much meruayle in mynde went" (1129–30).

The parallels between these two series of wonders are readily apparent. The landscape of the first series becomes the setting of the city in the second. The Maiden of the first series becomes the procession, of which she is a member, in the second series. The pearl of great price is transformed into the Lamb, who is described as the Maiden's "perle." The first sequence of wonders is a microcosm of the second; as in *The Confessions*, the elements of personal history and a private miracle are expanded until they encompass all of human history. In each of the two series, the narrative focus is on the growth of wonder, on *wonder* and *meruayl* as psychological states produced by Augustine's "difficult actions" rather than as isolated phenomena or events.

Nevertheless, the violation of nature, the "difficult act," acts as the proximate cause of that wonder. As the Dreamer says of the "maskeles perle": "Þy beauté com neuer of nature; / Pymalyon paynted neuer þy vys, / Ne Arystotel nawþer by hys lettrure / Of carpe þe kynde þese properté3" (749–52). Since miracles are beyond both human art and understanding, the *Pearl*-Maiden is miraculous because her "properté3" are praeter, if not supra naturam, or, in Augustine's words, "surpassing the faculty of nature." Yet for Augustine and Aquinas, even such a straightforward definition of the miraculous posed serious problems. For example, how might the laws of nature be suspended if, as the poet notes in *Purity*, Christ is the "Kyng of nature" (1087) and if all nature finds its first cause in God? Can God act *contra naturam* if all that God wills is, by definition, the natural order of things? Augustine raises just such perplexing questions in *Contra Faustaum Manichaeum* by first noting that "God, the Author and Creator of all natures, does nothing contrary to nature; for whatever is done by Him who appoints all natural order and measure and proportion must be natural in every case" (*Contra Faustaum Manichaeum* 26.3).[17]

Aquinas, again building upon Augustine, pushes the proposition even further in the *Summa* by remarking, "Further, as the order of justice is from God, so is the order of nature. But God cannot do anything outside the order of justice; for then He would do something unjust. Therefore he cannot do anything outside the order of nature" (*Summa theologicae*, prima pars, Qu. 105, art. 6).[18] The inability of God to act contra naturam is, it would seem, a corollary of the immutability of the divinity.

Interestingly enough, the *Gawain*-Poet appears in similar fashion to argue that the divinity is bound by his own nature or *kynde*. Paralleling Aquinas's argument concerning justice, the *Pearl*-Maiden argues that God simply "may do noþynk bot ry3t" (*Pearl*, 496). The same theme finds expression in *Purity*, first in the proem where God is similarly circumscribed by his own nature: "And 3f he nere scoymus and skyg and non scaþe louied, / Hit were a meruayl to much; hit mo3t not falle" (21–22), and later, in the "Exhortation to Purity":

> Bot sauyour, mon, in þyself, þa3 þou a sotte lyuie,
> Þa3 þou bere þyself babel, byþenk the sumtyme
> Wheþer he þat stykked vche a stare in vche steppe y3e,
> 3if hymself be bore blynde. Hit is a brod wonder.
> And he þat fetly in face fettled alle eres,
> If he hat3 losed þe lysten, hit lyfte3 meruayle;
> Trave þou neuer þat tale, vnntrwe þou hit fynde3,
> Þer is no dede so derne þat ditte3 his y3en.
>
> (581–88)

As the poet says in a similar passage in *Patience*, "Hit may not be" (124); such contradictions would be real wonders, the breaking of the covenant of *kynde* in the truest or ultimate sense. God's grace, then, constitutes a miracle, for that is a suspension of the contract. Justice, the keeping of the letter of the law, is not miraculous, though paradoxically the mercy that is the wellspring of grace is the *kynde* of God, as God informs Jonah.

Nevertheless, the *Pearl*-Maiden does appear to transcend nature through divine will, and miracles do seem to violate the laws of *kynde*, so that Augustine observes:

> There is, however, no impropriety in saying that God does a thing contrary to nature, when it is contrary to *what we know of nature*. For we give the name of nature to the usual common course of nature; and whatever God does to the contrary to this, we call a prodigy, or a miracle. But against the supreme law of nature, which is beyond the knowledge both of the ungodly and the weak believers, God never acts, any more than He acts against Himself. (*Contra Faustaum manichaeum* 26.3, emphasis added).[19]

Similarly, Augustine also argues that "When events happen, they do not happen against nature *except for us*, who have a limited knowledge of nature, but not for God, for whom nature is what He has made" (*De genesi ad litteram* 6.13, emphasis added).[20] For Augustine, then, miracles produce only the *appearance* of the violation of natural law. What are suspended in miracles are not these immutable laws but rather the laws or the patterns deduced by human reason, laws that are as limited in their scope as the faculty that produced them.

What emerges within *Pearl* is a similar sense of two distinct natures—one relative and one absolute. The violation of the former is the stuff of miracles, the "difficult acts" that seemingly violate *kynde*. Significantly, the very first words uttered by the *Pearl*-Maiden set forth this dichotomy:

> For þat þou lesteȝ watȝ bot a rose
> Þat flowred and fayled as kynde hyt gef.
> Now þurȝ kynde of þe kyste þat hyt con close
> To a perle of prys hit is put in pref.
> And þou hatȝ called þy wyrde a þef,
> Þat oȝt of noȝt hatȝ mad þe cler.
> Þou blameȝ þe bote of þy meschef;
> Þou art no kynde jueler.
>
> (269–76)

There are, then, two natures or *kyndeȝ*—"the kynde of the rose" and the "kynde of þe kyste."[21] If the Jeweler is not "kynde," it is because he is not sufficiently aware of the "kynde of Kryst" (55)—the "kyste" that he notes teaches "comfort" (55) and remains firmly anchored in the *kynde* of his worldly reason.

Of these two *kynde3*, one—represented by the waking world at the beginning of the poem—is fettered in time. There the emphasis is on the progression of the seasons, on the harvest. This is the *kynde* of the passing of the year that "3irne3" so relentlessly in *Sir Gawain and the Green Knight* where time is a function of reason. The other *kynde*, however, is eternal and immutable. The landscape of this atemporal world lacks all traces of seasons or the passage of time. Devoid of time, it is also devoid of change. Here the laws of biological time, embodied in the natural relationship between father and child, are inverted through the Maiden's premature death and subsequent glorification. In the transcendent world of the parable of the workers in the vineyard, chronological expectations and concepts, such as first and last, are repeatedly turned *vp-so-doun*.[22] Viewed through the lens of worldly logic, the realm of the *kynde* of the *kyste* must always appear to be a land in which "meruayles meuen." Viewed in its own light, as it is through the eyes of the *Pearl*-Maiden, it is a realm where everything is natural—that is, everything flows directly from God, the source of nature.

Such seemingly temporal reversals of the atemporal *kynde* are precisely what the Dreamer finds so confounding to his reason and, hence, miraculous. To be sure, the limits of human knowledge fuel the wonder generated by the miraculous. The ignorance of the fool leads him to see wonders where there are none, as in the response of the "lewed" man to the eclipse that his limited understanding perceives as a violation of the natural law he knows through his observations. Such fools, according to Augustine, are the very ones for whom wonders are created: "And I call a miracle anything which appears arduous or unusual, beyond the expectation or abilities of the one who marvels at it, of which kind there is nothing better suited for the people and in general for fools than what affects the senses" (*De utilitate credendi* 16.34).[23]

Moreover, as Benedicta Ward points out in regard to the wonder Augustine associated with miracles, "There were three levels of wonder: wonder provoked by the acts of God visible daily and discerned by wise men as signs of God's goodness; wonder provoked in the ignorant, who did not understand the workings of nature and therefore could be amazed by what to the wise man was not unusual; and wonder provoked by genuine miracles . . ."[24]

Part of the poet's comic genius is his ability to employ this idea of the mistaken marvel and its relationship to the fool or "babel," as he is called in *Purity* (582); even though human beings cannot judge marvels properly, their myopic vision is turned into a source of "solas" as well as of "sentence." Jonah, in *Patience*, comically finds his call to preach to the Ninevites a "meruayl message" (81), not because it is a message from God but because the calling violates his expectations of what is safe and, above all else, what is reasonable. On the other hand, in a statement bordering on litotes, we are informed that when Jonah is swallowed by the whale, "lyttel wonder hit watȝ, ȝif he wo dreȝed" (256). Similarly, in *Sir Gawain and the Green Knight*, Lady Bercilak comically finds it a "wonder" (1481) that her guest is Gawain because he "conneȝ not of compaynye þe costeȝ vndertake" (1483). The entire poem is, moreover, dominated by the ambiguous status of the Green Knight as divinely sent wonder or as product of witchcraft.[25] After noting Arthur's custom of not eating until he has been told "Of sum auenturus þyng, an vncouþe tale / Of sum mayn meruayle" (93–94) or witnessed a mortal combat as Fortune dictates (96–99), the poet focuses upon the court's bewildered response to the Green Knight's physical appearance.

Awestruck by the knight's greenness (147–50), Arthur and his guests "had meruayle quat hit mene myȝt . . . / . . . such a hwe lach" (233–34).[26] Then, once the court scrutinizes the Knight more intensely, "Wyth al þe wonder of þe worlde . . . , / For fele sellyeȝ had þay sen, bot such neuer are" (238–39), the company dismisses the knight's apparent physicality as "fantoum and fayryȝe" (240). In the same vein, we are amused in *Purity* by the foolish judgment of Belshazzar that the writing of the hand on the wall is merely an example of "wychecrafte" (1560) and by the failure of the "clerkes" that "con dele wyth demerlayk and deuine lettres" (1561).[27]

In *Purity*, the apocalyptic judgment of God assumes linguistic form in the mysterious writing on the wall, a divine "warnyng þat wonder . . . þoȝt" (1504) to Belshazzar and his retinue. Although Belshazzar correctly identifies the fist's "purtrayed lettres" (1536) as a "ferly" (1529, 1563, 1629), he fails to perceive that the miraculous "speche þat spredes in þise lettres" (1565) springs from God. After the court clerks who "con dele wyth demerlayk and deuine lettres"

(1561) are unable to decipher the message, the proud monarch enlists the aid of the prophet Daniel "Þat hatʒ þe gostes of God þat gyes alle soþes" (1598). Since Daniel represents a man of faith, "His sawle is ful of syence, saʒes to schawe, / To open vch a hide þyng of aunteres vncowþe" (1599–1600). Once Belshazzar implores Daniel to unveil "þe wytte of þe wryt þat on þe wowe clyues" (1630), for "here is a ferly byfallen" (1629), the foolish king still views a miracle in terms of reason (1633–35). Even when Daniel carefully recounts for Belshazzar events of Nebuchadnezzar's life, thereby illustrating graphically the proper ordering between faith and understanding (1651–60 and 1701–8), the prophet concludes that Belshazzar "Seʒ þese syngnes wyth syʒt and set hem at lyttel" (1710). Because Belshazzar lacks a firm belief in God, both the "syngnes" (miracles) of divine power and the actual explication of the words on the wall are meaningless to him. In this particular episode, then, linguistic failure—the inability to read signs—and moral failure are inextricably linked as noted in chapter 1. Words are not only the bonds that unite members of society, as explained in the first chapter, but also the means of linking human beings to God. Paradoxically, as in the case of the clerks at Belshazzar's court, the benchmark of the fool is his reliance on reason, not because reason is foolish, but because the causes of miracles are "hidden" and therefore not accessible to reason. But human art and logic are certainly not, as the fool thinks, the boundaries of nature, which, as we are reminded in *Patience*, is the "hondewerk" of God rather than of humanity. Throughout the poem, human endeavor and, especially, artistry, are characterized by incompleteness and finitude. The work of God is, simply put, beyond human language, art, and deed.

This failure of reason to unravel the miraculous is explored, likewise, in *St. Erkenwald*, a fourteenth-century work occasionally attributed to the *Gawain*-Poet.[28] In one key speech, the offshoot of vision and prayer rather than of logic or scholastic inquiry, Erkenwald addresses this problem:

Hit is meruaile to men þat mountes to litelle
Toward þe prouidens of þe prince þat paradis weldes,
Quen Hym luste to vnlouke þe leste of His Myʒtes.
Bot quen matyd is monnes myʒt and his mynde passyde,
And al his resons are to-rent and redeles he stondes,
Þen lettes hit Hym ful litelle to louse wyt a fynger

Þat alle hondes vnder heuen halde myȝt neuer.
Þere-as creatures crafte of counselle oute swarues,
Þe comforthe of þe creatore by hous þe cure take.
And so do we now oure dede, deuyne we no fyrre;
To seche þe sothe at oure selfe ȝee se þer no bote,
Bot glow we alle opon Godde and His grace aske
Þat careles is of counselle and comforthe to sende,
And þat in fastynge of ȝour faithe and of fyne bileue.
I shal auay ȝow so verrayly of vertues His
Þat ȝe may leue vpon longe þat He is Lord myȝty.
And fayne ȝour talent to fulfille if ȝe him frende leues.
(160–76)[29]

The saint thus responds directly to his people's ill-conceived notion of what constitutes a miracle. Erkenwald, however, offers a negative solution to the problem of defining the miraculous, for although he suggests that transrational signs exist, he claims that
human wit is too limited to distinguish between true and false
"meruayles." Furthermore, numerous ideas traced in Erkenwald's
speech serve to join what has happened (the actions of the people)
with what is about to be revealed (the disposition of the judge). Since
the "reason" that guides both the people and the judge is proven
worthless, reason cannot represent a suitable "fundement" for
"New Werke" just as good deeds based on natural reason cannot
trigger the salvation of the pagan judge.

At the heart of *St. Erkenwald*, then, lies the very problem with
which Augustine begins *The Confessions*, his own great act of memory and conversion: whether it is first necessary to pray in order to
know God or to know God in order to pray. The significant issue remains, of course, the proper ordering between faith and understanding, a relationship best reflected in the Augustinian maxim, "Credo
ut intelligam." Since religious belief represents the pathway to
knowledge of the divine, Erkenwald reacts to the wonder vexing the
reason of the "clerkes . . . with crownes ful brode"(55) by going to
the church, not to the tomb. Furthermore, he prays for spiritual illumination as he "beseche[ȝ] his souerayn of his swete grace / To
vouche safe to reuele hym hit by a visioun or elles" (120–21). Faith
thus leads to understanding as "so longe he grette after grace þat he
graunte hade / An ansuare of þe Holy Goste and afterwarde hit
dawid" (126–27). Erkenwald's speech to the people then concludes

with his juxtaposition of faith and "counselle" and with a promise
that belief will spark true enlightenment (173–76).

As we have already noted, the limitation of reason and the di-
minishment of language are signs of the disruption of the contract
of *kynde* that constitutes miracles. Especially significant is the appearance of a particular figure of logic, "Arystotel"—whose method
produces logically deduced laws as a result of empirical observation,
laws that have their first causes in phenomena rather than in Platonic ideals.[30] At the heart of *Pearl*, then, is the Dreamer's unswerv-
ing faith in his own reason and in his ability to rely on observations
of the phenomenal world or, more accurately, to mold natural phenomena into verities.[31] The Aristotelian/empirical method produces the principles, Augustine's "ordinary course of human experience" (*Contra Faustum manichaeum* 26.3),[32] which the Maiden
and her account of the *kynde* of heaven seem to violate.

The limits of such a method are made clear as the *Pearl*-Maiden
tells the Jeweler:

> I halde þat jueler lyttel to prayse
> Þat loueȝ wel þat he seȝ wyth yȝe,
> And much to blame and vncortoyse
> Þat leueȝ oure Lorde wolde make a lyȝe,
> Þat lelly hyȝte your lyf to rayse,
> Þaȝ fortune dyd your flesch to dyȝe.
>   (301–6)[33]

So firm is his belief in reason that, as the Maiden indicates, the
Dreamer goes so far as to believe that God would "make a lyȝe" and
violate divine *kynde* rather than doubt his own rationally based
sense of temporal propriety (and, more importantly, Aristotelian
noncontradiction)[34] concerning the Maiden's status as queen and
the location of the earthly Jerusalem. To the Dreamer, the Maiden
either *is* the Queen of Heaven, or she *is not*. Similarly, Jerusalem is
either in Judea or it is in heaven. Neither the Maiden nor the city
can, according to logical laws of noncontradiction, be both. The
Dreamer's logic is, of course, singular, that of the man who "sette
[the Pearl] sengeley in synglure" (8).[35]

In response to his question of the simultaneity of queenship in
heaven, the Maiden tells him that the kingdom of God has a logic
defying "property in hyt self" (446) whereby all are crowned but

none are displaced. This reasoning, of course, is not one of the "properte3" of which Aristotle spoke (752), for empirical observation can never fully describe the "kynde of kyste," but only "the kynde of the rose," which can be mistaken for that of the *kyste*.[36] Along the same lines, Augustine, in his reply to Faustus during their debate over miracles as a violation of natural law, says, "People in error, as you are, are unfit to decide what is natural, and what contrary to nature" (*Contra Faustum manichaeum* XXVI.3).[37] Such would also be the case with the Dreamer in *Pearl* whose reliance on reason to articulate what is and is not "natural" leads inevitably to his confusion concerning what is and is not a miracle of God.

If the atemporal "kynde of the kyste," emblematic of the New Jerusalem, constitutes the focal point of *Pearl*, the "historical" poems that follow have as their subject the unfolding of *kynde* in time and space. This second nature, "the kynde of the rose," is symbolized by the earthly Jerusalem that appears in *Purity*. Yet it would be a mistake to view any of these three works as devoted to one *kynde* to the exclusion of the other, for the poet's particular interest lies in those moments of hierophany or miracles where the two *kynde3* intersect. Thus, in *Purity* the poet narrates a biblical history punctuated by "wondere3" and "ferlyes" and "meschefes mony þat meruayl to here" (1164). And, of course, the marvel-filled *Sir Gawain and the Green Knight*, "Þat a selly in si3t summe men . . . holden / And an outtrage awenture of Arthure3 wondere3" (28–29) takes place during an age of "werre, and wrake, and wonder" (16) when "Mo ferlyes on þis folde han fallen here oft / Þen in any oþer þat I wot, syn þat ilk tyme" (23–24).

As *Pearl* so clearly demonstrates, to be taught the meaning of the miraculous is to study the complex relationship between the creator, the first cause of nature/*kynde*, and his creation. In *Purity*'s "Exhortation to Purity," the strength of that bond is made clear in the poet's depiction of the Nativity, especially in the instinctual homage rendered to the infant Christ by the ox and the ass that "knew hym by his clannes for Kyng of nature" (1087).[38] An analogous submission of nature to God is seen in the immediate response of the whale and the elements in *Patience*, the poet's retelling of the book of Jonah. In fact, the very subservience of the "doumbe beste3" (516) who "cnawe [God] for Kyng, and [his] carpe leue" (519) is cited by the voice from the whirlwind as a reason for the preservation of the repentant city of Nineveh. As the tale of that reluctant prophet demonstrates, history is portrayed largely as a series of violations of *kynde*, as the failure of human beings to render the subservience offered by other parts of Creation to the Creator. Hence *Purity* teaches the value of "clannes" by describing the fates of the unclean; *Patience* teaches that virtue through the negative exemplum of the impatient Jonah.[39]

History, as depicted in *Purity*, begins with the rebellion of willful Satan who, we are told, acted "vnkyndely" (208) toward God. *Wylle* unchecked, as we saw in chapter 2, leads inevitably to the violation of *kynde*, the natural order of things, as it does with Satan. The rest, as they say, is history—a history repeated in Adam and in his descendants for whom, the poet informs us, "Þer watȝ no law . . . layd, bot loke to kynde" (263) but who foolishly "controeued agayn kynde contrare werkeȝ" (266) and so "ferly fowled her flesch" (269). Within *Purity*, one next finds the violation of *kynde* at Sodom where Lot offers to "kenne" the Sodomites "by kynde a craft þat is better" (865) by offering his daughters to the angry mob at his gates. It is of that "craft" that God speaks to Abraham: "I compast hem a *kynde crafte*, and kende hit hem derne, / And amed hit in myn ordenaunce oddely dere . . . / Wel nyȝe pure paradys moȝt preue no better" (697–98, 704).

True *kynde* is equated with paradise, the realm of the *Pearl*-Maiden or, at least, the neo-Platonic reflection of the Edenic state. Even in the destruction of Sodom, an image of Eden is evoked: "He sende toward Sodomas þe syȝt of his yȝen / Þat euer hade ben an erde of erþe þe swettest, / As aparaunt to Paradis þat plantted þe Dryȝtyn; / Nov is hit plunged in a pit like of pich fylled" (1005–8).

Sodom, which was like paradise, has now become its unnatural antithesis. As a result of Sodom's destruction, all that is left is a landscape "ded in hit kynde" (1016) and "corsed of kynde" (1033) where "alle þe costeȝ of kynde hit combreȝ, vch one" (1024)—unequivocal signs, "teches and tokenes" (1049), which reflect the violence done to *kynde* by the Sodomites themselves: "For lay þeron a lump of led, and hit on loft fleteȝ, / And folde þeron a lyȝt fyþer, and hit to founs synkkeȝ, / And þer water may walter to wete any erþe, / Schal neuer grene þeron growe, gresse ne wod nawþer" (1025–28). Yet if the violation of *kynde* is the mark of the sinful, a return to na-

ture provides a model whereby man might attain grace and shine
again through "penaunce taken, / Wel bryȝter þen þe beryl oþer
browden perles" (1131–32). Interestingly enough, the very figure of
spiritual renewal within the poem is Nebuchadnezzar, who must
live with the wild beasts of the field—among them the ass and the
ox, the same beasts whose natural submission to God was depicted
in the Nativity.[40] As a result of that penance, Nebuchadnezzar
"loued þat Lorde, and leued in trawþe / Hit watȝ non oþer þen he þat
hade al in honde" (1703–4).[41]

As we have already noted in our discussion of the convergence of
the sorrow-filled time of the Jeweler and the eternal timelessness of
the *Pearl*-Maiden's New Jerusalem, the poet is interested in the
places where divergent time schemes come together or, at least, are
parallel, and especially in the wonder that results when the phenomena of one temporal perspective are viewed in the light of another antithetical one. Such an alignment of time schemes may be
found, for example, in the introduction to the poet's description of
the passing of the seasons in *Sir Gawain:*

> Gawan watȝ glad to begynne þose gommeȝ in halle,
> Bot þaȝ þe ende be heuy, haf ȝe no wonder;
> For þaȝ men ben mery in mynde quen þay han mayn drynk,
> A ȝere ȝerneȝ ful ȝerne, and ȝeldeȝ neuer lyke;
> Þe forme to þe fynisment foldeȝ ful selden.
> Forþi þis ȝol overȝede, and þe ȝere after,
> And vche sesoun serlepes sued after oþer.
>
> (495–501)

The progression is so subtle as to be overlooked. We move from the
individual, Gawain, at a fixed point in time (the "begynn[yng]" of
his adventure) to an indeterminate end, to the way the species (men
as a whole) view and pass time, to the passing of time in the world
through the seasons of the year. Remarkably, within the brief space
of seven lines, all of these time frames—the individual, the cultural,
the natural—are brought into alignment, so that each informs or
gives meaning to the other. The passing of the seasons, presented as
an impersonal constant, suddenly takes on new significance because
this cycle of seasons, theoretically no different from any other,
marks the rush toward a particular "fynisment." While the progression of the seasons serves as a reminder of the ongoing, impersonal

process of nature, it simultaneously suggests the temporal finitude
of the individual who will meet death, that most personal of experiences, at the end of the year.

As the poet's treatment of these coincidental cycles might lead
one to suspect, there are within the poem two *kynde3* in which
those times are passed—the *kynde* of nature and the *kynde* of man.[42]
The *kynde* of nature is, of course, evident in the passing of the seasons. Arthur's court, however, represents the *kynde* of civilization,
containing as it does "Þe wy3test and þe worþyest of þe worldes
kynde" (261). Interestingly enough, Gawain's assessment of his sin
is that "For care of þy knokke, cowardyse me ta3t / To acorde me
wyth couetyse, my kynde to forsake / Þat is larges and lewté þat
longe3 to kny3te3" (2379–81).[43] Human *kynde* is, then, equated with
the courtly code that dictates knightly behavior, and as with the
kynde3 of God and nature in the earlier poems, the violation of
kynde is wonder. Thus Lady Bercilak says, "Sir, 3if 3e be Wawen,
wonder me þynkke3, / Wy3e þat is so wel wrast alway to god, / And
conne3 not of compaynye þe coste3 vndertake" (1481–83).

Of course, the knight beside her is Gawain "the light-of-love,"[44]
but there seems little wonder in that, except in her somewhat mocking eyes. Moreover, the same comic, if not mocking, approach to the
defining of the marvelous is seen in the poet's treatment of the
marches, a middle ground between Camelot and Hautdesert that
has much in common with *Pearl*'s land where "meruayle3 meuen."
For example, during Gawain's journey through this netherworld, we
are told of the great wonders encountered by the questing knight:

> At vche warþe oþer water þer þe wy3e passed,
> He fonde a foo hym byfore; bot, ferly hit were,
> And þat so foule and so felle þat fe3t hym byhode.
> So mony meruayl bi mount þer þe mon fynde3,
> Hit were to tore for to telle of þe tenþe dole.
> Sumwhyle wyth worme3 he werre3, and wyth wolues als,
> Sumwhyle wyth wodwos þat woned in þe knarre3,
> Boþe wyth bulle3 and bere3, and bore3 oþerquyle,
> And etayne3 þat hym anelede of þe he3e felle.
>
> (715–23)

At every turn there is a foe, and the foes are all "meruayle3," the gi-
ants and the creatures who often populate the marches. But the poet

says, "He fonde a foo hym byfore; bot, ferly hit were," and presents
us with a conundrum: it would be a wonder if Gawain found no foe
(hence, marvel) there, an obviously self-contradictory statement. As
in God's final speech to Jonah in *Patience*, the poet mirthfully plays
with the notion of wonder through litoteslike understatement by assuring us that while Gawain awaits the third stroke of the ax, "No
meruayle þaʒ hym myslyke / Þat hoped of no rescowe" (2307–8).
And there is Gawain's comically self-serving assessment of his own
fault as he attempts to narrate his own tale: "Bot, hit is no ferly þaʒ
a fole madde / And þurʒ wyles of wymmen be wonen to sorʒe"
(2414–15). Once again, wonder is to be found in the eye of the be-
holder or, at least, in what that eye sees as natural.

Whom, then, are we to trust concerning wonder, especially in a
world where there is no *Pearl*-Maiden nor even a voice from a whirlwind to pronounce what is and is not ultimately a *meruayl?* The ambiguity of wonder is manifest from the outset. Although the poet reveals his intention to portray wonder, he does so in the most
equivocal of terms. The audience is told that there are more "fer-
leyes" in Arthur's time than in any time since and that the tale is
one "Þat a selly in siʒt summe men hit holden" (28). The line is a
masterstroke of noncommitment, for the event is a "selly" in the
sight of *some* unidentified readers. Presumably, it is not a "selly" in
the sight of others. To which group might we assign such characters
as the Dreamer of *Pearl* and the impatient prophet of *Patience* who
have such a difficult time sorting out such matters? Are the "summe
men" who deem this event a "selly" the same ones who at Arthur's
court speak openly of the event as a marvel and judge the green intruder who is "half etayn" (140) a "fantoum and fayryʒe" (240) or
wonder, like the presumably whole "etayneʒ" (723) of the marches?
For his part, the narrator states that, if he had to judge, he would say
that the half-giant is not an elf but a "mon" (141). Is, then, the tale
that we are about to hear a "selly" at all?

Clearly, Gawain, like the rest of the court, believes that he is deal-
ing with the forces of magic. The Virgin is, of course, his first refuge,
but the pentangle is his attempt to gild the lily, in the person of the
Virgin. In essence, the pentangle is a spell to use against a spell
should the Virgin fail. Taken as a whole, the dual-imaged shield is
emblematic of Gawain's inability or refusal to define the wondrous
hue of the Green Knight as the work of either God or man. The

knight's further adaptation of the green girdle is borne of the same imperfect faith and is perhaps no more than an attempt to gild the already gilded lily. What one encounters here is an overwhelming sense of "adubbement," a sense born of a fundamental distrust of the adequacy of what lies beneath the adornment. This seemingly omnipresent decoration, as Robert Hanning has demonstrated, calls so much of the poem into question and keeps the ambiguity, which is the poem's theme, at the forefront of the reader's attention.[45]

Such concern with the proper classification of miracles becomes an important recurring theme in much late medieval thinking. One finds theologians and philosophers alike attempting to determine what miracles spring from God and what miracles stem from the devil or magicians, both of whom are credited with the ability to fashion the appearance of "meruayles" or of an alteration of *kynde*. So real was the problem that by the thirteenth century the occurrence of "miracles" no longer constituted sufficient evidence for initiating the canonization of saints, especially since both angels and the devil were perceived as capable of apparent suspensions of the laws of nature.[46] A less scholarly, although more authoritatively firsthand view of the "problem" is offered by the green-clad northern demon of the *Friar's Tale*, who boasts,

> "But whan us liketh we kan take us oon [a figure . . . determinat]
> Or elles make yow seme we been shape.
> Somtyme lyk a man, or lyk an ape,
> Or lyk an angel kan I ryde or go.
> It is no wonder thyng thogh it be so;
> A lowsy jogelour kan deceyve thee,
> And pardee, yet kan I moore craft than he."
>
> (3.1462–68)

The rod of Aaron, the staves of the Pharaoh's magicians, or even the tricks of a "lowsy jogelour": How can one know the difference between the handiwork of God and the actions of the devil or magicians? The very essence of this dilemma is outlined in Caesarius of Heisterbach's *Dialogue on Miracles*, wherein a miracle is "anything contrary to the course of nature at which we marvel." While miracles spring ultimately from God, they are performed "proximately *through evil spirits as well as through saints*" (emphasis added).[47] Gawain's shield, with its dual emblems, Christian and magical, suggests that its owner is as uncertain in his own mind as the reason-flummoxed *Pearl*-Dreamer, transported to the realm where "meruaylez meuen."

Such ambivalence about the miraculous is implicit in the rash request that initiates the Arthurian wonder in the first place. As the poet states, Arthur ". . . wolde neuer ete / Vpon such a dere day er hym deuised were / Of sum auenturus þyng, an vncouþe tale, / Of sum mayn meruayle, þat he myȝt trawe . . ." (91–94).

The vow is, of course, foolish and is the product of the "brayn wylde" of the "childgered" king not only for the reasons critics have often noted but also for its self-contradictory nature. The king is requesting a "meruayle" that he might "trawe" or believe—a transrational event that accords with human reason. What Arthur seeks, then, is a wonder that will not, in the Green Knight's words, "wyttez . . . reue" (2459)—an action that is the very purpose of the miraculous. The ambivalence in Arthur's desire for a miracle is just as apparent in Arthur's immediate reaction to the very "meruayle" he has sought:

> Þaȝ Arþer, þe hende kyng, at hert hade wonder,
> He let no semblaunt be sene, bot sayde ful hyȝe
> To þe comlych quene wyth cortays speche:
> "Dere dame, today demay yow neuer;
> Wel bycommes such craft vpon Cristmasse,
> Laykyng of enterludez, to laȝe and to syng,
> Among þise kynde caroles of knyȝtez and ladyeȝ."
>
> (467–73)

Although admitting that he has "sen a selly" (475), he compares the event to interludes—events that, although remarkable, are not real violations of *kynde* but only manipulations of appearance.[48] By terming the "selly" an "enterlude," Arthur robs the event of its significance as a sign and reduces it to entertainment, the work of human rather than divine hands.

What is and is not a wonder? What is great and what is small? Such questions of proportion become, for instance, the focus of Jonah's debate with God at the climax of *Patience*. In a telling exchange, the disembodied voice from the whirlwind chides the outraged prophet by asking, "Why art þou so waymot, wyȝe, for so lyttel?" (492), to which Jonah replies, "Hit is not lyttel . . . bot lykker to ryȝt" (493).

The semantic battle thus becomes the essence of the debate. And because it is in reality but "lyttel," Jonah will be told to have "no wonder" (496). In the same fashion, such semantic bargaining over the term "lyttel" plays a significant role in *Sir Gawain and the Green Knight* when Lady Bercilak offers Gawain the green girdle as she tells the knight, "Lo! so hit is littel, and lasse hit is worþy" (1848) before explaining its lifesaving magical properties. To the lady's commentary the narrator then slyly adds, "Þen kest þe knyȝt, and hit come to his hert / Hit were a juel for þe jopardé þat hym jugged were" (1855–56).

In an act of radical inflation, the girdle goes from being "little" to being valued as a "jewel," only to be subsequently diminished and semantically redefined in the final meeting with the Green Knight. And, of course, *Pearl* contains the Maiden's lengthy and rather pointed discourse about the proper judging of jewels and the parallel perception of God's wonders. Clearly the world of the *Gawain* poems is a world of wonder where one must know "kynde" and place it in proper perspective. Wonders, then, are interruptions of the covenantal laws—including those of order and proportion—moments when "lyttle" becomes great and violates the limits of our expectations. Such moments should serve, as they do throughout the *Gawain* poems, to remind us of the laws of *kynde*—the bond between falcon and falconer, to return to Yeats—as well as the ambiguity of the language with which they are constructed. If the history that the four poems encapsulate is, again, all that potentially exists within the spoken words of Creation, then miracles, because they are not contra naturam, demonstrate that the medium of creation leaves room for providence and free will, for the "kynde of þe kyste" as well as the "kynde of þe rose" as "ȝirneȝ þe ȝere in ȝisterdayeȝ mony."

Four

TOOLS OF THE TRADE:
THE HAND OF GOD,
THE HAND OF MAN

"Þenne byþenk þe, mon, if þe forþynk sore, / If I wolde help my hondewerk, haf þou no wonder" (495–96): with these words from the whirlwind, God reminds Jonah of the reason for the preservation of Nineveh by suggesting to the intemperate prophet that the city as well as its inhabitants are both parts of God's Creation.[1] It is the nature of God to preserve the city ("I may not be so malicious and mylde be halden," 522). Not to do so—to violate God's *kynde*—would be a wonder, but that is not the case here. The city, itself "selly of brede" (353), is a wonder—although we may, in light of the semantic play and logical gamesmanship discussed in chapter 3, ask from whose perspective and in whose terms? And, in fact, the Creator continues his discourse on the relation of the craftsman to his "hondewerk" by upbraiding the wrathful Jonah for his lack of perspective in regard to another piece of divine "hondewerk": "Þou art waxen so wroth for þy wodbynde, / And trauayledeʒ neuer to tent hit þe tyme of an howre, / Bot at a wap hit here wax and away at anoþer" (497–99). The mocking "þy wodbynde" along with five other uses of the informal second person in the succeeding lines calls attention to the gulf between Jonah and his Creator. To be sure, the spiritual chasm between the prophet and God is brought into high relief by the counterpuntal "my" that precedes "hondewerk" (496) as well as by the prominence of the first person throughout God's speech. In chapter 5, we shall examine the poet's careful manipulation of such pronouns, but suffice it to say that at this point, the conflict between God and Jonah over the woodbine is reflected in the tension and conjunction of the personal pronouns as this question of ownership is mirrored in the possessive pronouns, *my* and *thy*.[2]

In opposition to Jonah's lack of time in tending and, hence, diminished claim to the woodbine, God stresses his own patience in

the craft of making, contrasting his own "trauayl . . . of termes so
longe" (505) with the efforts of the prophet who "trauayledeȝ neuer
. . . þe tyme of an howre":

> "Fyrst I made hem myself of materes, myn one,
> And syþen I loked hem ful longe and hem on lode hade,
> And if I my trauayl schulde tyne of termes so longe,
> And type doun ȝonder toun when hit turned were,
> Þe sor of such a swete place burde synk to my hert,
> So mony malicious mon as mourneȝ þerinne."
>
> (503–8)

What occurs in this passage is a virtual inversion of the *Pearl*-
Maiden's parable of the workers in the vineyard, wherein the heavenly lord reverses the temporally based claims of the workers who
arrived earliest and labored longest. But the world of the Dreamer
is not the heavenly kingdom; it is an earthly, temporal one. In fact,
the error of the "first" workers in the parable was to apply temporal standards to questions of heavenly justice. Arguably, the lit-
eral-minded Jonah commits the same error in his demand for the
destruction of the earthly city. As we have seen in chapter 2, the
possession (and quitclaiming) of earthly objects—whether "wodbynde,"[3] axes, or green girdles—is a matter of contractual and legal
propriety for this poet. In essence, Jonah is informed that he has no
valid claim on the woodbine, for it is not his "hondewerk" despite
the prophet's earlier characterization of the blissful bower as his
property:

> "A, þou Maker of man, what maystery þe þynkeȝ
> Þus þy freke to forfare, forbi alle oþer,
> Wyth alle meschef þat þou may? Neuer þou me spareȝ?
> I keuered me a cumfort þat now is caȝt fro me,
> My wodbynde so wlonk þat wered my heued;
> Bot now I se þou art sette my solace to reue.
> Why ne dyȝtteȝ þou me to diȝe? I dure to longe."
>
> (482–88)

Jonah may have "keuered" himself some comfort, but the woodbine
is part of the world that was earlier described as "ilk crafte [God] carf
wyth his hondes" (131). Such appropriation of God's "hondewerk"
as one's own is, likewise, the sin of Nebuchadnezzar in his boasts
about his creation of the city of Babylon (*Purity*, 1663–68).[4] History,

as the poet presents it, is thus the "werk" of hands. The hand of God, then, molds the order of Creation and often contravenes the natural progress of "kynde" in order to create miracles in the temporal world. Juxtaposed with the hand of God are the often ineffectual hands of "monkynde," which at times go so far as to violate the laws of "kynde." Yet when human hands alter the course of "kynde," the result of such manipulation is sin, not miracles.

The contrast between the hand of God and the hand of humanity in the realm of miracles is certainly not original with our poet, for in the contemporary *St. Erkenwald,* already seen to parallel the *Gawain*-Poet's emphasis on wonder and miracle, one finds a passage that not only emphasizes the transrational nature of miracles at the heart of *Pearl* but provides a direct contrast between the finger of God that works miracles and the all-but-useless mortal hands:

> Hit is meruaile to men þat mountes to litelle
> Towarde þe prouidens of þe prince þat paradis weldes,
> Quen Hym luste to vnlouke þe leste of His myȝtes.
> Bot Quen matyd is monnes myȝt and his mynde passyde,
> And al his resons are to-rent and redeles he stondes,
> Þen lettes hit Hym ful litelle to louse wyt a fynger
> Þat alle hondes vnder heuen halde myȝt neuer.
>
> (160–66)

The helplessness of human hands so strikingly portrayed here finds a counterpart in the description of the sailors of *Patience* who, caught in the storm directed at the reluctant Jonah, discover they had "noȝt in her honde þat hem help myȝt" (222).

To be sure, the image of the hand of God—a favorite iconographical motif in fourteenth-century art and literature[5]—serves as an important unifying theme in the *Gawain*-Poet's depiction of the miraculous. The tradition has a long and varied history before the fourteenth century, reaching back to early Semitic art and literature as well as to the classical world.[6] For example, Quintilian, whose rhetorical arts are an integral part of the trivium, speaks grandiloquently about the semantic possibilities of hands as a part of human rhetoric, so that in the absence of words, the pantomime of hands becomes a vocabulary unto itself:

> . . . the hands may almost be said to speak. Do we not use them
> to demand, promise, summon, dismiss, threaten, supplicate, express aversion or fear, question or deny? Do we not use them to

indicate joy, sorrow, hesitation, confession, penitence, measure, quantity, number and time? Have they not the power to excite and prohibit, to express approval, wonder and shame? Do they not take the place of adverbs and pronouns when we point at places and things? In fact, though the peoples and nations of the earth speak a multitude of tongues, they share in common the universal language of the hands.[7]

In patristic sources, likewise, the image of the *dextra Domini*, the metonymic hand of God, is likewise well known. Hugh of St. Victor, for example, states that "The entire sense-perceptible world is like a sort of book written by the finger of God,"[8] whereas Bernard Sylvestris portrays the hand of God as the very instrument for the creation of history: "The events written down by the finger of the Supreme Scribe can be read as the text of time, the fabled march of events, the disposition of the ages."[9] Moreover, in the visual arts, the motif of the dextra Domini springs from a reluctance on the part of early Christians to represent the form of God the Father.[10] Spanning both the geographical and temporal boundaries of the Middle Ages, the dextra Domini is evident in such widely divergent works as the figure of the hand of God on the cover of the *Codex Aureus of St. Emmeram* (figure 1), the depiction of the tomb of St. Thomas the Apostle in the early fifteenth-century English manuscript, *On the Passion of Our Lord* (figure 2), and in the elegant miniatures of Old Testament prophets in the eleventh-century illuminated prophet book (Vatican gr 1153). Spreading westward from its eastern Mediterranean origins, the dextra Domini had a firmly established insular tradition, illustrated, for instance, in the lavishly illuminated *St. Albans Psalter* of the twelfth century.[11] The *Sacra Parallela* (Parisinus Graecus 923) (figures 3–10), a ninth-century Greek manuscript, though far from the provenance of the *Gawain*-Poet, is of interest because it conveniently brings together so many of the biblical figures and events found in *Purity*.[12] Several features of the *Sacra Parallela* miniatures deserve special note. So pervasive is the tradition of the metonymous right hand of God the Father that in figure 4, *The Curse of the Serpent, Eve and Adam*, the divine presence is represented simultaneously by *two* right hands. Especially important is that while the dextra Domini appears as an emblem of divine presence or even action—for instance, in the destruction of Sodom

Figure 1. "Hand of God," completed 870 A.D. Codex Aureus of St. Emmeram, Clm 14000, fol. 97v. By permission of Bayerische Staatsbibliothek, Munich.

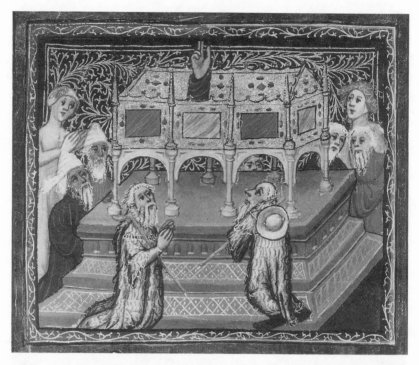

Figure 2. "The Tomb of St. Thomas the Apostle at Maabar," c. 1400. MS. Bodley 264, fol. 266v. By permission of the Bodleian Library, Oxford University.

(figure 8)—the divine hand is also an iconograph not just for the presence but for the voice of God as in figures 3–6 and 9.

As we have already seen in the debate between Jonah and the whirlwind concerning "hondewerk," this tradition of the dextra Domini is keenly felt in the Cotton Nero manuscript. Since the world, as ongoing instrument of "kynde," is viewed specifically as the "hondework" of God, frequent references to the creative power of God are presented in conjunction with the image of the hand. For example, in *Purity*, we are informed that Nebuchadnezzar, now a humble penitent, "loued þat Lorde and leued in trawþe / Hit watȝ non oþer þen he þat hade al in honde" (1703–4).[13] As already noted in *Patience*, when God calls upon the elements to bombard the ship carrying the fleeing Jonah, the Creator of "kynde" then "calde on þat ilk crafte he carf wyth his hondes" (131).[14] In both instances, Cre-

Figure 3. "Calling of Adam," early to mid-ninth-century. *Sacra Parallela,* Parisinus Graecus 923, fol. 149r. By permission of the Bibliothèque Nationale, Paris.

Figure 4. "Curse of the serpent, Eve and Adam," early to mid-ninth-century. *Sacra Parallela*, Parisinus Graecus 923, fol. 69r. By permission of the Bibliothèque Nationale, Paris.

Figure 5. "Covenant with Noah," early to mid-ninth-century. *Sacra Parallela,* Parisinus Graecus 923, fol. 356r. By permission of the Bibliothèque Nationale, Paris.

Figure 6. "Abraham Arguing with the Lord," early to mid-
ninth-century. *Sacra Parallela,* Parisinus Graecus 923, fol.
336r. By permission of the Bibliothèque Nationale, Paris.

Figure 7. "Lot Arguing with the Sodomites," early to mid-ninth-century. *Sacra Parallela*, Parisinus Graecus 923, fol. 307r. By permission of the Bibliothèque Nationale, Paris.

Figure 8. "Destruction of Sodom," early to mid-ninth-century. *Sacra Parallela,* Parisinus Graecus 923, fol. 307v. By permission of the Bibliothèque Nationale, Paris.

Figure 9. "Nebuchadnezzar Hearing a Voice," early to mid-ninth-century. *Sacra Parallela*, Parisinus Graecus 923, fol. 259r. By permission of the Bibliothèque Nationale, Paris.

Figure 10. "Nebuchadnezzar Praising the Lord." Early to mid-ninth-century. *Sacra Parallela*, Parisinus Graecus 923, fol. 259v. By permission of the Bibliothèque Nationale, Paris.

ation, itself the first miracle,[15] is expressly presented as the product of divine hands; moreover, the violation of the laws of Creation— unnatural storms, the whale swallowing and disgorging a man, the mysterious appearance of the woodbine—are, likewise, the products of the same divine instrument. Thus, in *Purity*, when Sarah laughs at the prediction that—contrary to nature—she will bear a son, God almost jokingly asks, "Hopeȝ ho oȝt may be harde my hondeȝ to work?" (663). Abraham also recognizes divine power, for, in bargaining with God concerning the destruction of Sodom, the patriarch first acknowledges the Creator who "al haldeȝ in þy honde, þe heuen and þe erþe" (734) before eliciting a provisional promise from the deity to "wythalde [His] honde for hortyng on lede" (740). Yet the hand of God not only punishes but spares humanity. When Jonah is cast into the sea in *Patience*, for instance, the power of God's mercy is revealed: "For nade þe hyȝe HeuenKyng, þurȝ his honde myȝt, / Warded þis wrech man in warlowes gutteȝ, / What lede moȝt lyue, bi lawe of any kynde, / Þat any lyf myȝt be lent so longe hym wythinne?" (257–60).

In some cases, however, the creative energy of God the Father is manifested by inhabitants of heaven—angels and beatified souls— who fulfill divine will. Through the protection of two angels in *Purity*, Lot is saved from a mob invading his home when the angels "by þe hondeȝ hym hent, and horyed hym wythinne / And steken þe ȝates ston-harde wyth stalworth barreȝ" (883–84). Then, just before the destruction of Sodom, the angels lead Lot, his wife, and daughters "by hande out at þe ȝateȝ" (941) of the city. Likewise, in *Pearl*, the Maiden is adorned with pearls "At honde, at sydeȝ, at ouerture" (218), emblematic of heaven and the immaculate nature of the beatified state. Finally, in *Purity*'s recapitulation of the parable of the wedding feast, the need for "schene schrowde of þe best" (170)— noble and pure actions—is emphasized in order for souls to gain *visio pacis*: "Þat þo be frely and fresch fonde in þy lyue, / And fetyse of a fayr forme, to fote and to honde, / And syþen alle þyn oþer lymeȝ lapped ful clene; / Þenne may þou se þy Sauior and his sete ryche" (173–76).

Yet if "monkynde" is made in the "forme"—both foot and hand— of the Creator, again we are reminded of the gap between "forme" and "fyniment" by the juxtaposition of the "hondewerk" of God and humanity.[16]

As with the dextra Domini, there is a rich visual tradition of the use of the human hand as both symbolic and "narrative" tool. An excellent example of such narrative iconography may be seen, for example, in the *St. Albans Psalter* where the often exaggerated, at times distorted, fingers and hand positions create a pantomimic action much in the tradition of the expressive hands described by Quintilian. In countless illuminations as well as carvings, the disposition of one's hands is an important symbolic indicator of one's disposition toward God and the words of his emissaries.[17] For example, the marginal sketch found in the eleventh-century manuscript Bodley 718 (figure 11) presents the traditional dextra Domini emerging from a nimbus/cloud, the two fingers extended in divine blessing. The human figure has his hands open, palms slightly upward in a gesture indicating a willingness to receive God's blessing. The placement of the human hands in relation to the dextra Domini, moreover, forms a visual circle that directs the viewer's eyes back to God. Similarly, the foregrounded figure in the early tenth-century depiction of Aldhelm presenting his book to the nuns at Barking (figure 12) stands hands open, ready to receive the codex. The fingers of her right hand, one might note, are slightly curled back, creating a sense of movement which directs the reader's eye back toward the recipients of the codex, thereby rendering the sense of "movement" or transmission of the text. A combination of these motifs is found in a mid-thirteenth-century illumination (figure 13) in which the hand of God directs the viewer's eye to the figure of Bernard or, more properly, the hands of Bernard. The saint's stylus, in turn, redirects our attention to two monks, one of whom holds a book, his own hands placed in a self-consciously "receptive" pose. The stylus then directs our line of sight to the heads of the two monks whose body lines, in turn, draw our eyes to the hands cradling the codex. The curiously placed right hand of the monk, with fingers curled slightly back, draws our eye upward, along the copying table, and back to the dextra Domini, thus again creating the dialogic circle of discourse with the divine. Yet despite their demonstrative function, the pose of these hands indicates willing reception as they are clearly cradling the text.[18] In a fourteenth-century historiated initial D(ixit Incipiens) (figure 14), one finds the hand of God directed at an unknown figure whose hands form another familiar pattern in medieval iconography. The right hand is raised toward the dextra Domini; the left is directed toward the intended audience, the fool. The hands of the presumably wise man thus serve as a conduit, a type of spiritual lightning rod that addresses or symbolically makes contact with the divine while the phenomenalizing left hand channels or redirects the divine to the world—the two fingers indicative of blessing being translated into the single extended finger that constitutes the pantomimic equivalent of human discourse. Yet the intended audience, the fool or, perhaps, the "babel" of chapter 3, stands not with hands open to receive but with the left hand raised, pointing away from the dextra Domini, in interruptive contradiction to the hand of the speaker.[19] The fool's right hand is awkwardly pulled away as far as possible from the instructive hand of the wise man, and is already filled, closed tightly around his fool's staff. The visual focal point of the illumination, then, is a triangle composed of the pair of human hands, consisting of the wise man's right hand and the fool's left, and completed by the dextra Domini.

A similar configuration of a costumed fool can be seen in another Bodleian manuscript (figure 15), wherein the fool again raises his hand, his index finger extended to a "superior," this time to a monarch. The fool here is not, as in King Lear, a sage because he speaks wisdom to his betters but, instead, is a fool precisely because he does speak. Here the iconographic fool inverts the natural order by raising his hand and partially closing his fingers to speak when they should be open to receive. In contrast to the fools of figures 14 and 15, the kneeling cleric in yet another historiated initial D (figure 16) extends one hand with its palm open to receive the word of God while the other hand, with finger extended not toward God in the attitude of the fool, but toward his own mouth, thereby directs the word of God to his own lips. This attitude on the part of this last figure is clearly a variation of the same pantomimic gestures exhibited by Moses as he speaks with the Lord in Sacra Parallela (figure 17), again demonstrating the transmission of the iconographic tradition from the early Christian eastern Mediterranean to late medieval western Europe. Even more significant for the study of Purity are two figures of Nebuchadnezzar contained in the Sacra Parallela (figures 9 and 10). In the first, the arrogant Nebuchadnezzar hears a voice but in his pride raises his hand, like the fool, as if to speak. In the second illustration, however, the now chastened king praises God with his own hands open in a posture of reception much like

Figure 11. Marginal figure, early eleventh century. MS. Bodley 718, fol. 28v. By permission of the Bodleian Library, Oxford University.

Figure 12. "Aldhelm Presents His Book to the Nuns of Barking," c. 1000. MS. Bodley 577, fol. 2v. By permission of the Bodleian Library, Oxford University.

Figure 13. Saint Bernard, mid-thirteenth-century. MS. Laud Misc. 385, fol.
41v. By permission of the Bodleian Library, Oxford University.

that seen in figure 11. In the intercourse between men, such as *Purity*'s Nebuchadnezzar, and the Word, it is clearly better to receive
than to offer, better to approach God with hands open than with a
lecturing finger extended, complaining and scolding like Jonah in
Patience.

  A late fourteenth-century depiction of Christ before Pilate (figure
18) demonstrates not the hands of the fool, but the hands of those

Figure 14. Initial D (*Dixit incipiens*), early fourteenth century. MS. Ashmole 1523, fol. 66. By permission of the Bodleian Library, Oxford University.

who would in the *Pearl*-Maiden's words do "hondelyngeʒ harme" (681). The illumination presents the judgment of a rather lifeless Christ who, positioned slightly right of center, stands with hands crossed in an almost passive, drooping manner. Indeed, the almost receding figure of Christ is virtually framed by the violent interlace of arms and accusatory hands that dominate the picture. In complete counterpoint to Christ's inert hands is the virtual cacophony of—in some cases—the grotesquely turned hands of his tormentors. Al-

Figure 15. Initial D (*Dixit incipiens*), early fourteenth century. MS. Douce
b. 4, fol. 4a. By permission of the Bodleian Library, Oxford University.

though almost all of the hands are worth noting, special attention
might be paid to the tension in the spread fingers of the hand placed
on Christ's left arm, thereby creating a stark contrast to the passive
hands of Christ. Moreover, those peculiarly twisted fingers direct
the viewer to Christ's head which is virtually ringed by hands cast
in grasping or accusatory poses. Christ's eyes then direct our atten-

tion toward Pontius Pilate and yet another knot of hands in conflict-ing and violent poses. The prominence of hands as a narrative, struc-turing device here is hardly surprising. Indeed, hands are so much a part of the story of the Crucifixion—whether Pilate's, Judas's, or the crucified hands of Christ—that they are frequently portrayed in the common medieval iconograph of the *arma Christi*, the instruments or elements of the Crucifixion (figure 19).[20]

That the rudiments of this pantomimic vocabulary of hands were known within the provenance of the poet is, in fact, evident within the Cotton Nero manuscript, although its illustrations clearly can-not be counted as the work of the poet. While the ten illuminations contained in the manuscript have consistently been described as "crude," both advancing and departing from the text of the works they illustrate, the majority of these pictures do demonstrate a con-sistent knowledge of the iconographic principles noted in our previ-ous figures.[21] For example, the four illustrations taken from *Pearl* employ a set of manual "gestures" in order to narrate pictorially the Dreamer's psychological movement from receptiveness, to foolish error, to repentance.

In the first of the illustrations (figure 20), the Dreamer lies asleep ready to receive his vision, his hands open in a receptive manner somewhat parallel to those of the open handed receptors of God's word in figures 9, 12–14, and 18. In the second Cotton illustration (figure 21), the Dreamer has awakened into the dreamworld and stands in the iconographically familiar pose of the wise man or me-diator as he extends his right hand with a finger pointing upward and the counterbalancing left hand motioning toward the ground.[22] In the third (figure 22), the Dreamer has adopted the position of the ba-bel or fool, with left index finger extended, presumably having his "tale mysetente" (257). The *Pearl*-Maiden's hands are raised, palms outward, in a clear gesture of rejection. In the poem's final illustra-tion (figure 23), the Dreamer's hands are in the posture of the orant/supplicant, a posture also displayed by one of Noah's sons (figure 24)[23] and by the repentant Ninevites (figure 25). While the *Pearl*-Dreamer's hands are in figure 23, likewise, extended in sup-plication, the Maiden's hands are posed like those of the wise man, who, as we have seen, extends his left hand to lecture while holding his right hand heavenward toward the source of his wisdom. In this case, the Maiden's left hand is directed toward the supplicant

Figure 16. Initial D (*Dixi custodium*), late fourteenth century. MS. Rawl.
G. 185, fol. 32v. By permission of the Bodleian Library, Oxford University.

Dreamer while the right is placed over her heart. The placement of
her right hand is singularly apt because, as a bride of Christ and a
Queen of Heaven, she already resides in the celestial Jerusalem, dis-
pensing rather than receiving the Word, in effect serving as a mirror
image or reversal of the kneeling figure in figure 18. The Maiden's
pose is similar to those of both Jonah and Daniel (figure 26), captured
preaching arms extended, with outsized hands and extended fingers.
Jonah, the dominant and, hence, disproportionately large figure,
much like St. Bernard in figure 13, directs his hands toward those of
the female orant. In figure 26, Daniel, with even more outsized

Figure 17. "Moses Speaking with the Lord," early to mid-ninth-century. *Sacra Parallela,* Parisinus Graecus 923, fol. 336r. By permission of the Bibliothèque Nationale, Paris.

Figure 18. "Christ before Pilate," late fourteenth century. MS. Lat. liturg. e 41, fol. 40v. By permission of the Bodleian Library, Oxford University.

hands, adopts the same two-handed pose as Jonah. Yet while Jonah's hands lead, almost meet, the hands of the repentant Ninevites and form a visual track that eventually leads back to the prophet, Daniel lacks an audience. Daniel's movements direct the reader's gaze toward the ground and away from Belshazzar for whom the message is, within the text, lost. For his part, Belshazzar stands in the mediating position, right arm raised, left hand and index finger extended toward Daniel. As in *Purity*, he is simply an intercessor through whose agency the writing is made available to Daniel for translation. Yet Belshazzar is, within the text of *Purity*, cut off from both God and the prophet, so in the illustration, he is outside the axis created by Daniel and the hand of God, clearly a dextra Domini,

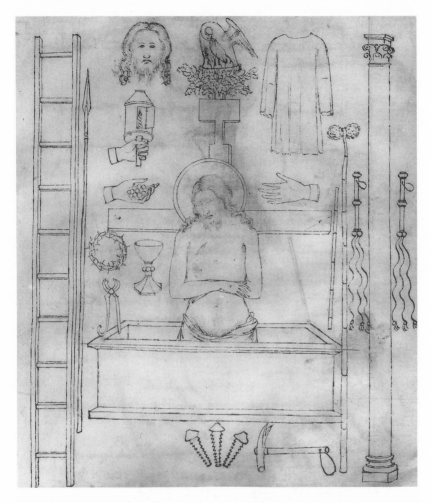

Figure 19. "Christ as Man of Sorrows with *Arma Christi*," 1400–1409. MS. Canon. Class. Lat. 80, fol. 36. By permission of the Bodleian Library, Oxford University.

which "faces" away from him and whose stylus likewise draws the viewer's line of sight to the upper left, away from the monarch. To Belshazzar's right is, as we have noted, Daniel who draws our line of sight to the lower right so that the dual eye tracks of the dominant hands lead away from Belshazzar, leaving him "isolated."

This same dichotomy between human hands and those of the Creator is strikingly in evidence in the poet's textual delineation of the "ferly," which occurs at Belshazzar's feast in *Purity:*

> His cnes cachches to close, and cluchches his hommes,
> And he, wyth plattyng his paumes, displayes his lerms,
> And romyes as a rad ryth þat rore3 for drede,
> Ay biholdand þe honde, til hit hade al grauen,
> And rasped on þe ro3 wo3e runisch saue3.
> $$(1541-45)^{24}$$

Although the mysterious "honde" appearing at the feast is certainly part of the poet's source, the explicit contrast between the impotent palms of Belshazzar pressed helplessly together and the handwriting on the wall is not to be found in the book of Daniel. In fact, of the nineteen references to hands, palms, and fingers, which recur throughout *Patience* and *Purity,* all but a scant three constitute the poet's presumably deliberate additions of this motif to his source and as such would seem to provide a striking piece of evidence indicating his thematic intent.

Specifically, Belshazzar's fear of the hand's fingers—"For al hit frayes my flesche, þe fyngres so grymme" (1553)—serves as a counterpoint to the poet's praise of the healing powers of Christ's "fyngeres" (1103), that perplexing symbol in the "Exhortation to Purity":[25]

> For whatso he [Christ] *towched* also-tyd tourned to hele,
> Wel clanner þen any crafte cowþe devyse.
> So clene wat3 his *hondelyng,* vche ordure hit schouied;
> And þe *gropyng* so goud, of God and Man boþe,
> Þat, for fetys of his *fyngeres,* fonded he neuer
> Nauþer to cout ne to kerue wyth knyf ne wyth egge.
> Forþy, brek he þe bred blades wythouten,
> For hit ferde freloker, in fete, *in his fayre honde,*
> Displayed more pryuyly when he hit part schulde,
> Þenne alle þe toles of Tolowse mo3t ty3t hit to kerue.
> $$(1099-1108)$$

Moreover, the image of the hand which so successfully draws together the seemingly disparate sections of *Purity* also links that poem directly with *Pearl.* The latter poem ends, appropriately enough, with the focus on Christ "Þat, in þe forme of bred and wyn,

Figure 20. "The Dreamer Asleep," late fourteenth century. MS. Cotton
Nero A.x., fol. 41. By permission of the British Museum, London.

Figure 21. "The Dreamer Awakens," late fourteenth century. MS. Cotton
Nero A.x., fol. 41b. By permission of the British Museum, London.

Figure 22. "The Dreamer Sees the Maiden," late fourteenth century. MS. Cotton Nero A.x., fol. 42. By permission of the British Museum, London.

Figure 23. "The Dreamer Debates the Maiden," late fourteenth century. MS. Cotton Nero A.x., fol. 42. By permission of the British Museum, London.

Figure 24. "Noah on the Flood," late fourteenth century. MS. Cotton Nero A.x., fol. 60. By permission of the British Museum, London.

Figure 25. "Jonah Preaching to the Ninevites," late fourteenth century. MS. Cotton Nero A.x., fol. 86b. By permission of the British Museum, London.

Figure 26. "Daniel and the Writing on the Wall," late fourteenth century. MS. Cotton Nero A.x., fol. 6ob. By permission of the British Museum, London.

/ Þe preste vus schewe3 vch a daye" (1209-10). The emphasis here seems to be on transubstantiation—Christ as bread and wine[26]—a subject that itself was an integral part of the medieval debate over miracles. Significantly, *Purity*—the poem that immediately follows *Pearl* in the Cotton Nero manuscript—begins with a consideration of the priests who "hondel [at the altar Christ's] aune body" (11), the Eucharistic wafer, the marguerite or "pearl." Moreover, the same image of the hand connects *Pearl* with *Patience,* especially since the *Pearl*-Maiden notes that those who shall enter the community of the saved include individuals who "Hondelynge3 harme . . . dyt not ille" (681). In *Patience,* one reason for the preservation of Nineveh is the existence of a group of innocents:

> And of þat soumme 3et arn summe, such sotte3 formadde,
> As lyttel barne3 on barme, þat neuer bale wro3t,
> And wymmen vnwytté, þat wale ne couþe
> Þat on hande fro þat oþer fol, alle þis hy3e worlde.
> Bitwene þe stele and þe stayre disserne no3t cunen,
> What rule renes in roun bitwene þe ry3t hande
> And his lyfte, þa3 his lyf schulde lost be þerfor.
>
> (509-15)

The inability to distinguish the right hand from the left is equated here with innocence of spirit. Such "unwytting" lack of reason identifies these people with the beast of "kynde" who knew God "for Kyng." Finally, since a number of Ninevites are unable to construct ethical distinctions—the choice of hands—these citizens are released from culpability, thereby staying God's hand. What emerges here is a seemingly antirational bias since salvation seems to be the property of those without reason (children and beasts) or those who have transcended it (ecstatics and visionaries).

So important is the question of the status of one's hands that this issue becomes the benchmark of morality in both *Purity* and *Patience.* Those who have clean hands—such as the sailors who in *Patience* specifically fear "blend[yng] her hande3" (227) with innocent blood—are set against those in *Purity* who "conterfete crafte" (13)—that is, who violate *kynde* by bearing the sacrament with unclean hands. It is perhaps worth noting that in the manuscript illustration of this scene (figure 27) the original visual focal point is not Jonah who is somewhat obscured by the water, but the outsized hands of the sailor lowering the prophet into the sea. Returning to figure 25, the illustration of Jonah preaching to the Ninevites, we see the same iconographic use of hands to separate the worthy from the sinful, this time as a means of classifying the members of the audience who listen to Jonah's prophecy. As Jonah, himself portrayed with out-sized hands, preaches, the two figures closest to him extend their hands either to pray or to receive his message, much as we saw in figures 3–5, 10–13, 16, and 17. What is of particular interest is the figure to their right who, though with face turned toward the speaking prophet, has his body and specifically his hands turned away from Jonah in a clear attitude of rejection where the earthly text stands in opposition to the spoken word of God. Indeed, one might explicitly contrast this figure's posture with that of the receivers of the Word in figure 13. Noting the blue fool's cap, Paul Reichardt has not only associated this figure with the "fool," but has further linked this figure of rejection with the sleeping Dreamer who in figure 20 is likewise portrayed as wearing a rather exaggerated blue hood.[27]

To be sure, in *Purity* the evildoers—those whose hands are bound by sin (155)—are explicitly portrayed as those with "handeȝ vn-waschen" (34), which are themselves equated with the "harlateȝ hod" (34). In contrast to the hands of the bishops who, we are twice told, created the vessels of the temple (1445, 1718) are the hands of the Babylonian king, Belshazzar, who, as we are told in *Purity*, wor-shipped idols of "stokkes and stones" (1343, 1523, 1720)—nature ("kynde") perverted—which constituted "fals fantummes of fendes, formed with handes" (1341). Thus, the conflict is framed between the hands of Belshazzar whose "werk" is the idols and the hands of the bishops whose "werk" is the vessels. Ultimately, the "honde-werk" of which the prince of Babylon is most proud, however, is the city itself which the narrator twice calls a "wonder" (1381, 1390). Yet there cannot help but be a touch of irony here, as in several other of the poet's uses of that term, especially since the poem that pre-cedes *Purity* has already presented an apocalyptic vision of the Heav-enly Jerusalem, a true city of wonder. Moreover, in the succeeding poem, *Patience*, God will point to the city of Nineveh and term it "my hondewerk" (496), a microcosm of the world that we have al-ready been told "he carf wyth his hondes" (131). So the "wonder" city of the Babylonian king of *Purity* is dwarfed on either side by re-

Figure 27. "Jonah and the Whale," late fourteenth century. MS. Cotton
Nero A.x., fol. 86. By permission of the British Museum, London.

minders of the unequal works of God and humanity. At the end of *Patience*, however, the message becomes especially clear. Not only does God claim the city, in the broadest sense of the term, as the work of his hands but he also asserts, "If I wolde help my hondewerk, haf þou [Jonah] no wonder" (496).

Included in the Cotton Nero manuscript's two overtly biblical poems, then, is a clear, conventional use of this iconographic motif of hands—the poet's deliberate addition to his source material. Although there is no immediate source for us to compare with *Pearl*, we find at the beginning of that poem the Dreamer clasping his hands (49) as a sign of human impotence and spiritual bleakness, an action somewhat reminiscent of Belshazzar (1542) in *Purity*. Even more strikingly, in *Pearl* the poet explicitly contrasts the sinful hands of the human shearer, the potential violator of the Lamb of God (802), with the martyred hands of the crucified Christ, "he on rode þat blody dyed, / Delfully þur3 honde3 þry3t" (705–6), thus recalling the visual contrast seen earlier in the portrayal of the judgment of Christ by Pilate (figure 18) and the *arma Christi* (figure 19).

To be sure, *Pearl*'s contrasts between the "clypper" as handheld weapon and the wounds of the Prince of Peace are strikingly brought together in the person of the Green Knight whose ax and holly bob constitute the embodiment of the conflict of *kynde3*, particularly in the "game" he offers to the court:

If any so hardy in þis hous holde3 hymseluen,
Be so bolde in his blod, brayn in hys hede,
Þat dar stifly strike a strok for anoþer,
I schal gif hym of my gyft þys giserne ryche,
Þis ax, þat is heué innogh, to hondele as hym lykes,
And I schal bide þe fyrst bur, as bare, as I sitte.

(285–90)

Like the mysterious words written on Belshazzar's wall, both the "lettre" and "tyxte" of this challenge—ostensibly an offer to exchange blows *with* the "giserne ryche"—need careful explication. Although the Green Knight's proposal is articulated forcefully, his reference to a particular weapon remains shadowy. There is, indeed, an offer of exchange of blows, but the weapon for exchange is unspecified. The ax is merely a "gyft," a reward or prize for participation in the "Christmas game"—like the "hondeselle"(66)/

"3iftes"(67) of the opening scene—and is not necessarily the
specified instrument for implementing the exchange. Indeed, that
such an exchange might be made without either violence to or ill
will on the part of the "loser" has already been made clear in the
poem's first reference to "hondeselle[s]":

> And syþen riche forth runnen to reche hondeselle,
> 3e3ed '3eres-3iftes' on hi3, 3elde hem bi hond,
> Debated busyly aboute þo giftes.
> Ladies la3ed ful loude, þo3 þay lost haden,
> And he þat wan wat3 not wrothe; þat may 3e wel trawe.
>
> (66–70)[28]

The ax is certainly an option in the "game" offered to the court,
but as the Green Knight states, it is the property of the challenger to
"hondele as hym lykes" (289).[29] Furthermore, the knight's sum-
mons, as we have argued in the second chapter, reflects the imprint
of a medieval covenant, whereas his ax suggests the romance equivalent of a *wed* or tally stick—a legal symbol of "the covenantor's voluntary acceptance of an obligation (indebtedness)."[30] In this light,
the ax's role in the "game" is diminished even further in its function as a sign of debt or obligation rather than as an actual instrument for the execution of the quid pro quo.

To appreciate the deliberate ambiguity in the game at hand, one
need only turn to the ceremonial restatement of the challenge and
the Green Knight's comments on equality. Gawain, for example,
initiates the transfer of covenantal indebtedness from the knight to
himself when he reiterates the terms of the bargain: "In god fayth
... Gawan I hatte, / Þat bede þe þis buffet, quatso bifalle3 after, / And
at þis tyme twelmonyth take at þe anoþer, / *Wyth what weppen fo
þou wylt,* ..." (381–84).

Although Gawain fails to perceive it, the choice of weapons offered to his opponent (384) reflects the implied selection of weapons
presented in the knight's original challenge. Somewhat later, however, the Green Knight underscores the concept of equal blows, for
he urges Gawain to "foch ... such wages / As þou deles me today"
(396–97) and "fotte / Such a dunt as þou [Gawain] hat3 dalt" (451–52).
Then employing a type of moral cause and effect argument, the
knight concludes by noting that Gawain deserves the type of stroke
he will receive—"disserued þou habbe3 / To be 3ederly 3olden"
(452–53)—because of the nature of the blow Gawain has dealt.

What, then, are the options for which Gawain is held so publicly accountable? What other "dunt" or "wages" might Gawain have offered? The answers to such questions, perhaps, may be found in the Green Knight's phrase, "to hondele as hym lykes" (289)[31]—a phrase that recalls the *Pearl*-Maiden's assertion that the saved include those who "Hondelynge3 harme . . . dyt not ille" (*Pearl*, 681). The ability to distinguish the right hand from the left has already been presented at the end of *Patience* (509–15) as a metaphor for the ability to make moral choices for which the individual is accountable. Many of the citizens of Nineveh, it will be recalled, were released from personal culpability for their behavior for the very reason that they could not formulate such ethical distinctions. Gawain, however, is both of an age and a state of mind that he bears responsibility for his actions and his choices. Thus, at Bercilak's court, Gawain "chooses" between his host's wife and "Anoþer lady . . . [that she] lad bi þe lyft honde" (947). Once Gawain leaves Hautdesert, the knight-errant again faces two alternatives—fleeing to Camelot or proceeding to the Green Chapel located "on . . . [his] lyfte honde" (2146). Similarly, when encountering the Green Knight at Arthur's court, Gawain must select either the right hand or the left, for, as the narrator informs us, the knight holds two objects in his hands: "Bot in his on honde he hade a holyn bobbe, / Þat is grattest in grene when greue3 ar bare, / And an ax in his oþer, a hoge and vnmete, / A spetos sparþe to expoun in spelle, quoso my3t"[32] (206–9). The narrative focus is clear, and, in fact, the poet continues on for another twelve lines describing the weapon. That the narrator should focus upon the ax is natural, for he presents the green intruder through the eyes of the court which, in effect, sees only the ax and assumes that the Green Knight has come to crave a fight similar to the one sought by Arthur before he sits down to his meal. Yet despite the descriptive imbalance in the narrative, there are two hands holding two objects.

Returning once again to the Green Knight's parting words concerning accountability and the equal exchange of blows, we should note that the holly bob, so trivialized by the narrator and ignored by the members of the court, may represent the solution to the open-ended game proposed by the Green Knight. As we have suggested, the knight's challenge is linked with identical blows, and the ax is designated as a "gyft" for participation in the "gomme," not as the instrument for the exchange of strokes. Presumably, then, Gawain could have wielded the holly sprig as a weapon. Certainly, then, his fetching of a "dunt as [he] hatʒ dalt" and "such wages as [he] deles" would have been a less somber affair. Whatever kind of fate this Yuletide emblem may suggest to Gawain, he is presented with a moral choice symbolized by a riddle whose solution requires that he differentiate one hand from the other, a fact confirmed by the description of Arthur's acceptance of the challenge as a response to the Green Knight's hand: "Lyʒtly lepeʒ he hym to, and laʒt at his honde" (328). Here, as when the Green Knight "Withhelde heterly his honde" (2291) at the second stroke, the narrative focus is on the hand, not on the ax. Within this poem, "honde[ʒ]" are the metonymic instruments that "dele . . . destiné (2285), as Gawain attests on his return to Camelot when he displays the nick "þat he laʒt, for his vnleuté, at þe leudes hondes" (2499). Moreover, when Arthur turns over the ax to Gawain during the initial challenge, the king gives the following ironic advice, " 'Kepe þe, cosyn,' quoþ þe kyng, 'þat þou on kyrf sette, / And if þou redeʒ hym ryʒt, redly I trowe / Þat þou schal byden þe bur þat he schal bede after' " (372–74). The surface meaning is plain enough; the king is urging Gawain to make the blow a lethal one so that receiving the return blow will not be a problem. The irony here is that Arthur unwittingly provides Gawain with the answer to the test that the king, himself, has just failed. The secret to being able to "byde þe bur" is, as we argued in chapter 1, to "rede" the Green Knight "ryʒt"—which, in this case, is to read the hands and see the holly bob. Thus, as he introduces Arthur's ironic advice, the narrator compounds the irony by wryly informing his audience that the king "lyfte vp his honde / And gef hym Goddeʒ blessyng, and gladly hym biddes / Þat his hert and his honde schulde hardi be boþe" (369–71).

As if to frame the king's advice with the very symbol the king has overlooked, the poet then reminds us of the proper handling of the game, "Gawan gotʒ to þe gome, wyth giserne in honde" (375). Moreover, this process of filling the hands ultimately becomes the source of wonder in the poem: Gawain fills his hand with the ax, whereas the Green Knight fills his hand with his own head. Indeed, one of the most striking features of the manuscript's depiction of the court scene is the fact that everyone's hands are filled (figure 28).[33] Moreover, the temptress tells Gawain, "I haf hit holly in my honde þat al desyres" (1257), and, in fact, such "handplay" is captured in the manuscript's depiction of the temptation scene. In particular, the temptress's two outstretched arms would seem to embrace the sleeping knight while her left hand is engaged in the iconographically significant action of "chin-chucking" (figure 29).[34] Moreover, since Gawain's sexual nemesis wishes, likewise, that "al þe wele of þe worlde were in my honde" (1270), her filled hand is identified with temptation, a form of moral choice. Finally, as if to underscore the importance of this central metaphor, the narrator concludes the first fitt with a warning: "Now þenk wel, Sir Gawan, / For woþe þat þou ne wonde / Þis auenture for to frayn / Þat þou hatʒ tan on honde" (487–90).

Such a warning is followed by a device reminiscent of the stanza linking in Pearl, for the image that is placed last ("honde") in the first fitt appears first ("hanselle") in fitt two: "This hanselle hatʒ Arthur of auenturus on fyrst / In ʒonge ʒer, for he ʒerned ʒelpyng to here. / Thaʒ hym wordeʒ were wane when þay to sete wenten, / Now ar þay stoken of sturne werk, staf-ful her hond" (491–94). Here too the adventure is one that fills the hand "staf-ful," a term that evokes the image of the ax with its long haft or staff. Like the ax, the appearance of the Green Knight is "hanselle." Noting the etymology of that term, one should recall that the adventure is a "selly," possibly the one promised in line twenty-eight, of the hand—a fact that is more evident in the orthographic form "hondeselle," which appears in line sixty-six.[35]

As we suggest at the close of the last chapter, one must ask whether this seemingly marvelous interruption of the Arthurian Christmas celebration is, in fact, a "selly" (475), ultimately wrought by God as a sign in the tradition of the hand at Belshazzar's court— a "warnyng þat wonder hem þoʒt" (Purity, 1504)—or a work of a human hand, most likely that of a magician. Clearly there is a controlling hand behind the "craft" witnessed at court. Its nature, however, is deliberately kept at arm's length. Within Purity, Belshazzar turns first to "wychecrafte" (1560) and "demerlayk" (1561), the work of human hands, as an explanation of the hand on the wall. Significantly, the knights of Arthur's court, likewise, suspect witchcraft as the source of the "meruayl" appearing before their eyes. In reality, the "palm" that presents itself at the Babylonian court is the hand of God, prepared for by the hand of Christ in the "Exhortation to Purity." In Gawain, however, we cannot be sure, and the half-gi-

Figure 28. "The Green Knight's Challenge," late fourteenth century. MS. Cotton Nero A.x., fol. 94b. By permission of the British Museum, London.

Figure 29. "The Tempation of Gawain," late fourteenth century. MS. Cotton Nero A.x., fol. 129. By permission of the British Museum, London.

ant who appears in Arthur's court "to dele . . . destiné "may be an
avatar of the opening stanza's ambiguous treacherous "tulk" who
was "trewest on erthe," and the wonder may be either a "miracle"
or a "crime." Arthur clearly has no idea whether the ax he mounts
on the wall is the rod of Aaron or the wand of the magician, the
"hondewerk" of God or of humanity. In circular fashion, then, we
return to the very dilemma faced by Jonah at the outset of this chapter: the need to know where human "hondewerk" ends and that of
the "Maker of man" begins, especially given the import of the relationship between "fynisment" and "forme."

Five

QUICKER THAN THE "I":
THE HAND OF THE POET AND
THE PRONOUNS OF NARRATIVE

In setting forth his beliefs about the foundations of the modern novel, the very unmedieval Gustave Flaubert once observed that the artist ought not to be seen in his work any more than God is to be found directly in nature.[1] In the preceding chapters, we have already seen just how frequently our very medieval poet's divine "Kyng of Nature" appears in just such a fashion within the works of the *Gawain* manuscript. Within the manuscript's four works, God not only establishes the laws of *kynde* but affects their miraculous suspension—whether in the recapitulation of biblical miracles, the allaying of a father's grief for a lost daughter, or even the providing of succor for a questing knight in search of a place to say Christmas Mass. Frequently apotheosized as "He who made" everything from eyes and ears to the "flood" and the firmament,[2] the Creator appearing throughout the *Gawain* poems is a Maker actively involved in his own "hondewerk," one whose hand is both felt and, in the case of Belshazzar, seen. In fact, to believe otherwise is tantamount to folly. Within *Patience*, for instance, Jonah's fundamental mistake is his belief in the remoteness of a Creator who is detached from his Creation: "Oure Syre syttes . . . on sege so hyʒe, / In his glowande glorye, and gloumbes ful lyttel / Þaʒ I be nummen in Nunniue and naked dispoyled, / On rode rwly torent wyth rybaudes mony" (93–96). In a sense, such belief in the remoteness of God precipitates miracles. The episode of Jonah's whale or the appearance of the "paum" in Belshazzar's court are reason-vexing wonders whose purpose is to remind humankind of the immanence or proximity of God to Creation.

Just as the God of the Cotton Nero poems violates Flaubert's "unseen" Creator by playing an active role in the unfolding events of his own Creation, so too, the narrator of the *Gawain* poems becomes an important first-person presence who frequently manipulates the events in the fictive world of the poems in order to establish his own function as "maker" of the text. Yet if the "Maker of Man" and the maker of the text are in many ways parallel, they are not identical. While the interventions of the divinity represent the wondrous display of miracles, the hallmark of the poet's intrusions is quite often their subtlety, for, as in the work of all skillful makers, the narrative seams in his art are invisible or, at least, deliberately hard to detect. The hand of the storyteller may be quicker than the reader's eye, but its gentle guidance is felt in shaping not only the content of his narratives but also his readers' responses to the events he describes.[3]

Just as Jonah receives corrective instruction from the voice of God because of the prophet's presumptions about divine remoteness, the chastened prophet, likewise, is judged and even admonished by the intrusive creator/narrator of the tale who belittles Jonah's separation of Creation from a Creator who "syttes . . . so hyʒe"[4] by asking, "Hope ʒe þat he heres not þat eres alle made? / Hit may not be þat he is blynde þat bigged vche yʒe" (123–24).

Interestingly enough, the same trope regarding the impossibility of separating the Creator from his handwork appears in *Purity* after the tale of the great Flood—again, through direct authorial intrusion:

> Bot sauyour, mon, in þyself, þaʒ þou a sotte lyuie,
> Þaʒ þou bere þyself babel, byþenk þe sumtyme
> Wheþer he þat stykked vche a stare in vche steppe yʒe,
> ʒif hymself be bore blynde. Hit is a brod wonder.
> And he þat fetly in face fettled alle eres—
> If he hatʒ losed þe lysten, hit lyfteʒ meruayle.
>
> (581–86)

Both passages illustrate the same denotative point: that the maker of eyes and ears must surely possess sight and hearing—that is, an awareness of creation that presages intervention by the Creator into Creation. In each passage, the narrator, by inserting such judgments, intrudes into the text of his tale. Making his presence felt by placing himself between the narrative action and his audience, the narrator, in each case, deliberately creates a second-person addressee set apart from both the third-person subject of his narrative and the first-person narrator. While the two passages have this much in common, the essential relationship between the three parties of the narrative—the subject of narration, the narrator, and the audience—differs in significant ways.

The narrator of *Purity*, in the second of the two passages we have just examined, clearly abandons his subject, the story of the Flood, in order to create a discourse with his reader who is addressed as "Mon . . . þou . . . þouself," thereby removing the subject, Noah, at least slightly from the audience and deliberately subverting the illusion of a direct, unbiased presentation of an uninterpreted, unbrokered history. As this brokering reminds us, the tale of the Flood, or any other tale, is a story already interpreted—that is, weighed in the balance and selected by the narrator—*before* it is presented to the reader.

The passage from *Patience*, although denotatively making much the same point as the passage from *Purity*, is, however, more interesting because of its ambiguous identification of its second-person audience. One might ask who exactly constitutes that formal, polite "ȝe"? Is its antecedent, as in the passage from *Purity*, the audience? Or does the "ȝe" have as its referent, perhaps, Jonah? To be sure, the poet is certainly capable of virtually turning his back to his audience as he does at the end of the first fitt of *Gawain*, where the narrator addresses his formerly third-person protagonist directly—first by name and then twice as "þou"—in order to warn the knight to consider the gravity of the adventure he has taken on: "Now þenk wel, Sir Gawan, / For woþe þat þou ne wonde / Þis auenture for to frayn, / Þat þou hatȝ tan on honde" (487–90). Unlike the second-person pronouns in the address to the audience in *Purity* or those in the address to Arthur's knight in *Gawain*, the "ȝe" of the *Patience*-narrator's observations on "he . . . þat bigged vche ȝe" remains ambiguous, for "you" may refer to audience, character, or both.

If the "ȝe" in the passage from *Patience* refers to Jonah, the narrator by joining with his character creates a "community" of discourse (character-narrator) that excludes the reader. Such interposition consciously creates a distance between observed and observer with a brokering narrator acting as the traditional medieval go-between.[5] One result of this technique is that the audience, as in the passage from *Purity*, is no longer told directly what occurs, but is merely allowed to eavesdrop on a private lecture delivered by an author to his own creation, just as the biblical reader indirectly overhears the words of God to Abraham, Jonah, or any other part of divine Creation. The dangers of such eavesdropping are evident in Sarah's reaction when she overhears the prophecy that she will bear a child. One might ask whether her skepticism is in some part the result of her marginalization, her position as audience outside the direct axis of the dialogue between Abraham and God. Were she part of that speech community, conversing directly with God as does her husband, would her skepticism be diminished? Is her position beyond the boundary of the discourse of which she is partly the subject like that in which Jonah finds, or at least imagines for, himself? More importantly, is her position reflective of the status of the "eavesdropping" reader when the narrator/maker addresses his own characters?

Conversely, if the "ʒe" in the passage refers to the audience, then the aside creates a counterbalancing community (narrator-reader) that excludes and, hence, distances the character from the discourse between author and reader. In the end, the essential ambiguity of "ʒe" creates both axes, producing a dual movement and complex interplay between the parts of the narrative in which the two communities—*character-narrator* and *narrator-reader*—overlap. The result is a referential tug-of-war whose tension creates an important part of the dynamic of the text. The type of inclusion/exclusion brought about by the shifting boundaries of the polyvalent "ʒe" perform the same function that Kelly and Irwin have found in parables that simultaneously create and minister to multiple audiences, an operation often reflecting acts of salvation and exclusion/damnation that are their subjects.[6]

To see just such a pronominal conflict between competing and at times overlapping communities that both include and exclude, one might well turn to the pronoun-laden debate at the heart of *Pearl* where the communities of humankind and the "gyng" (455) of heaven are both represented by the frequently ambiguous "we/us/oure" put into play by the *Pearl*-Maiden and the Dreamer. What is of interest here is the overlapping of the two communities. Both include the *Pearl*-Maiden who then becomes the mediatrix, just as the narrator acts as the common denominator between the two communities of audience-narrator and narrator-character. As in the case of the *Pearl*-Maiden, the poet transforms the narrator/poet, the common element, into the crucial hinge or fulcrum of the text. In short, the teller's intrusions into his story suggest to the reader the importance of poet as maker and thus serve the same purpose as divine interventions into history, intrusions that create the awe and wonder that remind humans of the Creator. The mediated text, the mediated Creation: in contradiction to Flaubert's dictum, the authors of text and of Flood not only appear in their respective "hondewerk" but are the essential mediating points of conversion within the dichotomous communities that they define.

The way in which the narrator presents himself not as a passive "instrument" for tale-telling but as a mediator brokering information and creating an expressly defined relationship between himself, his readers (both "ȝe" and "þou"), and the text is clearly within the tradition of the *ars praedicandi,* the generic core of both *Patience* and *Purity.*[7] To be sure, the legal and commercial implications of the term "brokering" are deliberately invoked here, for the *Gawain*-Poet's interest in legal contracts and covenants, as well as in *commercium* and exchange, has been amply demonstrated. Such preoccupation with commercium is evident in the poet's repeated offers to tell a tale in exchange for the audience's time or attention[8]—bargains echoed in *Purity* ("ȝif ȝe wolde tyȝt me a tom, telle hit I wolde" [1153]), *Patience* ("Wyl ȝe tary a lyttel tyne and tent me a whyle, / I schal wysse yow þerwyth, as Holy Wryt telles" [59–60]), and *Sir Gawain* ("If ȝe wyl lysten þis laye bot on littel quile, / I schal telle hit as-tit . . ." [30–31]; "And ȝe wyl a whyle be stylle, / I schal telle yow how þay wroȝt" [1996–97]). In each case, the yoking of the first person and the second deliberately evokes the type of formal exchange contracts that we saw at the heart of *Sir Gawain* in chapter 2.

To understand the poet/narrator's position, one need only return to the illumination of St. Bernard (chapter 4, figure 13), who, as mediator, receives the word of God and whose stylus visually leads us to the open hands of those waiting to receive his text. In fact, as already noted in the previous chapter, the visual pathway dominating the reader's viewing of the miniature forms a circle that, like Gawain's endless knot, ends where it begins. As the viewer moves from dextra Domini to the hand of Bernard, this last detail directs the reader's gaze to Bernard's audience, whose open hands lead the viewer's eyes to the copying table that, in turn, directs our line of vision back to the dextra Domini. In each half of the cycle, the writer and the copying table serve as copulae that link the human with the divine. The monks, it should be noted, do not have the dextra Domini within their own line of sight. At best, they will see only the written word—the approximation of the divine word—or even the hand of Bernard, which is in a pose different from that of the dextra Domini. The hand of the scribe or transmitter may imitate the hand of God but may never be identical with it. Hence the later western or Roman dextra Domini is presented traditionally in one attitude, two fingers extended in the gesture of blessing while the saintly transmitter demonstrates a different manual pose with one finger thrust forward in the act of teaching or preaching.

Similarly, one might consider the fourteenth-century miniature of Socrates and Plato that was the focus of Derrida's *The Post Card* (figure 30).[9] Leaving aside the complex chronological question of Plato dictating to Socrates, we might first view the figures in terms of their pantomimic gestures and positions, especially the verbal mediation of the scribe between rhetor and his text. To understand the relationship that exists between these two figures, one should examine the trio of hands above the copy-table (figure 31) in order to appreciate the contrast with the discordant trinity of hands in the illustration of the fool and the wise man (figure 32) or with the cacophony of hands in the judgment of Christ before Pilate (figures 33 and 34). Clearly, the hands of the two philosophers are acting in concert. Yet if there is a visual synchronicity in the cast or interplay of the hands of Plato and Socrates, who exactly are these two figures? More specifically, what is their relationship? In one possible "reading," the left hand of the dictator or rhetor (labeled "Plato") points upward to the right corner, the customary locus of the descending dextra Domini in religous art. The right hand, with finger extended, motions slightly downward, the small marks around the finger creating the suggestion of movement. This figure with one hand up and the other slightly downward suggests the act of transmission, of concretizing the abstract, of taking the transcendental and positioning it in the realm of the phenomenal.[10] The active role of this figure is further reinforced by his facial expression—possibly a grimace, although whether of concentration or of consternation is unclear. The second figure, though engaged in the act of writing, appears far more passive—his hands placed beneath and submissive to the active pointing finger of the rhetor who mediates between the scribe and the invisible, higher authority of unseen Truth. It is also important to note that the scribe's vision is limited to his downward gaze at the text while the rhetor's line of vision is directed upward. Yet, the

Figure 30. "Plato and Socrates," mid-thirteenth-century. MS. Ashmole 304, fol. 31v. By permission of the Bodleian Library, Oxford University.

Figure 31. Detail from "Plato and Socrates." MS Ashmole 304, fol. 31v. By permission of the Bodleian Library, Oxford University.

Figure 32. Detail from initial D (*Dixit incipiens*), early fourteenth century. MS. Ashmole 1523, fol. 66. By permission of the Bodleian Library, Oxford University.

Figure 33. (above). Detail from "Christ before Pilate." MS. Lat. liturg. e 41, fol. 40v. By permission of the Bodleian Library, Oxford University.

Figure 34. (right). Detail from "Christ before Pilate." MS. Lat. liturg. e 41, fol. 40v. By permission of the Bodleian Library, Oxford University.

relationship between rhetor and scribe is not quite as clear as in the depiction of St. Bernard and other mediating figures (figures 12, 14, 15). What is also revealed is the intrusive nature of the scribe whose larger body is interposed between rhetor and text. As a consequence, the dictator/rhetor is forced to stand on his toes and peer over the writer's shoulder in order to read what the scribe is writing.

Applying the names assigned to the two characters—Plato and Socrates—results in yet another reversal.[11] Perhaps Plato the rhetor is not the rhetor at all, but the audience, the particular Plato who observed and learned from Socrates. Suddenly, the axis defining the community of discourse is rewritten, and boundaries are redrawn. Such a reading, however, places the writer outside the axis of audience and text. If we accept the labeling as accurate, then the ostensible rhetor (Plato) now becomes the audience, not the writer marginalized or locked out of the discourse between the author and the text, eavesdropping much like the reader of *Gawain* during the "þenk wel" passage. Plato, the student who learned from Socrates, went on—as pupils, scribes, and all audiences do—to "wryte [Socrates] more trewe" as did Chaucer's Adam Scriven—to "correct" the subjective story of Socrates. For his part, Socrates—the author of the text—has become absorbed into the text. Certainly, the ambiguity of identification of author and audience in this portrayal of the two Greek philosophers is similar to the deliberate blurring of the "3e" in the authorial intrusion concerning "he þat bigged vche y3e." At the very least, such competing claims of authorship/ownership of the text raise important questions about art. Such aesthetic tension and uncertainty comprise an enigma, a call to interpretation, a confounding of reason similar to that produced by miracles.

Interestingly enough, the ambiguous visual identification and, hence, function of the narrator/audience are found, likewise, within the very confines of the Cotton Nero manuscript itself. As Paul Reichardt has recently reminded us, that manuscript contains five curious faces drawn within its margins.[12] Although Reichardt proposes "readings" of the various faces, suggesting ties between the marginal countenances and the content of the lines at which those faces appear to be gazing, crucial questions still remain: Are these the reactive faces of the physically marginalized audience, or are they the directive signals, or even representations, of the narrator/poet who habitually intrudes into his text to gloss and underscore significant

parts of his matter? While one's first instinct, as in the case of Reichardt, is to interpret such disparate faces as representations of the
poem's affective audience, there is the even more intriguing detail
involving the marginal hands drawn, index fingers extended, pointing to lines in *Pearl* and *Purity*.[13] In each case, the hand is clearly directive—authorial or at least scribal—rather than affective, but their
meanings have remained as elusive to contemporary scholars as the
mysterious "paum" was to Belshazzar. In the end, we are led to ask,
who is responsible for such marginalia? The author? The "owner"?
An unknown redactor? The scribe? If the scribe, was he acting as
maker or as audience?[14] Such questions, then, inexorably lead us to
the narrator's position vis-à-vis his audience and his text. Is he
standing aside in order to strengthen the reader-text relationship?
Does he interpose himself between viewer and text like Socrates
who forces Plato onto his tiptoes?

As the first-person presence of the narrator attests, the author is
not separable from text; he is interwoven into his text much as the
architects of the great medieval cathedrals placed their own images
inside the edifices they built. Bernard's great rival, Abbot Suger, in-
truded, if that is the appropriate word, into Saint-Denis with some
thirteen inscriptions and four likenesses, including his own image
at the foot of Christ on the tympanum.[15] No doubt if figure 13 were
a portrait of Suger rather than of Bernard, we would be reasonably
certain that part of what he was writing was his own name. Certainly Suger's cathedral is not an edifice built according to the aes-
thetics of Flaubert, for whether or not God appears in Saint-Denis,
Suger certainly does. Similarly, though not so dramatically, the possible author of the *Gawain* poems, one John Massey, may have
placed his own anagram within the poems of his making.[16] Like
Socrates who becomes a character both delivering and becoming a
part of his own text, or like the builders whose images appear in
their own "hondewerk," the fate of the literary maker seems to be
absorption into a text of one's own invention.

But what exactly is the audience to make of the author absorbed
into his own creation? In the end, we are never sure whether the
head of Henry of Reyns, first architect of Westminster Abbey, or that
of John of Gloucester who also worked on Westminster,[17] so carefully interwoven into the edifice, is watching the spectacle of the divine service *with* the praying faithful or simply gazing at them. Are

they praying *with* Henry, or *to* him? Or is he just observing from the sidelines? The communities/axes of object-maker-subject remain as slippery as ever, alternately including and excluding as well as generating the dynamic tension that lies at the heart of the subject's aesthetic experience of the maker's making. The point here is not to identify the author, whether Massey or not, or scribe, whether author or not, but to note that the relationship of maker to art, of Creator to Creation, was a complex subject for the medieval craftsman, one that was a source of conundrum and infinite self-reflexive play as well as philosophical speculation. Indeed, such relationships were far too complex to be easily dismissed by the all-encompassing notion of the artist as anonymous "instrument" or conduit for universal, rather than personal, truth.[18]

In the end, though, as interpreters of the Cotton Nero poems, we are ultimately left not with the manuscript illuminations or the marginalia, but with the poet's words. The poet's verbal ambiguity, however, serves to raise questions analogous to the visual conundrums concerning the connections between Creator and Creation, between maker and the made. The form of the poet's narrative manipulation of communities as well as his thematic foregrounding of his role as broker/maker reinforces his belief in the foolishness of the notion of the remoteness of God, who is after all the Creator, the author of the text that is Creation and the unfolding of the narrative that is history. In good medieval fashion, it is impossible for the maker to be divorced from the creation that takes his form. Indeed, the poet as maker of the text seems as inseparable from the fruits of his making as the God whom he portrays.

While the right hand of the poet does not appear explicitly within the text of *Purity*, like the salesman he is, the poet does manage to position his left foot within the door—that is, the text—in his rather remarkable interposition describing the befuddlement of Belshazzar's clerks: "And, alle þat loked on þat letter as lewed þay were / As þay had loked in þe leþer of my lyft bote" (1580–81). In its own way, such an intrusion is as remarkable as the hand appearing at Belshazzar's court. In fact, the poet's deliberate insertion of himself into the text is typical of this remarkably intrusive narrator, who insists on reminding his readers that this is a mediated vision. What begins with the allusion to the poet's left boot culminates in the presentation of the complete narrator as character in *Pearl*.

The question of mediation begins where chapter 1 began, with the binding power of language. Of course, we do well to remember that language is a *medium*, a term that implies the ability of language to join or couple ideas and objects. Yet language consisting of categories also separates, demarcates difference. For instance, an object is called a "chair" because it is perceived as being different from, say, a table. In circular fashion, perceived difference generates disparate categories such as chair and table, but distinct categories serve to denote and even underscore differences. As we have seen in passages from *Purity*, *Patience*, and *Sir Gawain and the Green Knight*, such linguistic mediation and separation are achieved through personal pronouns, especially through þe/þou and 3e/yow. Indeed, pronouns separate by creating mutually exclusive categories,"I" and "you," or pronouns can conjoin by resolving the "I/Thou" dichotomy into "we." Both movements are seen in microcosm at the close of *Purity*. In that poem's final lines, the narrator establishes the I/Thou relationship between himself and his audience and then dissolves the dichotomy by moving toward a strongly emphasized "us," wherein the second person is subsumed in the now plural first person. The poet thus concludes by turning from his description of Belshazzar to inform his audience that "vpon þrynne wyses, I haf yow þro schewed" God's anger at "vnclannes" (1805–6). Having established the "I/Yow" relationship, the narrator proceeds to trace the prospect of reconciliation, of drawing together the opposing communities, which he defined a few lines earlier: "Þat *we* gon gay in *oure* gere, þat grace he *vus* sende, / Þat *we* may serue in his sy3t, þer solace neuer blynne3" (1811–12). The poem thus ends with "we . . . oure . . . vus," the three parts and functions of the collective community of differentiated *I*'s and *thou*'s, taken together as a whole. Such pronominal "movement"—the progression from "I-You" to "we"— is, in fact, an integral part of the meaning of the text, thereby creating and reinforcing the poet's overt theme of the formation of the community of the saved.

As we already have seen in the passages from *Purity* and *Patience*, the second person is often the site of ambiguity and, hence, the starting point for the poet's dynamic pronominal progressions. Allan Metcalf, in his article "*Sir Gawain* and *You*," has convincingly demonstrated the poet's skillful employment of the formal or polite "Ye" or "you" for superiors and of the informal (and, at times, den-

igrating) "thee" used among equals, inferiors, and, curiously
enough, the divinity. Moreover, Metcalf traces Gawain's linguistic
evolution from his initial use of the informal "þou" as a referent for
the Green Knight at the poem's outset to the employment of the
more respectful "ȝe" at the poem's conclusion.[19] As with the competing first-person plurals of the Dreamer and Maiden in *Pearl*, a
character's selection of the familiar or of the formal automatically
creates categories that include and exclude individuals from defined
communities. Such actions are consonant with the worldview of a
poet whose poems concern judgment and damnation, the inclusion
and exclusion of people from the parabolic feasthall and the heavenly city of the Lamb. What appears to be true of pronominal exchanges between characters may, likewise, be applied to the very
"I/Thou" dialogue fashioned by the intrusive poet who, as we have
already noted, speaks in the first person to both his second-person
readers and characters, often mediating between the two.

Models for such acts of mediation—and such mediators—are, of
course, abundant within the Cotton Nero poems: The *Pearl*-Maiden
mediates between the Jeweler and the Lamb; the Green Knight between Morgan and Gawain; Jonah between God and the Ninevites.
However, the clearest illustration of such narrative brokering is
found in the figure of *Purity*'s Daniel, who not only interprets the
writing on the wall but also narrates the history of Nebuchadnezzar,
Belshazzar's father. Daniel's decoding of the writing on the wall provides an exemplar of the narrative techniques of the poet. Significantly, Daniel presents the entire history of Nebuchadnezzar in the
third person, never once intruding into the tale in the first person.
However, when it comes time to "rede"—that is, interpret—the
three words written by the mysterious hand, suddenly the prophet/
narrator becomes an invasive presence, interposing himself between
Belshazzar and the words Daniel would "malt [into Belshazzar's]
mynde": "Þise ar þe wordes here wryten, wythoute werk more, / By
vch fygure, *as I fynde*, as oure Fader lykes: / MANE, TECHAL, PHARES,
merked in þrynne, / Þat þretes þe of þyn vnþryfte vpon þre wyse"
(1725–28). As the prophet/translator continues some eight lines
later, "In PHARES *fynde I* forsoþe þise felle saȝes: / 'Departed is þy
pryncipalté. Depryued þou worþes. / Þy rengne rafte is þe fro and raȝt
is þe Perses. / Þe Medes schal be maysteres here, and þou of menske
schowued' " (1737–41). All three persons are at play here: There is

þou (Belshazzar) and the third-person text, but there is the speaker Daniel's first-person "I" interposed between the two. As is readily apparent, Daniel does not simply translate the writing on the wall but actively interposes himself between the text and Belshazzar, the would-be reader, the "thou." Certainly the "I/Thou" tension dominating the passage has been carefully anticipated, for in the very first line of his speech to the king, for example, Daniel states, "Ryche kyng of þis rengne, rede þe oure Lorde" (1642). To be sure, the virtual enjambing of these pronouns draws attention to their presence and significance in the narrative.

If we apply Metcalf's observations on the poet's deliberate use of the formal and informal second-person pronouns, we see that from the outset Daniel's speech delineates two clearly defined communities: that of the earthly king and that of "oure Lord." Not only are these communities established in the counterbalancing of king and Lord at their respective ends of the line in Daniel's speech, but, in particular, in the use of "oure," a pronoun that not only includes the community of the saved within the poem but reaches outward to the audience. The use of "þe," all the more noticeable because Belshazzar carefully emphasizes his rank as "highest," places him outside that community. The poet's method, then, is not merely to present Belshazzar as a degenerate but to create tension or distance between the reader and the character whose sins the author would have us eschew.

The "oure" in this passage both includes and excludes, constructing interpretive communities that in their very ambiguity generate the same tensions as the "ȝe" in the passage we have just examined from *Patience*. Whom does "oure" include? Does it include both Daniel and Belshazzar? As the poet makes clear, God, acknowledged or not, is Creator of both. Could "oure" in this context be restricted to the Hebrews' God, excluding Belshazzar as an unbeliever, as well as the reader who is outside the frame of the Old Testament discourse? Or does "oure" transcend its immediate discursive context, like several references to "oure Lord" in other parts of the canon, to include not only Daniel but the poem's audience? The shifting, sometimes conflicting, boundaries of these communities create a semantic tension, with a narrator whose self-created position at the center of discourse allows, perhaps demands, that he broker the results. The narrator thus becomes a type of porter, deciding who gains admittance and who does not, a principle of exclusion and inclusion fundamental to the parable of the wedding feast at the outset of *Purity*. Pronouns, then, are used to draw distinctions, to define communities that simultaneously include and exclude, which, of course, is the ultimate function of a community. We shall see the same possessive ambiguity in the *Pearl*-Maiden's reference to "my Lorde" in her debate with the Jeweler. As we noted in chapter 3's discussion of covenant-contracts, such questions of ownership are central to the manuscript as a whole, and in such conflicts, the virtual battleground is the possessive pronoun.

Such distancing—a "cinematic" manipulation of perspective[20]— represents the means by which the poet controls his reader's relation to the text either by allowing his reader to see action directly or to gaze at it from a consciously crafted remove. In film, this technique consists of permitting or not permitting the viewer to be aware of the narrative eye of the camera. Like the self-conscious camera, the narrator of the Cotton Nero poems—through intrusions like the "I trowe," "I fynde," and "fynde I" of Daniel—molds our thinking; he shapes our perceptions as to whether his narrative subjects or even his readers are inside or outside of the carefully established communities so skillfully delineated throughout his works. For example, the *Pearl*-Dreamer's description of his vision of the procession in the heavenly city across the river is punctuated with first-person intrusions,[21] which serve to prevent the visio from becoming an unmediated vision of the sort at the close of *Patience*. In *Pearl*, there is no Dante-like merging of mystic and godhead or of visionary and vision. But that is, in fact, the very point—the Dreamer's spiritual imperfection. His separateness from the subject of his vision is reflected in his dominant use of "I" throughout his debate with the Maiden as well as in his exclusive "we/us/our" categories that remove mankind from the "gyng" of heaven. The habitual "I" of the narrator is no less a boundary, a marker of separation, than the uncrossable river preventing the *Pearl*-Dreamer from entering the New Jerusalem.[22] Viewed in this light, the three landscapes or settings of *Pearl*—the earthly garden, the middle terrain of the dream, the separated world of the heavenly city—become characterized by their respective pronouns.[23] The waking world of the earthly garden is characterized by the Dreamer's dominant first-person "I." The land beyond the river is repeatedly cast in the commu-

nal "we/us" of "oure gyng." The middle ground is the site of the
great "I/Thou" debate comprising the core of the poem.

As we have noted, pronouns, by virtue of their status as acts of in-
clusion/exclusion, mirror the process of divine judgment. In this regard, one might consider the use of pronouns by Jonah and God in
five successive stanzas of *Patience* as the angry prophet attempts to
call down judgment on the city of Nineveh:

STANZA 104	PRONOUNS
I bīseche *þe*, Syre, now *þou* self jugge,	I . . . þe . . . þou
Watȝ not þis ilk *my* worde þat worþen is nouþe,	my
Þat *I* kest in *my* cuntré, when *þou þy* carp sendeȝ	I . . . my . . . þou . . . þy
Þat *I* schulde tee to þys toun *þi* talent to preche?	I . . . þi

                                                    (413–16)

The architectonics of this discourse deserve special note. Stanza
104 clearly delineates the I/þou tension underlying the conflict between Jonah and God. Although three of the four lines juxtapose the
first person with the second, the emphasis here is clearly on the first
person, which forms the leading part of the dichotomy.

STANZA 105	PRONOUNS
Wel knew *I þi* cortaysye, *þy* quoynt soffraunce,	I . . . þi . . . þy
Þy bounté of debonerté, and *þy* bene grace,	Þy . . . þy
Þy longe abydyng wyth lur, *þy* late vengaunce;	Þy . . . þy
And ay *þy* mercy is mete, be mysse neuer so huge.	þy

                                                    (417–20)

The second stanza (105) begins with the first person but quickly
becomes a discourse on þy (Jonah's view of God). By this time, the
perspective and the narrative alignments seem to be rather firmly
fixed.

STANZA 106	PRONOUNS
I wyst wel, when *I* hade worded quat-so-euer *I* cowþe	I . . . I . . . I
To manace alle þise mody men þat in þis mote dowelleʒ,	
Wyth a prayer and a pyne, *þay* myʒt *her* þese gete,	þay . . . her
And, þerfore, *I* wolde haf flowen fer into Tarce.	I

(421–24)

The third stanza (106) then begins a shift in focus and perspective. While the initial line is firmly rooted in the first person, containing three instances of "I," the fourth line returns to the first person. In between are the third person "þise mody men" . . . "þay" . . . "her." In the process of condemning the Ninevites, the prophet separates himself linguistically from those upon whom he would call down the wrath of God. Jonah has located himself in the first person, humankind in the third, with, interestingly enough, God in the middle as second-person "þou."

STANZA 107	PRONOUNS
Now, Lorde, lach out *my* lyf, *hit* lastes to longe;	my . . . hit
Bed *me* bilyue *my* bale-stour, and bryng *me* on ende	me . . . my . . . me
For *me* were swetter to swelt as-swyþe, as *me* þynk,	me . . . me
Þen lede lenger *þi* lore, þat þus *me* les makeʒ."	þi . . . me

(425–28)

The fourth stanza of the dialogue (107) calls attention to the return to the first person begun in the last line of the previous stanza. Yet more is going on here than initially meets the eye, especially since this stanza represents a virtual mirror or reverse image of the second stanza, analogous to the mirror reversals of the stanza-linking words in *Pearl*.[24] The second stanza opens with a single first-person, followed by seven second-person pronouns. Here, seven first-person pronouns are counterbalanced by a single "þi" in the last line.

STANZA 108	PRONOUNS
Þe soun of *oure* Souerayn þen swey in *his* ere;	oure . . . his
Þat vpbraydes þis burne vpon a breme wyse:	
"Herk, renk, is þis ry3t so ronkly to wrath	
For any dede þat *I* haf don oþer demed *þe* yet?"	I . . . þe

(429–32)

The final stanza (108) in this dialogue presents the type of am-biguous reversal seen before in the use of "oure," as the narrator breaks the frame of the Jonah-God dialogue to which we are mere eavesdroppers by noting: "Þe soun of *oure* Souerayn þen swey in *his* ere." In this instance, the antecedent of "oure" is clear. The narra-tor reaches out to his audience in an inclusive move that physically sets *our* community against Jonah who has been transposed from the active first person to the passive object of description through the use of the "his" and "þis burne." The prophet, having already sepa-rated himself from the Ninevites (422–23), has been set apart from us as well. God is now represented by the first-person "I" in line 432 with Jonah as the counterbalancing "þe." The perspective of the pro-nouns that initiated the discourse has been altered radically—set vp-so-doun, as it were.

Such dense stanzaic groupings of pronouns are, likewise, the defining feature of the debate in *Pearl*. In that poem, the Dreamer, by his own admission, is the type to "sette sengely in synglure"—which is to adopt the exclusive first-person singular. To sum up, the clusters of pronouns appearing throughout the speeches of Daniel, Jonah, and the dialogue in *Pearl* create ever-shifting axes of com-munity. As the pronouns assume protean forms, the relationships of characters to the narrator, the reader, the rest of humanity, and, most importantly, to God alter as the lines of inclusion and exclu-sion are redrawn.

What is true of the speeches of Daniel and Jonah is true of the narrators and their use of the first person in presenting their own

discourse. Most obviously, the rhetorical techniques and strate-
gies found in Daniel's sermon are employed skillfully in *Purity* as a
whole. From the outset, the poetic material is self-consciously mediated by a narrator whose informing consciousness binds together
disparate biblical sources and motifs in order to concretize *his* argument to *his* audience. That the narrator is acutely aware of his relationship with his audience is demonstrated when, at the end of *Purity*, he reintroduces this theme by stating, "Thus *I* have shown *you*
using these three stories. . . ." so that the distinction—and, hence,
the relationship—between speaker and receiver remains fixed even
unto the very end. What the narrator does not overtly append to this
statement, but what his intrusive presence indicates, is the implied
coda: "I have chosen these stories from among many that I could
have selected and have provided the organizing principle that unites
them, so the stories are mine. Since I have appropriated the text, I
am the meeting ground. You get the truth only through me."

In order to mediate between audience and text, the narrator of *Purity* must from the outset emphasize that the text is, in fact, his creation. Thus, addressing his audience directly, the narrator states
"Me myneʒ on one amonge oþer, as Maþew recordeʒ" (25). The text
about to be scrutinized is not simply the gospel of Matthew, but
rather the poet's interpretation, an almost Wordsworthian recollection ("myneʒ") of Matthew's words. As mental reconstruction, such
narrative is analogous to the middle ground in *Pearl*, wherein leaves
of silver and gravel of pearls represent the forms of the waking
world—trees, grass, stream—transfigured by the fantastic materials
of the world beyond. As such, that middle ground serves as a hinge
of a diptych,[25] very much like the narrator who stands between subject and object. As the poet concludes the first section of *Purity*, the
narrator, like Daniel, enters the text and tells us what he has heard
from clerks and what he must invent for himself, finally relying on
the locution, "As I fynde," already seen in Daniel's speech, as a
means of inserting himself into the text (193–205). As with Daniel,
the narrator's strategy, by virtue of his intrusion, consists of creating communities by distancing reader from text. Forming a relationship that reflects the ties between Daniel and his Babylonian audience, the narrator employs the familiar form of the second-person
pronoun in a warning to his audience, "War þe wel if þou wylt"
(165). Such an admonitory note is struck after the story of Noah

("war þe now" [545]) and is repeated two more times at the end of the "Exhortation to Purity" ("war þe wel" [1133], "war þe, then . . ." [1143]). Virtually ignoring the text, then, the poet interrupts his narrative to address his audience directly, not only to warn but to gloss the action he has described, as he does after Noah's flood (541) or after Lot's wife has been transformed into a pillar of salt (979–84).

The longest and most self-conscious of these narrative intrusions is, of course, the "Exhortation to Purity," where the poet's manipulative hand is busily at work. The poet begins the passage by calling attention to the rhetorically abstract "everyman" ("vch wyʒe") and his relation to "oure Lorde": "Þenne vch wyʒe may wel wyt þat he þe wlonk louies, / And if he louyes clene layk, þat is oure Lorde ryche" (1052–53); and then moves to the same denigrating informal second person used by Daniel to address Belshazzar: "And to be couþe in his courte þou coueytes þenne" (1054). The poet continues to employ the familiar second person some twenty-two times throughout the rest of the passage. What makes the exhortation of interest, however, is that in the midst of those second-person pronouns the poet sounds a note of hope for the community by switching to the first-person plural: "Nov ar *we* sore, and synful, and sovly vch one. / How schulde *we* se þen, may *we* say, þat Syre vpon throne?" (1111–12); the mediation between *I* and *thou* is "we." This brief sense of commonality achieved in these two lines coupled with the possibility of salvation is followed by a return to the familiar second person with a stern warning about the consequences of falling back into sin. Yet once the sermon is delivered and the exhortation is complete, the poet makes a remarkable effort to redefine his relationship with his audience by using the respectful "ʒe." He chastises us no longer but, like the divinity he portrays, seeks a new covenant—"If you will . . . I will," with the text ("hit") functioning as the bridge between the two: "ʒif ʒe wolde tyʒt me a tom, telle hit I wolde" (1153).

The relationship between reader and narrator is thus reformulated, and the distance between the two is minimized. As a result, first-person intrusions are eliminated, and we see directly through the narrator's eyes as he speaks *for* rather than *to* us through a series of interjections. Responding directly to the action of the poem, the narrator becomes part of the audience. No longer turning his back on his characters, the narrator then faces us directly. In fact, the narrator does not address the audience *as* audience until some 650 lines later when, at the end of the poem, he tells us, "Þus, vpon þrynne wyses, I haf *yow* þro schewed" (1805) and then ends with a prayer: "Þat *we* gon gay in *oure* gere, þat grace he *vus* sende, / Þat *we* may serue in his sy3t, þer solace neuer blynne3" (1811–12). Again, the mediation between "I" and "yow" is "vus," the "we" that apparently dominates the last third of the poem. And, indeed, the poet has demonstrated in three ways the anger of "oure Lorde" over sin. In the first two instances, he departs from his sermonized text to address a distanced reader, carefully kept at arm's length outside the circle of the saved. In the third, however, the narrator enables his audience to enter into the circle of the "we/us" of the text—the "our" of "oure Father"—by allowing the reader to peer over the shoulder of the narrator in order to share his perspective and to see the poem's action directly without mediation. Having been addressed as "thou" throughout the first two-thirds of the poem, we are now addressed as "ye" and transformed into covenantal partners like Noah and Abraham—asked for our patience and time before listening to Daniel's speech directed to "þou," Belshazzar, who is opposed to "oure Lord."

With such narrative relationships in mind, *Patience* clearly begins where *Purity* leaves off. As in *Purity*, the narrator of *Patience* brokers his tale, often by means of phrases such as "I herde" (9), "I trow" (127, 299), "I wene" (304), and "in myn vpynyoun" (40). In fact, there is probably no more overt example of such textual brokering of a text than the phrase "as I er sayde" (28), following the last of the Beatitudes, an interpolation that comes close to making the poet, rather than Christ, the author of the Sermon on the Mount. Moreover, like *Purity*, *Patience* is explicitly the product of an act of memory. The first section of *Patience* places the tale within the locus of the poet, an operation reflected in the placing of God's point with Jonah. Moreover, what is particularly noteworthy in the first sixty lines of *Patience* is that the use of pronominals closely parallels one aspect of *Purity's* exhortation. As we have just demonstrated, in *Purity* the plethora of "thous" is virtually bisected by the sudden adoption of "we" for two lines. Through this abrupt pronominal shift, the poet offers the hope of community before reverting to "I" and "þou," in order to remind the readers how far they are from the communal ideal. In *Patience*, the argument begins with the abstract "quoso," "For quoso suffer cowþe syt, sele wolde fol3e, / And quo, for þro, may no3t þole, þe þikker he sufferes" (5–6), and quickly moves from the

universal to the particular in the person of the narrator,[26] "Þen is
better to abyde þe bur vmbestoundes, / Þen ay þrow forth my þro,
þaȝ me þynk ylle" (7–8).

This progression from the universal to the personalized particular
is further reinforced as the narrator continues by stating, "*I* herde on
a halyday . . ." (9). Casting himself as the site of abstract virtues, the
narrator then presents the Beatitudes, which, as we noted earlier, he
appropriates with his "as I er sayde" (28). Like the narrator of *Purity*,
the preacher of *Patience* holds out the possibility of the reader joining with the narrator in the community defined by "we/us," "Þese
arn þe happes, all aȝt, þat vus bihyȝt weren, / If we þyse ladyes wolde
lof in lyknyng of þewes" (29–30).

Having presented the possibility of community, the narrator casts
his subject in some of his most personalized diction. Stressing that
his observation concerning the similarity between the first and last
Beatitudes is "*myn* vpynyoun" (40), the speaker discusses his own
"pouerté" and "destyné" so forthrightly that such references have
been taken as autobiographical. Employing some nineteen first-person pronouns, he ends the first section of *Patience* with a familiar
contractual offer couched in terms of "I" and "you," "Wyl ȝe tary a
lyttel tyne and tent *me* a whyle, / *I* schal wysse *you* þerwyth, as Holy
Wryt telles" (59–60). By holding out the ideal of community and
then separating himself from those whom he would join, the narrator makes it clear that the communion will be achieved when the
audience conforms to the spiritual views of the narrator. There will
be no movement on his part, no Hegelian meeting in the middle.

In making his offer of exchange with his reader, the poet of *Patience* frames the same contract between speaker and audience that
it takes him two-thirds of *Purity* to construct. From the outset,
however, the narrator of *Patience* closes with rather than distances
himself from his audience. The differences in the narrative strate-
gies of these two works reflect the poems' disparate perspectives on
the problem of judgment, for *Purity* is dominated by communities
judged, found wanting, and destroyed. The subject of *Purity* is the
separation of communities into "I/Thou" or "us/them." The clean
are distinguished from the unclean; Noah is separated from the rest
of humanity, Lot from the Sodomites. Only at the end of *Purity* does
the narrator appeal to "us," and even then, it is "us" as opposed to
Belshazzar. Conversely, *Patience* focuses on union rather than on
separation. Its subject is why Nineveh, in particular, and humanity,

in general, should be saved. Jonah's folly, as we saw in his use of pronouns, stems from his self-isolation, for he cuts himself off from the Ninevites and fails to embrace their general human condition as reflective of his own. In short, *Patience* has as its focus the "we" of community.[27] Failure to perceive commonality, the "we" of shared experience, is what leads the formerly sinful, albeit now repentant, prophet to view the regenerate Ninevites as separate and apart from himself, and, hence, to call for their destruction. As the Voice from the whirlwind tells Jonah, "Þenne byþenk þe, mon, if þe forþynk sore, / If I wolde help my hondewerk, haf þou no wonder" (495–96). As we saw in chapter 3, there is no wonder at all in the sparing of the city—that is, as long as one understands the proper bounds of community.

In *Patience*, Jonah's refusal to join the community of "we/us" leads inexorably to the separation of "I" and "thou" at the close of the poem. As we have already seen, the poem's prologue establishes the narrative point of view as the sanctified norm of the work and then offers the possibility of community, a "we/us" in which the audience attaches itself to the narrator and then returns to the existential "I/Thou" separation of narrator and reader. In short, the narrator is claiming, "these are my virtues, but we can all have them provided that you join me." If Jonah contends that God on his high throne is remote, God is not the one who has retreated from Jonah. If the gulf is to be closed, Jonah, not the fixed point of the circle's center, must move in order to achieve closure. Therein lies the dialectical movement of the poem.[28]

Throughout *Patience*, a strong narrative voice emerges, one that functions much like the "fixed foot" of Donne's famous "stiff twin compasses." As in *Purity*, the radius of the circle may change as the narrator defines and redefines the "us" of the saved, but the fixed foot keeps the circle as well as the judgment "just" in this poet who so frequently ends where he has begun. In large part, the poet's establishment of the narrator as the immovable focal point of the text is the means by which he associates himself with scripture. The poet's direct reference to "Holy Wryt" (244) as the source of *Patience* creates a narrative self-consciousness that distances the action and minimizes the reader's sympathy for Jonah.

As a means of fixing that narrative voice, scenes are shifted frequently as the narrator self-consciously changes his narrative vantage point. The effect of such legerdemain, as in the last third of *Pu-*

rity, is to distance the audience and the narrator from the subject of the narrative. For example, shortly after the sailors have cast Jonah into the sea and have made their own way to shore, they pray "to *oure* mercyable God, on Moyses wyse" (238). This particular use of "oure" defines a community that includes the sailors, the narrator, and the reader. Outside that community, however, lies Jonah, left suspended while the narrative eye follows the sailors to safe haven. And when he returns to telling the tale, the narrator then contrasts the reluctant prophet's terror with the joy of the sailors (241). The use of "our," along with the explicit contrast between Jonah and the sailors, constitutes a cinematic retreat that allows the poet to break his narrative perspective, which then switches from an external to an internal view of the whale.[29] Just as the prophet is about to be swallowed by the whale, the very moment when the reader's interest in Jonah is most intense, the poet chooses to shift the narrative perspective, thereby breaking the spell, reminding us of his own forgotten presence, and stealing the limelight from his own character. As with the "þenk wel" passage in *Gawain*, the shift in authorial point of view is employed to delineate sections in the poem, a technique comparable to the use of decorated manuscript capitals as indicators of narrative divisions. While the visual perspective may change, scenes may shift, or the narrator-reader axis may be redefined into one between narrator and character, the fixed foot of the narrator, the originating "I" at the center of the story, remains constant. This is, after all, a narrator who has not only associated himself with scripture but who has appropriated sacred text, as in the case of the Beatitudes or in the act of memory, the "myneȝ" at the outset of *Purity*. Internalizing such material, he has become as immutable as the scripture with which he has identified himself, just as Henry de Reyns in becoming part of Westminster Abbey cast off the mutability of his human condition in order to assume the permanence of his "hondewerk."

This identification of the narrator's perspective with that of God or his word is especially evident in *Patience*'s final stanza where the ambiguous first-person speaker may be God, Jonah, or the narrator:[30] "Forþy when pouerté me enpreceȝ, and payneȝ innoȝe, / Ful softly, wyth suffraunce saȝttel me bihoueȝ, / For þy penaunce and payne, to preue hit in syȝt / Þat pacience is a nobel poynt, þaȝ hit displese ofte" (528–31). The only one of the four poems that fails to end with the first-person plural, *Patience* concludes, nevertheless, by creating a sense of community through the mock union of all parties to the critical act. After the careful separation of persons in Jonah's complaint to God, all distinctions collapse into mystic unity, much as they do in the great visio at the end of the *Paradiso*,[31] and as they do not do in the "I"-dominated description of the Dreamer's vision at the end of *Pearl*.[32] The ambiguous identity of the speaker of *Patience*'s last lines presents much the same dilemma as the closing stanza of the Old English "Wanderer" in which the Anglo-Saxon poet follows the worldly complaint of the poem's central speaker with the wise understanding of the "snotter on mode," the wise man on earth. The reader is then forced to guess whether the speaker of the final lines is the now enlightened Wanderer, an omniscient narrator, or even a third party, who, unaware of the Wanderer's plight, utters universal truth.

As in the closing lines of the Old English poem, we are left at the end of *Patience* to wonder who exactly is speaking in the first person. Has the narrator suddenly turned his back on a mortified Jonah in order to address the audience directly? Is the first-person speaker here a properly chastened Jonah who has become one with the narrator and adopted his perspective? In the latter case, these lines represent closure of the "I/Thou" dichotomy through a conversion of Jonah's third person into a plural first person that defines the circle of the saved. The authoritative narrator's aim, like that of Chaucer's Parson, is to "draw folk to heaven"; that is, to draw the second-person "þe" into the circle of the first-person "we," and not the reverse. It is not the narrator's purpose to expand the boundaries of the circle of the saved, to extend the defined circumference until it encompasses everyone, in the fashion of Julian of Norwich. Rather, the poet would bring the reader into the circle of the narrator's "I" and, ultimately, the "I" of the whirlwind as its point of origin. The narrator, in whom the Beatitudes reside, acts as the fixed point of origin from which the poem's perspective emanates. Seeking beatitude, the reader must embrace the narrator's vision. To join with the narrator in the community of the faithful is, for the reader, to experience union with God, a union emulated in the final lines of the poem.

Such fixity and self-assurance in the narrator is exactly what is absent from *Sir Gawain and the Green Knight*.[33] Perhaps even rising

out of the ambiguous speaker of the last lines of *Patience*, the narrator of *Gawain* is more closely aligned with the preaching storyteller of *Patience* than the sermonizer of *Purity*, yet the narrator of
the Arthurian tale is, nonetheless, markedly different from what has
come before. In terms of its narrator, *Sir Gawain* is clearly a far more
decentered poem than either *Purity* or *Patience*. Despite that lack of
fixity, one does find the narrator assuming the role of mediator. No
less than five times he reminds us that the tale, one taken from the
"best book of romance," was "herde" (31) in town. This "boke"
(2521) is clearly a work far easier to appropriate than Matthew's text
of the Beatitudes in a single "as I er sayde." Its appropriation, however, does not grant the narrator who stands between that text and
the reader the same authority as scripture possesses.

Far from representing the distanced storyteller of *Purity*, the narrator of *Sir Gawain* breezily adopts the respectful "ʒe" (six times) in
addressing his audience. The deferential effect may be viewed as
comic or, at the least, as something other than authoritative, for the
narrator is more akin to the remarkably obtuse first-person narrator
of *Pearl* or perhaps even *Patience*'s Jonah than to the preacher/nar-
rators of the two homiletic poems. Such deference to an audience is,
however, not always a sign of perceptiveness as we see in Gawain's
first speech to Arthur as well as in his dalliance with Lady Bercilak.

Like the narrators of *Patience* and, especially, of *Purity*, the *Gawain*-
narrator would enter his text and gloss its action. But like the
Dreamer/narrator of *Pearl*, he misinterprets wildly. In fact, the narrator of *Gawain* is a storyteller who is remarkably adept in explaining the reason for the knights' silence, the meaning of the pentangle, the status of Gawain's soul. In such cases, he always assures us
of the facts, but assuredly those "facts" are not always correct, as in
the case of his overlong gloss of the pentangle, the very length of
which calls into question the narrator's powers of judgment. Filled
with "games" or verbal riddles, the poem, as we saw in chapter 1,
evokes a world in which language is deceptive, or at the least troublesome, rather than salvific, and the limitations of language trou-
ble the narrator no less than they do the characters. In the progression from *Purity* to *Patience* to *Gawain*, the poet waits until the
Arthurian romance to introduce the rhetorical device of *occupatio*,[34]
which signals the failure of language or of the narrator—or both. In
this tale, all words are "mervalous signals" in the sense that they

confound reason according to the Augustinian precepts set forth in chapter 3.

Within the text of *Gawain*, the narrator twice draws attention to his role as storyteller by noting what narrators are and are not capable of relating. In the first instance, he cannot describe the trefoils on the green intruder's surcoat; yet he can, so he claims, immediately after expressing this limitation, plumb the shadowy realm of the Arthurian knights' motivation in order to assure us that their silence is not due to fear but to courtesy, though clearly that is not the case. Later, at Bercilak's castle, the narrator reveals to us that he cannot verbalize the mirth at Bercilak's court, and then, in the very next line, assures us that nothing indecorous passed between Gawain and his hostess. Thus we are left to wonder if this observation is as valid as the one that followed his only other use of occupatio. As he tells his tale, he then sets up rules and subsequently breaks them. Like the divine violation of the laws of *kynde*, such ruptures call attention both to the creative process and to the presence of the hand of the Creator. For example, concerning Gawain's sleep the night before his fateful encounter with the Green Knight, the narrator tells us what reason will not allow him to say, although he is willing to say it anyway (1991–94). When the narrator focuses on the Green Knight, however, he tells us "Half etayn in erde I hope þat he were, / Bot mon most I, algate, mynn hym to bene" (140–41). What he "hope(s)" is not what is. Although his deferential manner softens the effect, this narrator, an intrusive force, stands between us and his characters, often presenting them as they are seen through the lens of his own peculiar values and assumptions. And it is an important part of his narrative strategy that when he would turn from his characters and speak almost confessionally to us, these are the times we as readers should keep him at arm's length.

At times this remarkably casual narrator has a way of pressing himself upon the reader when that reader would do well to maintain an objective perspective. At the end of the first fitt, for example, the narrator seemingly draws back from his character, addresses him as "þou," the informal second person reserved for peers and underlings, and warns him to "þenk well." As in the scene in *Patience* where the narrator shifts from outside to inside the whale, the formal interruption of *Sir Gawain* intensifies our sense of distance between the narrator and narrative. At the same time, as the poet struts forth at his mock homiletic best, he earnestly addresses his reader as "ᴣe." Similarly, the narrator can divorce his audience from his character by telling the reader to let Gawain "lie" and then by following quickly with the deferential "ᴣe." Or he can, when he so desires, virtually abandon the reader by participating in an almost Pirandellian dialogue with his protagonist as he does in the third temptation. Such changes suggest remarkable fluidity rather than fixity. The real pronominal progression, as Metcalf has shown, resides in the characters' use of pronouns, in Gawain's change from "þou" to "ᴣe" in denoting the Green Knight. The changing dynamic between narrator and reader as presented in the pronominal progression in *Purity* and *Patience* finds itself incorporated into *Sir Gawain* as the evolving relationship between the poem's principal characters.

In many ways, *Gawain* remains elusive because critics fail to reconcile the narrator's judgments and assertions with the action he describes. He intrudes into his narrative to proclaim that Gawain is absolved as surely as if Judgment Day were tomorrow (1883–84), despite the questionable nature of Gawain's confession. He asserts that the pentangle symbolizes that Gawain was faultless in the flesh, a notion directly contradicted by Gawain himself (2435).[35] Part of the difficulty here is that the narrator's remarks have generally gone unchallenged, his ironies too frequently taken as the exception rather than as the rule as though his view were the authoritative, fixed perspective possessed by the narrators of *Purity* and *Patience*. Assuming such a fixed narrator for *Gawain* results in taking all parts of the narrative as equally valid as they are in the homiletic poems. In the end, part of the interpretive problem is that we are not allowed the distance to put this narrator into relief. Long recognized as a poem about disguise and identity, *Gawain* is a work whose narrator, like Bercilak, is made over, disguised, or masked. Yet unlike the Green Knight, the narrator of *Gawain* has never been asked to reveal his true self, and the reader thus remains as unable to describe the narrator as the narrator remains powerless to depict the trefoils of the Green Knight's surcoat. The problem of the identity of the narrator is reflected in the action of the poem itself, which continually raises the question of exactly whose hand is determining events. Gawain believes that he controls his own destiny, only to find out that he is manipulated by the Green Knight who, in turn, is controlled by Morgan Le Fay. Accordingly, Morgan's desire to affect the fate of Camelot by frightening Guinevere to death is thwarted by Fortune and/or God, who oversees the world of the poem. Standing somewhere behind or to the side is the amiable but ambiguously defined narrator.

Finally, if *Gawain* is decentered slightly by a deferential narrator whose reliability is suspect and whose powers are at times limited, *Pearl* may be viewed as completely decentered as a result of its shifting narrative voice. As such, *Pearl* completes the narrative progression from the homiletic poems, *Purity* and *Patience*, through *Sir Gawain and the Green Knight*. As we have demonstrated earlier, the homiletic poems emanate from a stable, strongly positioned narrator who speaks with scriptural authority. For the reader of those poems, the perspective of the first-person narrator is never in doubt since, as we saw in passages from *Purity* and *Patience* at the opening of this chapter, such ambiguity is situated in the second person rather than in the "I" of the narrator. Throughout *Purity* and up to the final lines of *Patience*, neither the identity nor the authority of the speaker is in doubt. Only the audience and its ability to join the community of the saved remain unclear. Because the first-person narrator of each of those poems is immutable, the homiletic works are built around the metamorphosis of the second person, the changing status of the reader who moves from "þou" to "ȝe" in order to become absorbed into the collective "we/us" of the saved.

Gawain presents a deferential, nonauthoritarian narrator who, although outside and even above the action he relates, is no longer capable of anchoring the pronominal dialectic found in the two homilies. The narrator of *Pearl*, however, is now a character, making him the subject of his own narration.[36] Like Henry de Reyns, he has entered his own work, and having become part of the fictive world of his own creation, the narrator of *Pearl* has lost his omniscience as well as any illusion of fixity. The Maiden, as a character, assumes the authorial function of glossing the action while the narrator suffers repeatedly from the inability to perform his assigned duties. This reversal is reminiscent of the miniature of Plato and Socrates in which Socrates, the subject of Plato, now seems to have displaced the author. Indeed, the chronological reversal of Plato dictating to Socrates is as difficult and destabilizing for the modern viewer as the unexpected reversals of temporal and familial relations are for the Dreamer lectured by his two-year-old daughter in *Pearl*—or for that matter, the workers in the vineyard who expect the first arrivals to be the best paid. Within the illustration of the two philosophers, Plato seems to be active, inserting words in the mouth of Socrates. Or is it Socrates, drawn larger than Plato and seeming to dominate the woodcut, who is in control? Instead of narrator lecturing character, is it the other way round? Instead of *Patience's* narrator admonishing Jonah, in *Pearl* the character reproves the narrator. Just as Socrates, the chronologically older of the two figures, has been absorbed into Plato's text, so the older father of *Pearl* has been assimilated into the dreamworld. If, as Lukács states, the history of the modern novel involves the gradual disappearance of God from the text, the progression in the *Gawain* manuscript is the evolutionary absorption of the narrator into the text until he becomes as problematic as the architects embedded in the cathedrals of their own making. The process begun with the narrator's insertion of his left foot into the text has now become complete. Just as the narrator of *Patience* appropriated the text of the Beatitudes with his "as I er sayde" (28), the text, like the dreamworld in *Pearl,* has subsumed the narrator/poet. To be sure, the *subject* of *Pearl* is no longer someone else—Noah, Abraham, Daniel, Jonah, Gawain—but the narrator himself. Whereas in *Purity* and *Patience* the poem concerned the metamorphosis or the redefinition of the "thou" in the face of the immutable "I," in the visionary world of *Pearl,* the singular first-person "I" seems to shift.

Part of that illusion of change occurs because *Pearl* is built around the dynamic juxtaposition of two conflicting first persons, each vying for a position at the center of the poem. Both the Dreamer and the *Pearl*-Maiden are characterized by the first person. Each "I," in turn, generates a second-person "thou" as audience. If the "I" of the *Pearl*-Maiden stands at the center of the poem, as it eventually does, then the poem focuses on the process by which the "you/thou" of the narrator comes to join the "we/us" invoked at the poem's conclusion. In that case, the pronominal dialectic is identical with that of *Purity* and *Patience,* the movement of the second person to the first-person plural. What complicates the dialectic, however, is the evolution of the narrator's first person to the character's first person as normative, fixed center of the poem. Of course, such transference could not have been possible were it not for the intermediate narrator of *Gawain,* one who, while not displaced, is certainly no longer omniscient nor even very steadfast in his point of view.

This emphasis on the first-person singular is clear from the outset of *Pearl*. The first stanza, for instance, both presents and offers a solution to a dichotomy between the first-person narrator and the lost pearl through linking pronouns for the Dreamer and his daughter. The narrator tells us that "I neuer her precios pere" (4) and that "her syde3 . . . I jugged" (6–7) so that "I sette her sengeley" (8). Yet the dichotomy is resolved in favor of the predominant first person, used an additional three times while the pearl is reduced to the less personal "hit" (10). The second stanza then juxtaposes that "hit" (13) with some ten first-person pronouns, the most important of which is the possessive "my." The fifth stanza of the first group serves as a virtual microcosm of the themes and images we have studied so far. There we encounter reason struggling with *wylle* over the laws of *kynde*, the essential conflict of miracles. Located amidst the cluster of first-person pronouns, we find the image of his expressive hands pressed together:

Bifore þat spot my honde I spenud,
For care ful colde þat to me ca3t.
A deuely dele in my hert denned,
Þa3 resoun sette myseluen sa3t.
I playned my perle þat þer wat3 spenned,
Wyth fyrte skylle3 þat faste fa3t.
Þa3 kynde of Kryst me comfort kenned,
My wreched wylle in wo ay wra3te.
                    (49–56)

"My honde . . . my perle . . . my wylle": Possession reveals identity. In *Sir Gawain*, the Green Knight reveals himself by announcing his ownership of the green girdle: "For hit is my wede þat þou were3, þat ilke wouen girdel; / Myn owen wyf hit þe weued . . ." (2358–59). In the same way, the Dreamer identifies himself by stating his ownership of the pearl—claiming its mutability, since she has fallen victim to death, and his own seeming immutability and superiority, since he has survived. These are the very claims that the Maiden refutes, explaining that the Dreamer has confused the transitory rose and the eternal "perle of prys" (269–76).

The debate between the Dreamer and Maiden is thus a battle of ownership, of defining the *possession* of eternal reward or beatitude.[37] The poem thus becomes a contest to see where the competing boundaries of perception and salvation are drawn, to ascertain which of the competing *our*'s or *we*'s used by both the Dreamer and the Maiden has existential reality. In that sense, *Pearl* with its parable of the workers in the vineyard is very much like *Gawain* in its emphasis on contracts and the ownership they create. In *Pearl*, the dominant question of ownership becomes obvious in stanza groups 5–7 that form the core of the "I/thou" debate of the poem. Here stanzas are dominated either by the first or the third person, both used as often as twelve or thirteen times in the poem's twelve-line stanzas, thereby reflecting the type of juxtapositions that we saw earlier in stanzas 105–8 of *Patience*. In these stanzas, the *Pearl*-narrator uses the first person to refer to himself, his true subject, but rarely uses the third to refer to the Maiden. But curiously, the *Pearl*-Maiden tends to minimize the first person and to allow second-person pronouns denoting the Dreamer to dominate her speech. Her subject, apparently, is also the Dreamer. Both, at least, are talking about the same thing.

The Dreamer begins the fifth stanza group by asserting his ownership of the *Pearl*: " 'O perle,' quoþ I, 'in perleȝ pyȝt, / Art þou my perle þat I haf playned, / Regretted by *myn one* on nyȝte?' " (241–43). Self and ownership: these represent the mainstays of the Dreamer's point of view. For her part, the Maiden, shifting from the formal "ȝe" to the informal "þou" much like the narrator in the "Exhortation to Purity," throws the Dreamer's words back at him in a fashion which not only demarcates the "I/Thou" gulf between them but stresses the folly of possessiveness:

"Sir, ȝe haf *your* tale mysentente,
To say *your* perle is al awaye . . ."
(257–58)

"Bot, jueler gente, if *þou* schal lose
Þy joy for a gemme þat *þe* watȝ lef
Me þynk *þe* put in a mad porpose . . ."
(265–67)

And *þou* hatȝ called *þy* wyrde a þef,
Þat oȝt of noȝt hatȝ mad *þe* cler.
Þou blameȝ þe bote of *þy* meschef;
Þou art no kynde jueler."
(273–76)

Beyond the plethora of second persons, there is a clear and mocking emphasis on possession, along with a movement from 3e (your) to þy (thou), a progression that the narrators of *Purity* and *Patience* employ so often to lecture the reader.

The Jeweler's response to the Maiden's lecture is like Arthur's to the Green Knight when, in spite of the visual evidence to the contrary as well as the knight's repeated insistence that he comes in peace, Arthur persists in asking the green intruder if he has come "to fy3t." In short, the Dreamer's first-person-dominated reply compounds his perceptual/linguistic error with his reference to "my Lorde" (285), in spite of his being told that to speak in such terms is folly.

The *Pearl*-Maiden, no longer turning the Dreamer's possessives on him, responds by defining a community that excludes the Dreamer and thereby nullifies his claim to ownership:

I halde þat jueler lyttel to prayse
Þat loue3 wel þat he se3 wyth y3e,
And much to blame and vncortoyse
Þat leve3 *oure* Lorde wolde make a ly3e,
Þat lelly hy3te your lyf to rayse,
Þa3 fortune dyd your flesch to dy3e.
(301–6)

The *Pearl*-Maiden's "oure Lorde" clearly stands in deliberate counterpoint to the Dreamer's "my Lorde." Moreover, "oure," strategically placed between the first- and second-person pronouns, is juxtaposed to the double "your," thus suggesting the exclusion of the Dreamer. Both the sense of the lines—the self-alienating nature of the Jeweler's belief that God would lie—as well as their structure, serve to draw the boundary of salvation and place the Dreamer outside its circumference.

As to commonality, all that the two characters share, according to the Maiden, is "oure 3orefader" (322), the source of Original Sin. As to salvation, the Maiden speaks with the fixed authority of the narrators of *Purity* and *Patience*, making holiness her personal property as she successively refers to "My Lorde" (403), "my Lorde þe Lamb" (407), "my Lorde þe Lombe" (413). Indeed, some four hundred lines later, she appeals to "My Lombe, my Lorde, my dere juelle, / My joy, my blys, my lemman fre . . ." (795–96), in a virtual litany of possessives that further reinforce the same point. In the earlier passage, having so firmly established her possession of and identification with her Lord, the Maiden then ends her speech with lines clearly designed to stress God's reciprocal possession of the Maiden: "And sesed in alle hys herytage / Hys lef is. I am holy hysse: / Hys pyese, hys prys, and hys parage / Is rote and grounde of alle my blysse" (417–20). The Maiden possesses the Lord; the Lord possesses the Maiden. The narrator of *Purity* possesses Matthew in recollection; the narrator of *Patience* possesses the Beatitudes. Only the *Pearl*-Dreamer does not really possess what he claims, for a legal claim of possession can only be made by, among other things, a clearly defined or fixed entity. In both *Purity* and *Pearl*, God is the immutable, fixed point from which the circle of salvation emanates. How far from *Purity* the narrator of *Pearl* has come. In the earlier poem, the narrator's absorption of and identification with scripture made him the "I" at the center of the poem. All those who did not join him in the "we/us" at the end of the poem risk exclusion from beatitude. The reflexivity of possession between the *Pearl*-Maiden and her Lord are clearly designed to demonstrate the narrator's exclusion. The Dreamer's response to the community defined here is to counter with his own first-person plural community, explaining that his disbelief in the Maiden's claims springs from the perspective of "*We* [who] leuen on Marye, þat grace of grewe" (425), again insisting on earthly community to authorize the name: "*We* calle hyr Fenyx of Arraby" (430). Clearly the Dreamer's "we" is an exclusive term—a term that sets him apart from the "we/us" of the community of heaven.

As the verbal give-and-take continues, the Maiden responds with a counterclaim of ownership, "my Lady of quom Jesu con spryng" (453), and then adds that Mary's sovereignty displeases none of "oure gyng" (455), a group that clearly excludes the Dreamer. As she proceeds to refer to that "gyng" as we ("Al arn we membreȝ of Jhesu Kryst" [458]; "So fare we alle" [467]), she formulates a counterbalancing "we" in opposition to the "we" previously invoked by the Jeweler. In many ways, the Dreamer's community is analogous to the false "we/us" of the complaining workers in the Maiden's parable of the vineyard (549–56), a "we" meant to exclude those who have come lately into the vineyard. And that selfish first-person exclusion has its own poetic antecedent in *Patience*, specifically in the complaining Jonah's "I" that, in turn, sets him apart from the Ninevites.

Exactly how the "I" of the individual becomes included as a part of the "we/us" of heaven is a mystery at the thematic center of the poem that becomes a philosophical exploration of the pronomial progression that structures the other three works in the manuscript. Describing the process, the Maiden says,

"Among vus commeȝ no noþer strot ne stryf,
Bot, vch on enlé we wolde were fyf . . .
Þe mo þe myryer, so God me blesse!
In compayny gret our luf con þryf
In honour more, and neuer þe lesse.

Lasse of blysse may non vus bryng
Þat beren þys perle vpon oure bereste,
For þay of mote couþe neuer mynge,
Of spotleȝ perleȝ þa beren þe creste.
Alþaȝ oure corses in clotteȝ clynge,
And ȝe remen for rauþe wyþouten reste,
We þurȝoutly hauen cnawyng;
Of on deþe ful oure hope is drest.
Þe Lombe vus gladeȝ, oure care is kest;
He myrþeȝ vus alle at vch a mes.
                                    (848–62)

Set against the "we/us/oure" of that community is the single "ȝe" of line 858. Such separateness is maintained throughout the poem, not only in the vision but as the narrator/Dreamer attempts to cross the river boundary and enter the circle of the saved:

Delyt me drof in yȝe and ere,
My maneȝ mynde to maddyng malte.
Quen I seȝ my frely, I wolde be þere,
Byȝonde þe water, þaȝ ho were walte.
I þoȝt þat noþyng myȝt me dere
To fech me bur and take me halte,
And to start in þe strem schulde non me stere,
To swymme þe remnaunt, þaȝ I þer swalte.
Bot, of þat munt I watȝ bitalt.
When I schulde start in þe strem astraye,
Out of þat caste I watȝ bycalt;
Hit watȝ not at my Prynceȝ paye.
                                    (1153–64)

Hit payed hym not þat I so flonc
Ouer meruelous mereȝ, so mad arayde.
Of raas, þaȝ I were rasch and ronk,
ȝet, rapely þerinne I watȝ restayed.
For ryȝt as I sparred vnto þe bonc,
Þat brathe out of my drem me brayde.
Þen wakned I in þat erber wlonk;
My hede vpon þat hylle watȝ layde
Þeras my perle to grounde strayd.
I raxled and fel in gret affray,
And, sykyng, to myself I sayd:
"Now al be to þat Prynceȝ paye."
                                    (1165–76)

That the Dreamer's impulsive charge into the river represents an act of uncontrolled ego is evident in the ubiquitous first-person pronouns.[38] Rarely does one see such persistence in the first person, even in Jonah at his most willful. The refusal to abandon "I" and hence join the inclusive "we/us" of the previous passage—rather than the magical properties of the river—keeps the Dreamer out of the New Jerusalem. Not until the poem's concluding lines does the narrator finally evoke the "us" of the faithful: "Þe preste vus scheweȝ vch a daye. / He gef vus to be his homly hyne / And precious perleȝ vnto his pay" (1210–12).

His perspective thus turned inside out, the narrator, the "I" of the poem, has finally moved into the circle, crossed the boundary into the parameter of the community drawn by the character, the Maiden. In doing so, he has completed the progression from *Purity* to *Gawain*. If *Pearl* culminates in the progressive metamorphosis of the narrator, it also begins that progression anew and in circular fashion leads back to *Purity*. The plea to "us" at the end of *Pearl* recalls the priest of the introduction to *Purity* who shows us the Eucharist. More importantly, the Jeweler, returned to the waking world still grieving and locked into the first person, is like the man in the dirty garment, invited into the hall only to be cast out in the end. In fact, the final lines with their sudden reversal in their abandonment of the first-person singular and their adoption of the Maiden's first-person plural, come as a complete surprise,[39] creating the type of ambiguous speaker found in the final quatrain of *Pa-*

tience. Is this the narrator suddenly made over? Or is the poet dropping the mask of persona to become the instructive author standing
behind the fictive narrator, just as God stood behind the "klerk"
Merlin who, in turn, taught "koyntyse" to Morgan, and Morgan behind the Green Knight, who taught humility to Gawain? If *Pearl*'s
final shift from the singular to the plural first person is evidence of
such an emerging author, then we as readers become aware that the
still unenlightened first-person narrator, continuing to grieve and
lament as he does in the penultimate stanza, is very much in need
of the sermon that is *Purity,* which itself focuses on what it means
to be cast out in such a fashion. In its ending, then, *Pearl* both
prefigures and concludes, is both initiator and capstone, beginning
and end of the sequence of poems that progress from *Pearl* to
Gawain, from *forme* to *fynisment*—which is, in turn, why beginnings and endings have always been of special importance to students of the anonymous fourteenth-century *Gawain* manuscript.

NOTES

INTRODUCTION

1. All textual references to and citations from *Pearl, Purity, Patience,* and *Sir Gawain and the Green Knight* are taken from *The Pearl Poems: An Omnibus Edition,* vol. 1, *Pearl and Cleanness,* vol. 2, *Patience and Sir Gawain and the Green Knight,* ed. William Vantuono (New York: Garland, 1984). All emphases in the text are added. Despite Vantuono's decision to follow the current practice of entitling the manuscript's second poem *Cleanness,* we have chosen to retain its "trwe tytel," *Purity.* While Stanbury provides the most cogent and practical reasoning for retaining its "original" title (*Seeing,* 66, n. 1), our usage is a matter of unabashed sentimental attachment both to the poem as we first knew it and to the times in which we first read it. We follow the practice of using "Belshazzar" rather than the currently popular "Baltasar" because Julian learned it that way in Sunday School.

For the most recent annotated bibliographies on the Cotton Nero poems, see Foley, "*Gawain*-Poet," 251–82; and Blanch, "Supplement," 363–86. For the most current survey of *Gawain* scholarship, see Stainsby, *Sir Gawain.* For a discussion of current trends in *Gawain* scholarship and of potential areas for future research, see Blanch and Wasserman, "Current State," 401–12.

2. On the circular form of *Gawain, Patience,* and *Pearl,* see, for example, Ebbs, "Stylistic Mannerisms," 522–25; Burrow, *Ricardian Poetry,* 58, 60, 64–65; Nelson, *The Incarnate Word,* 25–49; Benzon, "Sir Gawain," 267–93; Huntsman, "The Celtic Heritage," 179; Lenz, *The Promised End,* 29–34; and Davidoff, *Beginning Well,* 189–94.

3. See Irwin and Kelly, "Way and the End," 33–55.

4. Davenport notes that while critics write of a single author for all four poems, a "caution . . . keeps creeping in" studies that treat more than one of the Cotton Nero A.x poems (*Art,* 1). Such caution is perhaps best seen in Spearing's self-assessment of having produced chapters that "would not . . . be invalidated if it should eventually be proved by objective evidence that the poems were the work not of a single poet but a school of poets" (*Gawain-Poet,* 40). Echoing Davenport, Lynn Johnson writes that the poems "deserve to be studied as a group," citing Charles Moorman's statement, "Our greatest need seems now to be for studies in which the works of the *Pearl*-Poet are taken as a whole" (*Voice of the Gawain-Poet,* ix). In good *Gawain*-Poet fashion, Johnson ends her study where she begins by taking up her introductory concerns with unity, effectively discussing the themes, structures, and images that unite the four poems (see especially 213–14).

Still, despite the undoubted quality of Johnson's chapters, they are in many ways separable treatments of separate poems—although each adds an important element of the "voice" of the poet. A. Hieatt ("Symbolic and Narrative Patterns," 125–43), as his title indicates, treats a series of common elements that unite the poems in the manuscript.

5. For recent advocates of the single authorship hypothesis, see Derolez, "Authorship and Statistics," 41–51; Vantuono, "*Patience, Cleanness, Pearl, and Gawain,*" 37–69; as well as Cooper and Pearsall, "The *Gawain* Poems," 365–85.

Some critics, however, claim that the question of common authorship remains open. See, for example, Lawton, "Middle English Alliterative Poetry," 8–9; and McColly and Weier, "Literary Attribution," 65–75. For studies arguing the case for multiple authorship, see, for instance, Kjellmer, *Did the "Pearl Poet" Write Pearl?*; and Tajima, "Additional Syntactical Evidence," 193–98.

6. Reichardt, "Paginal Eyes," 22–36.

7. See Crawford, "Structure," 29–45, whose argument is considerably strengthened by the realization that medieval architects, lacking Euclidian geometry and instruments of the modern architect, relied on similar proportional design to plan and construct the great cathedrals of medieval Europe. See Coldstream, *Masons and Sculptors,* 34–39, as well as Gimpel, *Cathedral Builders,* 98–108.

8. Lee, "Illuminating Critic," 17–46, calls the poem's illustrator its "first critic" (18), but that title should more accurately go to the manuscript's compiler.

9. For the "unified vision" of the Middle Ages, see Chenu, *Nature, Man, and Society* (1–48), concerning the discovery of natural law and growing new Aristotelianism which, in turn, led to what Chenu terms "the symbolist mentality" (99–145). See also Chenu, 6–9, 24; as well as Mâle, *Gothic Image,* 1–22, in reference to the allegorical mind and its concomitant belief in the interconnectedness of parts of Creation. It should be noted that Mâle arranges his study according to the medieval concept of the *speculum* or mirror. The notion of mirrors and the concept of reflection serve to reinforce the idea of the similarly reflective relationship between microcosm/macrocosm as well as the interconnectedness and, hence, unity of the various parts of creation that serve as mirrors/reflections of one another. See Gradon's brief remarks on Vincent of Beauvais in *Form and Style,* 27, notably her discussion of signs and metaphor. Also instructive is the discussion of metaphor by Nims, in "Translatio," 215–30. Obviously, the metaphoric relationship presumes an interconnectedness between its various, often seemingly dissimilar, parts. Finally, for an illuminating discussion of the medieval concept of "unity," see the introduction to Allen and Moritz,

Distinction of Stories. Much of what Allen and Moritz argue may be applied profitably to questions of unity in the Cotton Nero A.x manuscript.

10. "Omnis mundi creatura / Quasi liber et pictura / Nobis est et speculum / Nostrae vitae, nostrae mortis / Nostrae status, nostrae sortis / Fidele signaculum," *Rhythmus alter* (*PL* 210.579A–B).

11. For example, see Savage, "Significance of the Hunting Scenes," 1–15, for a reading of the poem based on the interconnectedness and mutual referentiality of the poem's seemingly separate parts.

12. History and time have long been focal points of criticism of all four poems. Representative examples would include Lynn Johnson, *Voice,* 218–19, who, seeing concern with, and perhaps fear of, time as one of their unifying themes, devotes specific sections to cyclic, degenerative, and regenerative time in *Gawain;* Shichtman, "*Sir Gawain,*" 3–15, who treats the "movement from mythic time to historical time" (12); Stanbury, *Seeing,* 42–70, who examines *Purity* largely in the light of "History"; Schleusener, "History and Action," 959–65, who views *Patience* in terms of history as a providential plan. Other essays on time and history include Bishop, "Time and Tempo," 611–19; Blamires, "Turning of the Year," 21–37; Newman, "Sin, Judgment, and Grace," 3027–28A; Rhodes, "Vision and History," 1–13; and Stanbury, "In God's Sight," 105–16. Finally, see Sheila Fisher, "Leaving Morgan Aside," 129–51, who sees *Gawain* as a poem "that tries to revise history in order to make it come out right" (129).

13. For a discussion of providential history as the unfolding of divine will, see Schleusener, "History and Action." As we shall note in the study of miracles in chap. 3, Augustine views historical events as deriving from "hidden causes" (*De Genesi ad litteram,* 9.18.33–34, *PL* 34.406–7), or "semina" that are "planted" during the working of the first and greatest miracle, Creation. Thus, the world is described as being "pregnant" with events yet to be brought into being (*De Trinitate,* 3.9.16, *PL* 42.877–78).

14. For a treatment of time in *Pearl,* especially the poet's use of August and the parable of the workers in the vineyard, see Lynn Johnson, "*Pearl* Dreamer," 3–15.

15. On the order of composition of the Cotton poems, Vantuono states in *Pearl Poems:* "Scholars generally agree that the poems were not written in their order of appearance in the manuscript" (vol. 1, *Pearl and Cleanness,* xix; see also xx–xxii). Early assessments of the "order of composition" were based largely on two assumptions: (a) the greater complexity/sophistication of *Gawain* and *Pearl* in comparison with the two homiletic poems and (b) the assumption that the complexity of an artist's work grows rather than diminishes. Both of these assumptions have been challenged. In fact, it is interesting to note that the question of the order of composition is now a topic significant in its omission rather than in its presence. Davenport, *Art,* 5–6,

argues that the only ordering that can be deduced is that of the compiler, stating that hypothetical ordering and extrapolated "biographies" based on those findings are, in his words, "a game anyone can play." On dating, see also Horrall, "Notes," 191–98.

16. On felix culpa see Haines, *Fortunate Fall*, as well as Clark and Wasserman, "*Purity*: The Cities," 284–306.

17. Here, as elsewhere, we adopt Menner's subtitle for the section, including lines 1049–1156 in *Purity*.

18. Shichtman, "*Sir Gawain*," sees *Gawain* as subverting traditional temporal cycles. For a discussion of cyclical history in *Sir Gawain and the Green Knight*, see Lynn Johnson, *Voice*, 40–46. For a discussion of the life cycle of the individual and the larger scheme of history, see Stanbury, *Seeing*, 52–54, et passim.

19. For the rise and fall of cities, see Clark and Wasserman, "*Pearl*-Poet's City," 297–309.

20. For the significance of city imagery, see the Clark and Wasserman essays, "*Pearl*-Poet's City" and "*Purity*: The Cities."

21. The Old English text is taken from Wyatt, ed., *Anglo-Saxon Reader*, 144.

22. The word *childgered* has fueled a critical controversy. See, for example, Schnyder, "Aspects of Kingship," 289–94; John Fisher, "Wyclif," 151; Burrow, *A Reading*, 7; Campbell, "Character of King Arthur," 26–30, 40; Moody, "*Childgered* Arthur," 173–80; Lynn Johnson, *Voice*, 49; Wasserman, "Weavers and Wordsmiths," 112; Dean, *Arthur of England*, 77–79; and Piehler, *Visionary Landscape*, 144–62.

For differing, and we would argue essentially "romantic," views of the poet's appreciation of the child, see Attreed, "Medieval Children," 390–94, who argues for viewing the *Pearl*-Maiden in light of what she deems the medieval esteem for children as symbols of innocence; and Pattison, *Child Figure*, 21–24, 45, who views the Maiden in *Pearl* as the "first true child figure" in English literature.

23. For discussions of a medieval concept of history, see Chenu, *Nature, Man, and Society*, 110–11, 116–19, and especially chap. 5, "New Awareness of History," 162–201; as well as Mâle, *Gothic Image*, 131–76, 332–89.

24. For a good summary of early critical treatments of *Pearl*, especially of the elegy versus allegory controversy and of the poem's theology, see Wellek, "*Pearl*."

25. On the structure of *Purity*, see Crawford, "Structure"; Brzezinski, "Conscience and Covenant," 166–80; Davenport, *Art*, 56, 98–100, et passim; Spearing, *Gawain-Poet*, 41–50; Matsumoto, "Structure," 75–90.

26. Schnyder, "Aspects of Kingship," 289–94, has argued for the similarities between the courts of Arthur and Belshazzar.

CHAPTER 1

1. For the Word as the medium of Creation, see Augustine, *Confessiones*, 11.5–6 (*PL* 32.811–12); and *De genesi ad litteram*, 9.10.17 (*PL* 34.398–99); as well as Hugh of Saint-Victor, *De arca Noe morale*, 2.13 (*PL* 176.644B). The notion of expressly verbal Creation leads naturally to the ubiquitous metaphor of Creation as a book: Augustine, *Sermonum mai* 126.6 (*PL* 38.699–702) and Hugh of Saint-Victor, *De eruditione docta* 7.3 (*PL* 176.814B). Also see Wasserman, "Language and Destiny," 196–98.

2. See Clark and Wasserman, "*Pearl*-Poet's City," 297–309.

3. For a discussion of approaches to the Otherworld, see Dinzelbacher, "Way to the Other," 70–87. For an extended discussion of this *locus amoenus*, see Curtius, *European Literature*, 183–202; and Patch, *Other World*.

4. See, for example, Matsuda, "Linear View," 1–23; Spearing, "Medieval Narrative Style," 1–21; and Clark and Wasserman, "Passing of the Seasons," 5–22.

5. See, for example, Gross, "Telescoping in Time," 130–37.

6. See, for example, two essays by Stanbury: "*Pearl* and the Idea," 117–31; and "Visions of Space," 133–58.

7. Lynn Johnson, *Voice*, notes that *Gawain* "evokes the theme of fallen cities, placing Sir Gawain and Arthur's court against a background of waste" (219). On the series of kingdoms in *Gawain*, see Chapman, "Ticius to Tuskan," 59–60.

8. For some representative studies of time in *Gawain*, see Crane, "Four Levels of Time," 65–80; Ordelle Hill, "Sir Gawain's Holidays," 17–26; Boitani, "World of Romance," 60–70; Patrick, "A Reading," 27–33; Lock, *Aspects of Time*, 206–21; Lynn Johnson, *Voice*, 37–96, 243–53; Bishop, "Time and Tempo," 611–19; and Shichtman, "*Sir Gawain*," 3–15.

9. On the liturgical calendar in *Gawain*, see Savage, "Feast of Fools," 537–44; Pace, "Gawain and Michaelmas," 404–11; Neaman, "Sir Gawain's Covenant," 30–42; Keenan, "Feasts and Fasts," 34–35; and Ordelle Hill, "Sir Gawain's Holidays," 17–26.

10. For an explanation of the poet's accurate naming and depiction of deer, see Ong, "Green Knight's Harts," 536–39; and Savage, "Hunting Terms," 216. See also Savage's notes for *hertteȝ* (1154), *hindeȝ* (1158), *bukkeȝ* (1155), and *does* (1159), in "Notes on *Sir Gawain*," 169–76.

11. For a sampling of interpretations of "first age," see Hussey, "*Sir Gawain*," 161–74, especially 162; Stevens, "Laughter and Game," 65–78, especially 66–67; Tristram, *Figures of Life*, 28–34; Burrow, *Ages of Man*, 173–77; and Dove, *Perfect Age*, 134–40.

12. See lines 1412 and 2008. On the symbolism of cockcrow and the potential link with St. Peter, see Burrow, *Reading*, 114.

13. On the poet's apocalypticism see Pollard, "Images of the Apocalypse," 85–93; Clark and Wasserman, "Passing of the Seasons"; Prior, "*Patience*—Beyond Apocalypse," 337–48; Russell, "*Pearl*'s Courtesy," 183–95.

14. Blanch, "Imagery of Binding," 53–60.

15. The "semiotic" matter of *Gawain*, especially the influence of this romance's language, signs, and multivalent imagery, has been examined carefully within recent years. See, for example, Hanna, "Unlocking What's Locked," 289–302; Shoaf, *Poem as Green Girdle*; Gertz, "Green Knight Teaches," 73–83; Gertz, "*Translatio studii et imperii*," 185–203; Arthur, *Medieval Sign Theory*; Ashley, "*Trawthe* and Temporality," 3–24; and Shoaf, " 'Syngne of Surfet,' " 152–69. For more recent explorations of the semiotic issues raised in *Gawain*, see the following essays in *Text and Matter*, ed. Blanch, Miller, and Wasserman: Plummer, "Signifying the Self," 195–212; Ashley, "Bonding and Signification," 213–19; and Arthur, "Gawain's Shield," 221–27. Finally, in one of the more challenging and perceptive of the recent readings of the "semiotic" matter of the poem, Heng, "Feminine Knots," 500–514, presents a feminist reading in which the pentangle represents a "static" or "finished" male sign that attempts to announce "Gawain's attributes and his actual possesion of them" (504), in short, a direct, nonarbitrary identification of signifier and signified. In contrast to the abstract pentangle and its "fantasy of the uncut knot," Heng sets the feminine green girdle, which imprints the body of its wearer.

16. For studies of the "privatization" of language, see Ferster, "Writing on the Ground"; and Wasserman, "Language and Destiny," 179–224.

17. See Liuzza, "Names, Reputation, and History," 41–56; and Blanch, "Name and Fame of Gawain," 141–47.

18. On the Realist position on signs in regard to grammatical categories, see Colish, *Mirror of Language*, 69, 84–85. For helpful and brief overviews of the Nominalist/Realist debate over the existence of "Reality" *ante res* or *in res*, see the introduction to *Problem of Universals*, ed. Landesman, 3–17, as well as Copleston, *History of Philosophy*, 136ff.

19. On the crucial question of names and identities, see Taylor, "Gawain's Garland," 6–14.

20. See Vantuono, ed., *Pearl Poems*, vol. 2, *Patience*, 2.238, n. 11, for a brief history of the editorial debate over "Ticius."

21. Interestingly enough, Finucane, *Miracles and Pilgrims*, notes "a document posted on the doors of Parliament in 1395" in which Lollards specifically "condemned offerings to 'blind roods and deaf images of wood and stone' as idolatry" (200). Whether the poet's repeated condemnation of the mute idols of "stokkes and stones" reflects this contemporary Lollard attitude is uncertain.

22. On Belshazzar's inability to read signs, see, for example, Stanbury, *Seeing*, 59–66.

23. For the importance of sloth in *Patience*, see Stock, " 'Poynt' of *Patience*," 163–75. As Stock points out (169–70), the king's speech may represent "a clear warning against and repudiation of . . . *acedia*."

24. For an application of Bakhtin's theories to *Sir Gawain and the Green Knight*, see Levine, "Aspects of Grotesque Realism," 65–75.

25. This rather concise formulation of Bakhtin's concept of the purpose of carnival and the grotesque is taken from Krystyna Pomorska's foreward to Bakhtin's *Rabelais and His World*, ix. For a discussion of Bakhtin's concept of the way "parody in its narrow sense [as well as] all the other forms of grotesque realism degrade, bring down to earth, turn their subject into flesh," see Bakhtin's own introduction to this work, especially 20–25.

26. The ambiguous and frequently appearing laughter in *Sir Gawain* has attracted a good deal of critical attention which has, in turn, produced a variety of interpretations. See Butturff, "Laughter and Discovered Aggression," 139–49; Christmas, "A Reading," 238–47; Stevens, "Laughter and Game," 65–78; Longsworth, "Interpretive Laughter," 141–47.

27. Vantuono, Andrew and Waldron, Moorman, and Tolkien, for example, all gloss "steuen" as "noise" and "terme" as "place," "goal," and/or "time limit," yet all recognize the poet's use of these terms to mean "voice" and "word," respectively, in other places within the canon. None sees the possibility of a pun on the linguistic denotations associated with these words elsewhere in the manuscript. See Joseph Bosworth, *An Anglo-Saxon Dictionary; Based on the Manuscript Collections of Joseph Bosworth* (London: Oxford University Press, 1972), s. v. "steven," and s. v. "term."

28. For the importance of sound in *Gawain*, see Renoir, "An Echo to the Sense," 9–23.

29. For example, see *Gawain*, lines 46, 47, 116–18.

30. The noise of Sodom specifically offends God: "The grete soun of Sodamas synkkeȝ in myn ereȝ" (*Purity*, 689). For noise as a characteristic of Sodom, see also lines 849, 862, 873–74. For a recent study of rhetorical games in *Gawain* and other works, see Troyan, "Rhetoric without Genre," 377–95.

31. For the knight as instructor, see Gertz, "Green Knight Teaches," 73–83.

32. See Blanch and Wasserman, "Medieval Court," 176–88.

33. See Augustine, *De Ordine*, 2.12.1011–12, for a discussion of communication as the purpose of language.

34. Andreas begins the second book, whose subject is the retention of love, with an explicit warning about the need to keep love secret: "The man who wants to keep his love affair for a long time untroubled should above all things be careful not to let it be known to any outsider, but should keep it hidden from everybody" (*Art of Courtly Love*, 151). For discussions of the influence of Andreas and courtly love on *Sir Gawain and the Green Knight*,

see Gallagher, "*Trawþe* and *Luf-talkyng*," 362–76, wherein he sees the two qualities in his title as being opposed to each other. See also Kiteley, "*De Honeste Amandi*," 7–16; Wright, "*Luf-Talkyng*," 79–86.

35. See two important essays by Hanning: "Sir Gawain and the Red Herring," 5–23; and "Poetic Emblems," 26–28.

36. "*Sir Gawain* and You," 165–78.

37. On the Arthurian court's reaction to Gawain's adoption of the girdle, see Bruten, "Gawain's Green Girdle," 452–54.

CHAPTER 2

1. All quotations from the works of Chaucer are taken from *The Riverside Chaucer*, ed. Larry D. Benson (Boston: Houghton Mifflin Co., 1987).

2. On the force of law, see Blanch, " 'Al was this land fulfild,' " 41–51. On the link between Gawain's pentangle and medieval legal-chivalric tradition, see Richard Green, "Gawain's Five Fingers," 14–18.

3. For studies of the pledged word and covenants in *Gawain*, see Machann, "Structural Study," 629–37; Blanch, "Religion and Law," 93–101; Arthur, "Head for a Head," 178–94; Blanch and Wasserman, "Medieval Contracts," 598–610; Cole, "Purpose and Practice," 1274A; and Canfield, *Word as Bond*, 13–21.

4. Despite the number of contracts formed and executed in *Gawain*, critics generally ignore the influence of English common law upon the poem's content. Furthermore, the token attention that has been paid to the legal coloring of *Gawain* focuses upon legal phraseology rather than upon the poem's employment of medieval legal theory and practice. See, for example, Burrow, *Reading*, 22–23 and 66–69; and Wilson, *Gawain-Poet*, 119–20. Some recent scholars, however, have examined in nontechnical ways humanity's covenants with God or the impotence of linguistic forms as mirrors of *trawthe*. See, for example, Brzezinski, "Conscience and Covenant," 166–80; and Ashley, "*Trawthe* and Temporality," 3–24. For the imprint of a medieval legal maxim, "quod principi placet," upon the beginning and end of *Pearl*, see Schless, "*Pearl*'s 'Princes Paye,' " 183–85.

For an analysis of legal conventions, motifs, and formulas in Chaucer—a study that includes some references to the *Gawain*-Poet—see Hornsby, *Chaucer and the Law*. For the significance of covenants both in medieval life and in *Gawain*, see Shoaf, *Poem as Green Girdle*.

5. While scholars have been nearly unanimous in citing Gawain's failure to surrender the green girdle, critical assessments of the seriousness of Gawain's fault have varied widely. For example, Blenkner, in "Sin, Psychology, and the Structure," 354–87, perceives the psychological development of sin as an important structural element in the poem, whereas Engelhardt in "Predicament of Gawain," 218–25, discusses Gawain's failure to

conform to the virtues symbolized by the pentangle. See also Burrow, "Two Confession Scenes," 73–79; Shedd, "Knight in Tarnished Armour," 3–13; W. O. Evans, "Case for Sir Gawain," 721–33; and Christmas, "A Reading," 238–47. For more recent moral-religious approaches to Gawain's flaws, see the following important studies: Thomas Hill, "Gawain's Jesting Lie," 279–86; Arthur, "Head for a Head," 178–94; Hamilton, "Chivalry as Sin," 113–17; and Morgan, "Validity of Gawain's Confession," 1–18.

6. For the free exercise of will as a condition for the construction of a binding contract—"a voluntary transaction between debtor and creditor"— see Simpson, *History of the Common Law*, 186. Furthermore, Brundage, *Canon Law*, 56, underscores the necessity of "mindful consideration" in the making of a vow and notes that the primary means of assessing vows is the oath taker's intention at the moment of swearing (62). Similarly, Henry, *Contracts*, 172–73, contends that a voluntary promise is necessary for both the creation and execution of a contract and that contracts made under duress are invalid.

Perhaps the best indication of the centrality of will may be found in Sir William Blackstone's definition of this legal term. See his *Commentaries on the Laws of England*, 20–21: "An involuntary act, as it has no claim to merit, so neither can it induce any guilt: the concurrence of the will, when it has its choice either to do or to avoid the fact in question, being the only thing that renders human action either praiseworthy or culpable. Indeed, to make a complete crime cognizable by human laws, there must be both a will and an act."

Blackstone contends that the commission of a crime requires a "vicious will" and an illegal act precipitated by the vicious will (21). Furthermore, the will is not fused with the unlawful act when a "defect of understanding" exists: "For where there is no discernment, there is no choice; and where there is no choice, there can be no act of the will, . . . he, therefore, that has no understanding can have no will to guide his conduct" (21). Moreover, when actions are committed "by chance or ignorance" (21), although sufficient comprehension of the nature of the act is posited and the will is ordered properly, then "the will sits neuter" (21). Deficiency of will, however, is represented when a man's illegal act is shaped by "misfortune or chance," not by design (26). Another type of defective will springs from "*compulsion* [Blackstone's italics] and *inevitable necessity* [Blackstone's italics]," for these forces represent "constraints upon the will" (27). Finally, see Stephen, *New Commentaries*, 106–7, who notes that will is a crucial consideration in determining the punishment of a lawbreaker: ". . . to make a complete crime [legally] . . . , there must be both a will and an act. . . . And as a vicious will without a vicious act is no civil crime, so, on the other hand, an unwarrantable act without a vicious will is no crime at all."

7. The traditional division of a contract into the oath ("forwarde") and the stipulations (quid pro quo) parallels Blackstone's (*Commentaries*, 21) and Stephen's (*New Commentaries*, 106–7) division of a crime into its two components, will and act. See also Henry Campbell Black, *A Law Dictionary*, 2d ed. (St. Paul, Minn.: West Publishing, 1910), 99; and Woodbine, ed., *Bracton*, 2: 290. For a discussion of oaths in contracts, see Pollock and Maitland, *History of English Law*, 2: 187–98; and Henry, *Contracts*, 35, 227, and 241–42. For discussions of the quid pro quo, see Henry, *Contracts*, 245; Pollock and Maitland, *History of English Law*, 2: 211; and Simpson, *History of the Common Law*, 153, 193, and 424.

8. All of the contracts in *Gawain* are divided into their constituent parts—the "forwarde" (lines 378, 409, 1105, 1395, 1405, 1636, 1934, and 2347) and the "couenaunt" (lines 393, 1123, 1384, 1408, 1642, 2242, 2328, and 2340). In English common law, the "couenaunt" may represent either the quid pro quo or the contract as a whole, including the oath.

9. Henry, *Contracts*, 207.

10. See Vantuono's note on "wylle," *Pearl Poems*, vol. 2, *Patience and Sir Gawain*, 295, line 76. Brzezinski, "Conscience and Covenant," equates clean conscience or *imago dei* with "good wylle," an equation that has important ramifications for the dubious status of Gawain's confession.

11. Lopez, "Proxy in Medieval Trade," 187–94.

12. For a brief outline of the development of patristic thought on the nature and status of vows, see Brundage, *Canon Law*, 33–48.

13. Brundage, *Canon Law*, 37ff.

14. Brundage, *Canon Law*, 36 and 41.

15. An obligation is called a covenant whenever a contract entails "an agreement [binding transaction] to do [or not to do] something in the future." See Simpson, *History of the Common Law*, 19.

16. See Gordon, ed., introduction to *Pearl*, xx–xxi.

17. For a thorough explanation of "entente" ("intention" or "will") in Chaucer's *Friar's Tale*, see Passon, " 'Entente' in Chaucer's *Friar's Tale*," 166–71. For a discussion of Walter's "irrepressible freedom of will" (*Clerk's Tale*) in terms of the nominalist distinction between "potentia dei absoluta" and "potentia dei ordinata," see Steinmetz, "Late Medieval Nominalism," 38–54; for more recent readings of Walter's behavior, see Van, "Walter at the Stake," 214–24; Cramer, "Lordship, Bondage, and the Erotic," 491–511; and Lynch, "Despoiling Griselda," 41–70. For a study of "entente" in Chaucer's *Friar's Tale*, see Williams, "From Grammar's Pan," 77–95.

18. See lines 1390, 1406, 1678, and 1939. It should be noted that the exchange contracts in *Gawain* are depicted in expressly mercantile terms. For a discussion of mercantile imagery and themes, see Taylor, "Commerce and Comedy," 1–15; and Curley, "Note on Bertilak's Beard," 69–73. Recent explorations of commerce in *Gawain* include Mann, "Price and Value," 294–318; and Shoaf, *Poem as Green Girdle*.

19. The concept of gift giving as a molder of contractual obligation is as ancient as the Anglo-Saxon foundations of English common law. See, for example, Wiglaf's speech in Klaeber, ed., *Beowulf*, lines 2633–38: "Ic ðæt mæl geman, þær wē medu þēgun / þonne wē gehēton ūssum hlāforde / in bīorsele, ðē ūs ðās bēagas geaf, / þæt wē him ðā gūðgetāwa gyldan woldon, / gif him þyslicu þearf gelumpe, / helmas ond heard sweord."

For an appropriate English translation of this passage, see Crossley-Holland, trans., *Beowulf*, 108, lines 2637–41: "I think of that evening we emptied the mead-cup / in the feasting-hall, partook and pledged our lord, / who presented us with rings, that we would repay him / for his gifts of armour, helmets and hard swords, / if ever the need, need such as this, arose."

See also Simpson, *History of the Common Law*, 153; and Pollock and Maitland, *History of English Law*, 245. For the gift-giving activity as the thematic center of *Gawain*, see Harwood, "*Gawain* and the Gift," 483–99.

20. Henry, *Contracts*, 241.

21. For a comparison of the pride or willfulness of Arthur in *Gawain* and of Belshazzar in *Purity*, see, for example, Hans Schnyder, "Aspect of Kingship"; and Ackerman, " 'Pared out of Paper,' " 410–17.

22. For comments upon medieval man's antipathy toward governance by willfulness rather than by rule, see Southern, *Making of the Middle Ages*, 107: "The supremacy of Will was itself an evil, whether the will was one's own or another's . . . ." As Southern notes further (108), when true freedom is embraced and/or sought, individual actions are not ruled by will but by law: "The higher one rose towards liberty, the more the area of action was covered by law, the less it was subject to will." For differences between the two courts, see Nicholls, *Matter of Courtesy*, 112–38; and Bergner, "Two Courts," 401–16. See also two essays in the Haymes collection, *Medieval Court in Europe:* Blanch and Wasserman, "Medieval Court," 176–88; and Lepow, "Contrasted Courts," 200–208.

23. For reason as the traditional restraining influence over will, see Robertson, *Preface*, 74. It is especially important to note that in *Purity* Noah is spared because he has lived by reason (328–29): "For þou in reysoun hatʒ rengned and ryʒtwys ben euer: / Þou schal enter þis ark . . . ." For recent critical commentary on Noah's adherence to "natural law" and his "unique covenant with God," see Stanbury, *Seeing*, 56–57.

24. Black's *Law Dictionary*, 940, cites the principle of "Prior tempore potior jure" [He who is first in time is preferred in right] and notes that the concept of "priority," rooted in Anglo-Saxon law, denotes "a legal preference or precedence": "When two persons have similar rights in respect of the same subject-matter, but one is entitled to exercise his right to the exclusion of the other, he is said to have priority."

25. For recent studies of the hunts and temptations in *Gawain*, see Blenkner, "Three Hunts," 227–46; Roney, "*Sir Gawain*," 33–34; Margaret Ward, "French Ovidian Beasts," 152–61; D. H. Green, *Irony in the Medieval*

Romance, 352–57; Kean, "Christmas Games," 9–27; Barron, "*'Trawthe' and Treason*"; Garner, "Gawain and the Green Goom," 34–41; Maxwell, "Ritual and Aggression," 33–35; Goodlad, "*Gamnes* of *Sir Gawain*," 45–58; Morgan, "Action of the Hunting," 200–216; and Morgan, *Sir Gawain*, 106–23.

26. Brundage, *Canon Law*, 54, cites a Cambridge manuscript marginal gloss that notes that the breaking of a vow is a more serious sin than adultery. For the view that the temptations present tests of Gawain's *mesure*, see McClure, "Gawain's *Mesure*," 375–87; and Solomon, "Lesson of Sir Gawain," 599–608.

27. For the legal use of courtesy, see, for example, Reisner, "*Cortaysye* Sequence in *Pearl*," 400–403. For a spirited refutation of Reisner's legal interpretation of "the curtesy of England," see Alford, "Literature and Law," 942, 946–47; for an excellent study of medieval references to the law, see Alford and Seniff, eds., *Literature and Law*.

28. See *Gawain*, 1642; and *Purity*, 564. For a discussion of the symbolism of knots and the theme of binding, see Blanch, "Imagery of Binding." See also Shoaf, " 'Syngne of Surfet,' " 152–69; and Ashley, "Bonding and Signification," 213–19.

29. See lines 2456–58. For discussions of the theme of felix culpa in *Gawain*, see Haines, *Fortunate Fall*; Sims, "Gawayne's Fortunate Fall," 28–39.

30. In the first oath, Gawain swears "Bi God," whereas the other two oaths in the exchange of winnings are described as adhering to the form of the first night's agreement. For a discussion of oaths offered to God as surety and an explanation of the pledging of one's faith, see Pollock and Maitland, *History of English Law*, 186–87 and 190–91; and Henry, *Contracts*, 202.

31. For pertinent comments upon contrition, see Neuner and Roos, *Teaching of the Catholic Church*, 314: "Contrition, which has the first place among the aforesaid acts of the penitent, is a sorrow of mind and a detestation of sin committed, *together with the purpose of not sinning in the future*" [our italics]. Although the phraseology employed here ultimately stems from the Council of Trent (1551), the theological principle had been established as early as the writings of Tertullian in the second century. For a brief survey of early patristic thought on contrition, see Berington and Kirk, *Faith of the Catholics*, 24–128. For a discussion of the imperfect nature of Gawain's confession, see Burrow, "Two Confession Scenes," 73–79. See also Braswell, *Medieval Sinner*, 95–100; and Goltra, "Confession in the Green Chapel," 5–14.

32. As a covenantal partner in the Old Testament, God consistently displays contractual largesse toward man even though man fails to uphold his part of the binding transaction. As Steinmetz points out, "The God of the

late medieval nominalists, like the God of the Old Testament, is a God who remembers His covenants and who keeps them, even if He finds from time to time no faithful covenant partners among the children of men" ("Late Medieval Nominalism," 41). In giving Gawain only a nick (2311–12) on the neck and in "quitclaiming" his rights (2341–42), the Green Knight clearly acts with such largesse, especially in the light of Gawain's repeated literal-mindedness in the performance of his contractual duties (1395–97 and 2322–30). Furthermore, the Green Knight's behavior toward Gawain is linked with the performance of vertical or monopleuric contracts, another reflection of Old Testament covenants framed between God and man. See Steinmetz, "Late Medieval Nominalism," 42 and 53, n. 16; and Cantor, *Meaning of the Middle Ages*, 61–63. On the Green Knight's magnanimity in *Gawain*, see Borroff, "*Sir Gawain*," 105–28.

CHAPTER 3

1. See, for example, Ganim, *Style and Consciousness*, 55–78, 161–64.

2. Although word counting by itself proves little, it does reveal the ubiquitousness of the miraculous in the poet's work. For example, forms of "ferly" (as "wonder") occur two times in *Pearl*, seven times in *Purity*, seven times in *Gawain*; "selly"—one time in *Pearl*, one time in *Purity*, two times in *Patience*, six times in *Gawain*; "wonder"—two times in *Pearl*, nine times in *Purity*, four times in *Patience*, thirteen times in *Gawain*; meruayl ("marvel")—five times in *Pearl*, three times in *Purity*, one time in *Patience*, seven times in *Gawain*. For the importance of *selly, meruayl,* and *aventure* in *Gawain*, especially in fitt 1, see Barron, "Ambivalence of Adventure," 28–40.

3. For the poet's wordplay on *kynde,* see Wendell Johnson, "Imagery and Diction," 34; as well as Glenn, "Dislocation of *Kynde,*" 77–91; Tambling, "More Powerful Life," 1–23; Schmidt, " 'Latent Content,' " 145–68; Spearing, *Readings in Medieval Poetry,* 173–94; Baldwin, "Sacramental Perfection," 125–40; Schmidt, "*Kinde Craft,*" 105–24; Twomey, "*Cleanness,* Peter Comestor," 203–17; Twomey, "Sin of *Untrawpe,*" 117–45; and Twomey, "Anatomy of Sin," 5046A.

4. For studies referring to the Sodomites' sin, see, for example, Clark and Wasserman, "*Purity:* The Cities"; O'Bryan, "Sodom and Gomorrah," 15–23; Clark and Wasserman, "*Purity* and *Das Neunfelsenbuch,*" 179–84; Kelly and Irwin, "Meaning of *Cleanness,*" 232–60; Lynn Johnson, *Voice,* 117–30; Morse, *Pattern of Judgment,* 129–99; Matsumoto, "Structure"; Brzezinski, "Conscience and Covenant"; and Purdon, "Sodom and Gomorrah," 64–69.

5. For an effective presentation of historical patterns in *Purity,* see Morse, *Pattern of Judgment,* 129–99.

6. For a discussion of the essential differences between Augustine and Aquinas on miracles, see Benedicta Ward, *Miracles and the Medieval Mind*, 18, 24, 221 n. 4; as well as Louis Monden, *Signs and Wonders*, 42–48. Both scholars emphasize Augustine's treatment of miracles as "signs." This aspect of Augustine's thought is evident in *De Genesi ad litteram*, 9.18; and especially in *In Joannis evangelium*, 24.2.

7. "[Miraculum voco,] quidquid arduum aut insolitum supra spem vel facultatem mirantis apparet" (*De utilitate credendi ad honoratum*, 16.34, *PL* 42.90).

The translation is taken from *Advantage of Believing*, trans. Meagher.

8. "Miraculum autem dicitur quasi admiratione plenum, quod scilicet habet causam simpliciter et omnibus occultam. Haec autem est Deus. Unde illa quae a Deo fiunt praeter causas nobis notas, miracula dicuntur" (*Summa Theologicae*, prima pars, ed. Petri Caramello [Rome: Marietti, 1950]). All additional Latin quotations from the *Summa* are from this text.

9. The difference between miracles and magic is one of purpose. Augustine defines the difference between pagan magic and true miracles of God in terms of their divergent "ends": "quaedam vero etsi nonnullis piorum factis videantur opere coaequari, finis ipse quo discernuntur, incomparabiliter haec nostra ostendit excellere" (*De civitate Dei*, 10.16, *PL* 41.295). "It is true that some of those miracles may seem in externals to equal many of those performed among true worshippers; the distinction lies in the difference of the end, and here our miracles show incomparable superiority" (*De civitate Dei: Concerning the City of God*, trans. Bettenson). Among the various ends that Augustine ascribes to the miraculous are the generation or strengthening of faith and "giving testimony to the Law" (*De civitate Dei*, 10.16–17); demonstrating a "divine message" (*De Trinitate*, 3.10.19; *De utilitate credendi*, 14; *In Joannis Evangelium*, 24.1).

10. "Miracula quae fecit Dominus noster Jesus Christus, sunt quidem divina opera, et ad intelligendum Deum de visibilibus admonent humanam mentem. . . . Secundum ipsam suam misericordiam servavit sibi quaedam, quae faceret opportuno tempore praeter usitatum cursum ordinemque naturae, ut non majora, sed insolita videndo stuperent, quibus quotidiana viluerant . . . . ut invisibilem Deum per visibilia opera miraremur, et erecti ad fidem et purgati per fidem, etiam ipsum invisibiliter videre cuperemus, quem de rebus visibilibus invisibilem nosceremus" (*PL* 35.1592–93).

The translation is taken from *Lectures or Tractates*, trans. John Gibb, vol. 1. For a discussion of the medieval view of miracles, see Finucane, *Miracles and Pilgrims*, 49–52.

11. See Bogdanos, *Pearl, Image of the Ineffable*; as well as Watts, "*Pearl*, Inexpressibility," 26–40; and Schotter, "Vernacular Style," 23–34.

12. Part of those expectations as well as their violation is due to the poem's status as a dream vision. On the visionary tradition and the dream

landscape of *Pearl*, see, for example, Constance Hieatt, *"Pearl* and the Dream-Vision," 139–45; Kean, *Pearl*, 27–30, 31–52; Bogdanos, *Pearl, Image of the Ineffable*, 35–63; and Niemann, *"Pearl* and the Christian," 213–32. For the most recent significant analyses of the dream vision form, see Michael D. Cherniss, *Boethian Apocalypse*; Lynch, *High Medieval Dream*; and Russell, *English Dream Vision*.

13. For analysis of the spiritual journey in *Pearl*, see, for example, Blenkner, "Theological Structure," 43–75; Finlayson, *"Pearl,"* 314–43; Baldwin, "Tripartite Reformation," 140–43; and Blanch, "Color Symbolism," 58–77.

14. "Sed rursus haec in duo dividuntur: quaedam enim sunt quae solam faciunt admirationem; quaedam vero magnam etiam gratiam benevolentiamque conciliant. Nam si quis volantem hominem cernat, cum ea res nihil spectatori afferat commodi praeter ipsum spectaculum, miratur tantummodo. Si quis autem gravi et desperato morbo affectus, mox ut jussum fuerit convalescat, admirationem sanitatis suae, sanantis etiam charitate superabit. Talia facta sunt illo tempore quo Deus in vero homine, quantum sat erat, hominibus apparebat" (*De utilitate credendi ad honoratum*, 16.34, PL 42.90).

The translation is taken from *Advantage of Believing*, trans. Meagher.

15. On the different "meanings" of the pearl, see Schofield, "Symbolism, Allegory," 585–675. On the pearl as symbol, see Robertson, "Pearl as a Symbol," 155–61; Fletcher, "Allegory of *The Pearl*," 1–21; as well as Blenkner, "Pattern of Traditional Images," 26–49. On the significance of the pearl symbolism, see Kean, *Pearl*, especially 138–61; Bishop, *Pearl in Its Setting*, 92–98; Spearing, "Symbolic and Dramatic Development," 1–12. See also Baldwin, "Tripartite Reformation," 140–43; and Warren Ginsberg, *Cast of Character*, 144 and 184.

16. See Bogdanos, *Pearl, Image of the Ineffable*, 64–98.

17. "Deus autem creator et conditor omnium naturarum nihil contra naturum facit; id enim erit cuique rei naturali, quod ille fecerit, a quo est omnis modus numerus, ordo naturae" (*Contra Faustum manichaeum*, 26.3, PL 42.480).

All translations of *Contra Faustum manichaeum* are taken from *A Select Library of the Nicene and Post-Nicene Fathers of the Christian Church*, ed. Philip Schaff, vol. 4, *St. Augustine: The Writings Against Manichæans and Against the Donatists* (Grand Rapids, Mich: William B. Eerdmans, 1979).

18. "Praeterea, sicut ordo iustitiae est a Deo, ita et ordo naturae. Sed Deus non potest facere aliquid praeter ordinem iustitiae: faceret enim tunc aliquid iniustum. Ergo non potest facere aliquid praeter ordinem naturae" (*Summa theologicae*, prima pars, Qu. 105, art. 6).

19. "Sed contra naturam non incongrue dicimus aliquid Deum facere, quod facit contra id, quod novimus in natura. Hanc enim etiam appellamus

naturam, cognitum nobis cursum solitumque naturae, contra quem deus cum aliquid facit, magnalia vel mirabilia nominantur" (*Contra Faustum manichaeum*, 26.3, *PL* 42.481).

20. "Nec ista cum fiunt, contra naturam fiunt, nisi nobis quibus aliter naturae cursus innotuit; non autem Deo, cui hoc est natura quod fecerit" (*De genesi ad litteram*, 6.13, *PL* 34.349).

21. See Bogdanos, *Pearl, Image of the Ineffable*, 75–81; Blenkner, "Pattern of Traditional Images," 26–49; Kean, *Pearl*, 53–85, 167–72; Bishop, *Pearl in Its Setting*, 19; and Alfred L. Kellogg, "*Pearl* and the Augustinian Doctrine," 406–7.

22. See Braeger, "Interpretation in Poetry," 97–116. For discussion of the parable, see, for instance, Bishop, *Pearl in Its Setting*, 122–25; Bogdanos, *Pearl, Image of the Ineffable*, 91–95; Robert W. Ackerman, "Pearl-Maiden and the Penny," 615–23; Spearing, *Gawain-Poet*, 158–59; Robertson, "Heresy of *Pearl*," 152–55; Marti, *Body, Heart, and Text*, 83–99; Wood, "*Pearl*-Dreamer and the *Hyne*," 9–19; Borroff, "*Pearl*'s 'Maynful Mone,' " 159–72; and Schless, "*Pearl*'s Princes Paye," 183–85.

23. "Miraculum voco, quidquid arduum aut insolitum supra spem vel facultatem mirantis apparet. In quo genere nihil est populis aptius et omnino stultis hominibus, quam id quod sensibus admovetur" (*De utilitate credendi ad honoratum*, 16.34, *PL* 42.90).

The translation is taken from *Advantage of Believing*, trans. Meagher.

24. Benedicta Ward, *Miracles and the Medieval Mind*, 3–4.

25. For the knight as an apocalyptic symbol, see Pollard, "Images of the Apocalypse"; for the knight as a fusion of benevolent and malevolent natures, see Besserman, "Idea of the Green Knight," 219–39. For the Green Knight as devil, see Randall, "Was the Green Knight a Fiend?" 479–91; Levy, "Gawain's Spiritual Journey," especially 79–83; Puhvel, "Art and the Supernatural," 1–69; Luttrell, "Folk-Tale Element," 105–27; and Schmidt, " 'Latent Content,' " 145–68.

26. On the significance of the knight's greenness, see Blanch, "Games Poets Play," 64–85; Bachman, "*Sir Gawain*," 495–516; Hoffman, "Re-Hearing of *Sir Gawain*," 66–85; Puhvel, "Art and the Supernatural," 1–69; and Nickel, "Why Was the Green Knight Green?" 58–64. See also Besserman, "Gawain's Green Girdle," 84–101.

27. Morgan, it should be noted, derives her own knowledge, "koyntyse of clergye" (2447), from that "conable klerk," Merlin (2450).

28. We tend to resist the ascription of *St. Erkenwald* to the *Gawain*-Poet, although Savage, in his 1926 edition of *St. Erkenwald*, argued for common authorship with the *Gawain* poems. For a persuasive argument for the exclusion of the poem from the *Gawain* canon, see Larry D. Benson, "Authorship of *St. Erkenwald*," 393–405.

29. All citations of *St. Erkenwald* are taken from Clifford Peterson, ed., *St. Erkenwald*, Haney Foundation Series, vol. 22 (Philadelphia: University of Pennsylvania Press, 1977).

30. On the discovery of natural law and the growing new Aristotelianism of the twelfth century, see Chenu, *Nature, Man, and Society*, 1–48, as well as 49–98 on medieval neo-Platonism. For these topics in the *Gawain*-Poet, see Wallace, "*Cleanness* and the Terms," 94–96, who discusses *Cleanness* in light of the intellectual struggle between what he terms the "realists" and the *moderni*. See also Reeves and Medcalf, who treat the theme of the ideal versus the actual in both *Pearl* and *Gawain* in "Ideal, the Real and the Quest," 76, 79–80, 85, 90.

31. See, for example, Finlayson, "*Pearl*," 314–43.

32. ". . . contra naturae usum mortalibus" (*Contra Faustum manichaeum*, 26.3, *PL* 42.480).

33. See Blenkner, "Theological Structure," 43–75.

34. Aristotle states that given two mutually contradictory propositions— such as (a) Mary is the Queen of Heaven and (b) the *Pearl*-Maiden is the Queen of Heaven—only three possibilities exist: (a) that the first proposition is true and the second is false; (b) that the first proposition is false and the second is true; (c) that both are false. What Aristotelian logic will not permit is the fourth possibility, that the two contradictory propositions are both true, that Mary is the Queen of Heaven *and* that the Maiden is also the Queen of Heaven. Yet the latter situation is exactly the case argued by the *Pearl*-Maiden in describing a heavenly kingdom where all souls are brides of Christ and yet none displaces another.

35. On the difference between the logic of the Dreamer as opposed to that of the Maiden, see Clark and Wasserman, "Spatial Argument of *Pearl*," 1–12.

36. See, for example, Chance, "Allegory and Structure," especially 45–47.

37. Quid sit autem secundum naturam, quid contra naturam, homines, qui sicut vos errant, nosse non possunt (*Contra Faustum manichaeum*, 26.3, *PL* 42.480).

38. See Stanbury, *Seeing*, 45–50.

39. See C. David Benson, "Impatient Reader," 147–61.

40. Doob, *Nebuchadnezzar's Children*, 81–87.

41. See Lynn Johnson, *Voice*, 130–33, 135–36.

42. On the theme of civilization versus nature, see Bachman, "*Sir Gawain*," 495–516; Hanning, "Poetic Emblems," 1–32; Petroff, "Landscape in *Pearl*," 187; Stiller, "Transformation of the Physical," 405; as well as Bogdanos, *Pearl, Image of the Ineffable*, 48.

43. For a good summary of the moral-religious implications of *Gawain*, see Vantuono, ed. and trans., *Sir Gawain*, xiii–xiv, xvii–xxi.

44. The epithet "Light-of-love" comes from Tennyson's *Idylls of the King*, "Pelleas and Ettarre." For Gawain's reputation as a lover, see Larry D. Benson, *Art and Tradition*, 95, 103, 198–99. Also see Sheila Fisher, "Leaving Morgan Aside," 132 and especially 148, n. 6; as well as John Matthews, *Gawain, Knight of the Goddess*, 19.

45. See Hanning, "Sir Gawain and the Red Herring."

46. Finucane, *Miracles and Pilgrims*, 51.

47. Caesarius of Heisterbach, *Dialogus Miraculorum*, 2.217–18. Also see Finucane, *Miracles and Pilgrims*, 50–51.

48. See, for example, Kean, "Christmas Games," 9–27; Barron, "Ambivalence of Adventure," 28–40; Weiss, "*Laykyng of Enterludez*," 189–99; and Weiss, "*Sir Gawain*," 229–41.

CHAPTER 4

1. See, for example, C. David Benson, "Impatient Reader," 157–58.

2. For the significance of pronouns in *Patience*, see, for example, Lynn Johnson, *Voice*, 16, 20–21; and C. David Benson, "Impatient Reader," 150–51.

3. On the woodbine, see Lynn Johnson, *Voice*, 18–20; and Stanbury, *Seeing*, 87–91.

4. On Nebuchadnezzar's character, see Wilson, *Gawain-Poet*, 108–11; and Davenport, *Art*, 67–68, 71–77, 94–96.

5. For the hand of God as an emblem of the voice of God, see Gertrude Schiller, *Iconography of Christian Art*, 1: 148–51, plates 405, 409, 412, 414, and 416.

6. Art historians generally trace the transmission of the emblem from the East to the West, in particular citing Byzantine adoption of the motif and subsequent copying in the West; for example, Calkins notes the influence of Byzantine texts in frontispieces (some of which contain the dextra Domini) of Carolingian bibles—in *Illuminated Books*, 113. Of course, the Hindu tradition of mudras, symbolic hand positions, predates the Mediterranean iconographic tradition.

7. ". . . prope est ut dicam, ipse loquuntur. Annon his poscimus, pollicemur, vocamus, dimittimus, minamur, supplicamus, abominamur, timemus, interrogamus, negamus; gaudium, tristitiam, dubitationem, confessionem, paenitentiam, modum, copiam, numerum, tempus, ostendimus? Non eaedem concitant, inhibent, probant, admirantur, verecundantur? Non in demonstrandis locis ac personis adverbiorum atque pronominum obtinent vicem? Ut in tanta per omnes gentes nationesque linguae diversitate hic mihi omnium hominum communis sermo videatur" (*Institutio Oratoria*, 11.85–87).

Both the Latin text and the translation are taken from H. E. Butler, *The Institutio Oratoria of Quintilian.*

8. "Universus enim mundus iste sensibilis quasi quidam liber est scriptus digito dei," *De tribus diebus,* 3 (*PL* 176.814B).

9. "Illic exarata supremi digito dispunctoris textus temporis, fatalis series, dispositio seculorum." The Latin text is taken from Bernardis Silvestris, *De Mundi Universitate.*

10. See Ferguson, *Signs and Symbols,* 27. For a discussion of the development of this motif, see Didron, *Christian Iconography,* 1: 201–10. Didron notes that as late as the twelfth century there are no portraits of God the Father (201). Instead, one finds the metonymic hand, which Didron traces back to early Judaic and, in some instances, classical art, and which occurs as late as the seventeenth century (205). Didron provides both scriptural references on which the icon is based as well as examples of the hand of God in various media. For samples of the dextra Domini, including photographic examples of the various gestures and postures of the hands of Christ, as well as of various Old and New Testament figures in early Christian art, see Walter Lowrie, *Art in the Early Church.*

11. In regard to the "prophet book" Vatican GR 1153, see John Lowden, *Illuminated Prophet Books: A Study of Byzantine Manuscripts of the Major and Minor Prophets* (University Park: Pennsylvania State University Press, 1988), 32–39. See especially color plates 2, 4, and 8 and figures 76–87 and 89 for excellent examples of the dextra Domini. A remarkable facsimile of the St. Albans Psalter is available: *The Saint Albans Psalter (Albani Psalter): The Full Page Miniatures by Otto Pächt, The Initials by C. R. Dodwell, Preface and Description of the Manuscript by Francis Wormwald* (London: Warburg Institute, University of London, 1960). The psalter contains numerous examples of exaggerated, pantomimic hand gestures.

12. Containing "over 400 scenic illustrations and more than 1,200 portrait figures," many of which depict the dextra Domini, the Sacra Parallela has been described as "the most lavishly illustrated Byzantine manuscript still in existence." Fortunately, many of these portraits are accessible in Weitzmann, *Miniatures of the Sacra Parallela.*

13. See Lynn Johnson, *Voice,* 135.

14. See Stanbury, *Seeing,* 78–79.

15. For Creation as the primary miracle, see Benedicta Ward, *Miracles and the Medieval Mind,* 3; and Grant, *Miracle and Natural Law,* 135ff, especially 153.

16. See Stanbury, *Seeing,* 43–45; and Lynn Johnson, *Voice,* 99–105.

17. Most recently, scholars have begun to examine the visual techniques in the *Gawain* poems, notably the relationship between descriptive passages in the works and the philosophical problems of knowledge and vision

in the fourteenth century. See, for example, Stanbury's "Visual Hermeneutics" as well as *Seeing*. In the latter work, Stanbury does a particularly admirable job of demonstrating the visual "paths" that define the mechanics of "viewing" both pictorial and literary scenes in regard to several fourteenth-century apocalypses (24ff).

18. One might note the same pantomimic positions of the hands discussed here in the central figures of the apocalypses in Stanbury, *Seeing*, 29, figure 3.

19. Savage links *Gawain*, specifically "noel," with the fool in "Feast of Fools."

20. See Schiller, *Iconography of Christian Art*, for the development of the *Arma Christi* (instruments of the Passion), 189–97. Plates include two fourteenth-century examples, one from a small book of devotions (figure 654), either English or French, and the second, Bohemian, dated 1320, from the passional of Abbess Kunigunde. Schiller also provides a number of plates depicting the Agony in the Garden in which the descending hand of God the Father forms a trinity of hands with the hands of Christ raised in prayer (see especially figures 143 and 144).

21. Horrall, "Notes," observes that the pictures have been "often assailed," adding that "most observers consider them to be the crude drawings of a rank amateur" (195). In particular, Horrall cites Greg, Review of Gollancz, 227–28, and Turville-Petre, *Alliterative Revival*, 45, as examples of critics holding this view. In contrast to that position, Horrall observes that "some elements in the drawing and painting, however, are very competently executed" (195), noting in particular that the leaves on the trees in the *Pearl* landscapes are "meticulously drawn and carefully shaded" (195).

Lee, "Illuminating Critic," also comments on the illustrations' initial "crude appearance" and "muddy colors" (17) but—like Horrall, who notes that the illustrations are an "extremely rare phenomenon in a fourteenth-century Middle English manuscript" (191)—she claims that Cotton Nero A.x is one of the earliest illustrated fourteenth-century English manuscripts. Lee adds that the artist is "noteworthy in that he carefully considered his texts and chose his pictures truly to illustrate the four poems" (18). While some critics have argued that the manuscript's illustrations deviate significantly from the text, Horrall demonstrates how details of the illustrations conform to the poems (196–97).

Lee distinguishes between the "draftsman" who developed the illustrations that follow the text to a remarkable degree and the "painter" who often violated the lines set down by the draftsman (21). Both the drafting and the coloring, in Lee's opinion, took place some years after the composition of the poems. Finally, and most importantly for our study of the iconography of hands, Horrall terms the Cotton Nero A.x illustrator's Jonah "conventional, reflecting centuries of iconographic tradition" (196), since the artist "clearly . . . had a good grasp of contemporary iconographic conventions" (196).

22. The positioning of the hands so that one points skyward while the other is directed downward toward the earth is frequently found in the portrayal of angels, those mediators par excellence between heaven and earth. See, for examples, figures 469d, 469c, and 542 in Pächt and Alexander, *Illuminated Manuscripts*. Again, the same pose can be seen in figure 3 ("St. John Worshiping the Angel") of Stanbury, *Seeing*, 9.

23. In vol. 1 of *Pearl Poems*, Vantuono, 244, n. 434, describes the debate among the poem's editors over the Maiden's hand movement: "Gollancz thought the maiden was covering her face in the hanging folds of her garment. Andrew and Waldron followed Gordon who rendered *folde vp hyr face* 'with her face upturned.' Moorman agreed with Hillmann who suggested the Maiden was 'covering her face with her hands,' in 'horror at the jeweler's ignorant but blasphemous question' " (423). Hillmann's gloss is fitting, but the Maiden's movement may be taken as a gesture of humble adoration for Mary, not horror over the Dreamer's question.

24. On Belshazzar's feast, see Kelly and Irwin, "Meaning of *Cleanness*," 232–60; and Lynn Johnson, *Voice*, 133–37.

25. See, for example, Stanbury, *Seeing*, 47–50. On the Eucharistic connotations of this episode, see Kelly and Irwin, "Meaning of *Cleanness*," 250; and Wilson, *Gawain-Poet*, 74–75.

26. For Eucharistic symbolism in *Pearl*, see Garrett, *Pearl*; Lynn Johnson, *Voice*, 176–77; Spearing, *Readings in Medieval Poetry*, 213–15; Bogdanos, *Pearl, Image of the Ineffable*, 146; and Phillips, "Eucharistic Allusions," 474–86.

27. Paul F. Reichardt also notes the blue-hooded miller of the General Prologue as another example of a blue-hooded rascal in an unpublished paper, "Several Illuminations, Coarsely Executed: The Illustrations of the *Pearl* Manuscript," delivered at the Twenty-eighth International Congress on Medieval Studies on May 7, 1993.

28. For a detailed explanation of *hondeselle*, perhaps a game of sexual forfeits, see the note for lines 66–70 in Barron, ed. and trans., *Sir Gawain*, 169–70. For a summary of critical-editorial opinions on gifts and *hondeselle*, see the note for lines 66–70 in Vantuono's dual-language edition of *Sir Gawain*, 151.

29. See Weiss, "Gawain's First Failure," 361–66. Also see Bergner, "Two Courts," 404, n. 25, who notes that the Green Knight glosses the holly bob but not the axe. We would argue that such glossing serves to underscore the holly bob as an overlooked option in the game.

30. See Blanch and Wasserman, "Medieval Contracts," 598–610.

31. Vantuono, ed., *Sir Gawain*, 157, argues, however, that "an analysis of the content of lines 265–300 favors the view that the Green Knight carried the holly to show he did not want all-out war but that he did expect the axe to be used for the exchange of blows."

32. For comments on these lines, see Vantuono, ed., *Sir Gawain*, 156–57.

33. See Lee's comment that all hands are filled in the illustration of Arthur's court, in "Illuminating Critic," 21.

34. On chin chucking, see Lee, "Illuminating Critic," 22, as well as Robertson, *A Preface*, 113. On the Maiden's hand movements, see above, n. 23. See also Stanbury, *Seeing*, 29, figure 3, in which the angel takes St. John's chin in his hand.

35. See *Old English Dictionary*, s. v. "Handsel," which provides the following etymology emphasizing the root word "hand": "The form corresponds to OE. *handselen* glossed 'mancipatio' (giving into the hands of another), or to the ON. *handsal*, 'giving of the hand, promise or bargain confirmed by joining of the hand, promise or bargain confirmed by joining or shaking hands.' " On the poet's ironic use of *hondeselle*, see Burrow, *Reading*, 31. See Barron's edition of *Sir Gawain*, 172, for an explanation of lines 491–99.

CHAPTER 5

1. *Selected Letters of Gustave Flaubert*, trans. Francis Steegmuller (New York: Farrar, Straus, and Young, 1953), 195.

2. See J. W. Clark, "Paraphrases for 'God,' " 232–36. See also Menner's introduction to his edition of *Purity*, xvi–xviii.

3. While numerous scholars have written about the narrators of the individual poems, there has been very little criticism on the narrator of the whole manuscript. Lynn Johnson (*Voice*, ix) notes that her own title implies a unified overarching *Pearl*-Poet/narrator. Stanbury, *Seeing*, 1, refers to the poet's "impressively fictional persona," a "fiction out of the fabric of fiction." On the narrator of *Pearl*, see Milroy, "*Pearl*," 195–208, as well as Moorman, "Role of the Narrator," 73–81; see also Astell, "*Sir Gawain*," 188–202. Yet while Astell's perceptive and thorough study alludes to and compares the *Gawain*-narrator with the "I" of "Gower's Amans, Chaucer's pilgrim narrator, Juan Ruiz's sinner, Boethius' prisoner, and Langland's dreamer" (188), Astell makes no comparison with the narrators of any of the other Cotton Nero A.x poems—something that again attests to the habit of separating the poems (see intro., n. 3). For a further sampling of studies of this first-person narrator, see Russell, "Meaningless Dreams," 20–32; Finlayson, "*Pearl*"; Sklute, "Expectation and Fulfillment," 663–79; Spearing, *Medieval Dream-Poetry*, 111–29; Clark and Wasserman, "Spatial Argument"; and Luttrell, "Introduction to the Dream," 274–91.

4. See Vantuono, ed., *Pearl Poems*, vol. 2, *Patience*, 212, note on lines 93–94—who contrasts the language here with that of line 261 in order to demonstrate Jonah's pride.

5. A number of critics have noticed the distancing of the audience although they have disagreed as to both the method and the purpose of such distancing. See Shichtman, *"Sir Gawain,"* who describes the audience of *Gawain* as "distanced" although by history rather than by patterns of address. Shichtman argues that the poet's literate milieu "removes the reader from the sort of character identification only oral formulaic poetry may have required," adding that the "freedom derived from historical distance . . . allows the reader to judge the characters more clearly" (7). Wallace, *"Cleanness* and the Terms," 102, n. 10, refers to the poet's "terrorization of his readers," thereby creating a theological separation of reader and character. A number of writers have seen the poet's use of ambiguity as a means of distancing the audience from the text. Ashley, "Bonding and Signification," argues that the poet's deliberate ambiguities distance the reader from the poem. Similarly, Bragg, *"Sir Gawain,"* 482–88, argues that the narrator deliberately "eludes clarity" in order to show that no code of social behavior is adequate. See also Ganim, "Disorientation, Style, and Consciousness," 376–84. Hunt, "Irony and Ambiguity," 1–16, argues that irony and ambiguity represent a means of preventing the reader from making simple judgments concerning the complex issues treated in the work. Bridges, "Sense of an Ending," 81–96, makes a similar argument for *Pearl*, observing that the poet deliberately frustrates the audience's expectations concerning closure. See also Hendrix, "Reasonable Failure," 458–66.

6. See Kelly and Irwin, "Meaning of *Cleanness."*

7. The homiletic structure of the poems has long been recognized. For representative studies examining the poet's use of the ars praedicandi tradition, see Means, "Homiletic Structure," 165–72; Kittendorf, *"Cleanness,"* 319–30; Vantuono, "Structure and Sources," 401–21; Chance, "Allegory and Structure"; Brzezinski, "Conscience and Covenant."

Ordelle Hill has argued that the intended audience was a clerical one—in "Audience of *Patience,"* 103–9—a view supported by R. H. Bowers, *Legend of Jonah*, 61–67.

See Astell, *"Sir Gawain,"* an excellent survey of the classical and medieval foundations of the *Artes Praedicandi* (190–92). She cites Caplan's "Rhetorical Invention," 284–95; and "Classical Rhetoric," 73–96.

8. See Shoaf, *Poem as Green Girdle;* and Mann, "Satisfaction and Payment," 17–48.

9. See Derrida, *Post Card.*

10. See, for example, figure 3 ("Saint John Worshiping the Angel") in Stanbury, *Seeing*, 29; as well as above, chap. 4, nn. 23 and 33. Also note in Stanbury, figure 3, the trio of hands.

11. Derrida, *Post Card*, 13, et passim, ad nauseam.

12. See Reichardt, "Paginal Eyes."

13. The three marginal hands appear at the upper left margin of fol. 53b, the middle left margin of fol. 59b, and the middle left margin of fol. 66b. Such marginal hands are a relatively common occurrence in fourteenth-century manuscripts.

14. Doyle, "Manuscripts," 92, suggests that the hand of the scribe belongs to the last quarter of the fourteenth century while the illustrations are later. Doyle's view is supported by Horrall who, based on the costumes, dates the illustrations as produced after 1400, most likely between 1410–20. See also Lee, "Illustrating Critic"; and Horrall, "Notes."

15. Gimpel, *Cathedral Builders*, 17. See also 9–18, especially 9–11. Amazingly, in all of these inscriptions, Suger failed to make any reference to the architects of Saint-Denis (Coldstream, *Masons and Sculptors*, 16).

16. For the identification of John de Mascy of Sale with the *Gawain*-Poet, see Vantuono, "John de Mascy of Sale," 77–88; Kooper, "Case of the Encoded Author," 158–68; Nolan and Farley-Hills, "Authorship of *Pearl*," 295–302; and Peterson, "*Pearl*-Poet and John Massey," 257–66.

17. Gimpel, *Cathedral Builders*, 110.

18. On the relationship of the medieval artist in general and the Gothic architect in particular to the modern artist whose hallmark is self-expression, see Mâle, *Gothic Image*, 392–96, who responds to Victor Hugo's "modern" portrayal of the medieval architect/artist as an "independent and restless spirit" in our own image. While Mâle provides an excellent corrective, the very presence of master builders in cathedrals shows that he perhaps overcorrects Hugo. For a similar argument, in part, founded on Mâle, see Robertson, *Preface*, 10–15.

19. Metcalf, "*Sir Gawain* and *You*." See also Evans, "Dramatic Use," 38–45; as well as Nicholls, *Matter of Courtesy*, 106, 119; Johnston, "Significance of the Pronoun," 34–36.

20. Stanbury, *Seeing*, uses the term "cinematographic." Stanbury also notes "the drawing out or foregrounding of a visual detail as the background fades" (99). See also Renoir, "Descriptive Technique," 126–32.

21. While a number of critics have written about the narrator as an important shaping force in the poet's works, few have recognized the extent of his intrusiveness. Astell, "*Sir Gawain*," who argues that the narrator creates an "I," a "performing self" to mediate between poet and audience, observes that scholars have "paid little attention to the narrator" of *Gawain*, but asserts that the narrator "only rarely intrudes with his 'I'" (188). Wallace, "*Cleanness* and the Terms," 98, claims that "the *Cleanness*-Poet is sometimes a troublesome presence, but is mostly a troublesome absence, merging with the God he represents in some distant, absolute realm."

22. Fowler argues that although the stream is not an impassable boundary the Dreamer's own limited perception keeps him from discovering a ford where the water might be crossed. See "On the Meaning of *Pearl*, 139–40," 27–29.

23. On the three landscapes of *Pearl*, see Blenkner, "Theological Structure," as well as Finlayson, "*Pearl*."

24. On the linkwords in *Pearl*, see Wilson, "Word Play," 116–34; Macrae-Gibson, "*Pearl*," 54–64; and McGalliard, "Links, Language, and Style," 279–99.

25. The image of the diptych has been applied to *Pearl* by Harwood, "*Pearl* as Diptych," 61–78.

26. See Lynn Johnson, *Voice*, 3: "Structurally, the poet's use of a first-person narrator unifies [*Patience*]; thematically, the presence of a narrator links the concerns of the poem to those of a contemporary audience, since the narrator intrudes upon the action of the poem, providing us with a contemporary point of view." On the narrator of *Patience*, see 3–4, 24, 31, 34.

27. See Clark and Wasserman, "Jews, Gentiles, and Prophets," 230–55.

28. We rely on a geometric metaphor to describe the poet's sense of the boundaries of community. Several critics have discussed geometric symbolism within various poems in the manuscript. For a discussion of the "geometric implications" of the point in *Patience*, see Eldredge, "Late Medieval Discussions," 90–115. See also Fleming, "Centuple Structure," 81–98; and Gilligan, "Numerical Composition," 7–11. Other studies include Stanbury, "Space and Visual Hermeneutics," 476–89, which discusses the motif of enclosed structures in each of the four poems and which sees the poet as essentially a "spatial thinker"; and Stanbury, "Visions of Space," 133–58. See also Clark and Wasserman, "Significance of Thresholds," 114–17, as well as "City Imagery"; and Nelson, "*Pearl*," 25–49.

29. A number of critics have noted that such scene shifting, as well as the use of multiple perspectives, is typical of Ricardian poetry. There has, however, been little discussion of this as an affective device or the resulting distance created between observer and observed. Bergner, "Two Courts," describes "a consciously-fashioned multi-dimensionality" (401) and "multiple perspective, that is, the perception of one and the same thing from different view-points" (402) as features of Ricardian poetry. Indeed, Wallace, "*Cleanness* and the Terms," notes that the poet presents the tale of the flood from outside the ark in contrast to the usual narrative perspective in which the tale is told (93). See also Clark and Wasserman, "Jonah and the Whale," 1–19. Hamilton, "Repeating Narrative," 182–88, argues that *Cleanness* is structured in a fashion consonant with Gérard Genette's theories of time and narrative and notes that the story of Nebuchadnezzar's life is told five times from five different perspectives (183). Similarly, Reed,

" 'Boþe blysse and blunder,' " 140–61, notes the poet's "multiple narrative points of view" in regard to *Gawain*, refering to Larry D. Benson, *Art and Tradition*, 185–97. See also Stanbury, *Seeing*, 2.

30. See Vantuono, ed., *Pearl Poems*, vol. 2, *Patience*, note on line 524.

31. "I asspyed" (979); "I forth dreued" (980); "I syȝe" (986); "I . . . con wale" (1000); "I knew" (1019); "saȝ I" (1021); "I syȝe" (1033); "I con asspye" (1035); "I blusched" (1083); "I stod" (1085); "I nawþer reste ne trauayle" (1087); "watȝ I rauyste" (1088); "I dar say" (1089); "I watȝ war" (1096); "I wot" (1107); "I laȝt" (1128); "þoȝt I" (1138); "I wende" (1148).

32. On the traditional link between mystical experience and poverty of ego, see Underhill, *Mysticism*, 239–78, especially 266, as well as Riehle, *Middle English Mystics*, 59–64. On human will and mysticism, see John Bowers, "*Patience* and the Ideal," 1–23, who sees Old Testament prophets as prototypes of mystics.

Themes of pride, humility, and poverty of ego have dominated discussion of all four poems, especially *Patience* where the question of the poet's meaning of "poverté" so impresses the narrator. Of course, such problems of ego are particularly germane to considerations of the use of the first person and the intrusive narrator. On spiritual poverty, see Moorman, "Role of the Narrator," as well as Williams, "*Poynt* of *Patience*," 127–36; and Wilson, *Gawain-Poet*, 6. See also Kelly and Irwin, "Meaning of *Cleanness*"; Brewer, "*Gawain*-Poet," 130–42, sees controlling selfish desire as a recurring theme in all four poems. On the theme of pride, see Braswell, *Medieval Sinner*, 96–97; as well as Schnyder, "Aspects of Kingship," 289–94.

33. For recent studies of the narrator in *Gawain*, see Astell, "*Sir Gawain*"; Bragg, "*Sir Gawain*," 482–88; Freed, " 'Whoso shal telle a tale,' " 80–93; Ashley, "*Trawthe* and Temporality," 3–24; Barron, "Chrétien and the *Gawain*-Poet," 255–84; Sharon-Zisser, "Endless Knot," 67–99; and Flint, "*Sir Gawain*," 157–60.

34. For a concise discussion and definition of occupatio in Chaucer, see Knight, "*Rhyming Craftily*," 136–37, 240.

35. On Gawain's failure and the virtues of the pentangle, see Horgan, "Gawain's *Pure Pentaungel*," 310–16, as well as Spearing, *Gawain-Poet*, 208–9, who argues that Gawain specifically offends against virtues of the fifth pentad.

36. As Stanbury, *Seeing*, notes, "Although many studies have focused on the plight of the narrator, few have looked at the mechanics of his perceptual process" (36, n. 4). Lynn Johnson, *Voice*, contends that most studies of the *Pearl*-narrator have focused almost exclusively on his spiritual condition (see especially 161–65, 175–79.) See also Moorman, "Role of the Narrator," who—using Henry James's term, "the central intelligence"—refers to "the 'I' of the poem" as "the quickest way to come to the heart of the poem" (104).

37. See Clark and Wasserman, "Spatial Argument."

38. Madeleva, *Spiritual Dryness*, sees the Dreamer's charge into the river as representative of the desire of the mystic to forsake the material world (46–47), while Hillmann, ed., *Pearl*, views the act as the "folly of uncontrolled passion" (xxi). Assessments of the final status of the Dreamer are equally varied. Lynn Johnson, *Voice*, sees the *Pearl*-narrator's experience as a "success" resulting in "spiritual renewal" (176). Bishop, *Pearl in Its Setting*, sees a change in the Dreamer, particularly when one compares his first speech to the Maiden with that of lines 1182–88. Bogdanos, *Pearl, Image of the Ineffable*, interprets the end of *Pearl* as an intimation of radical alienation (145).

39. See Kean, *Pearl*, 230, who argues that in the last sixty lines the poet "speaks in *propria persona*," dropping the persona of the Dreamer.

BIBLIOGRAPHY

PRIMARY SOURCES

Alanus de Insulis. *Rhythmus alter.* PL 210.579A.

Andreas Capellanus. *The Art of Courtly Love.* Trans. John Jay Parry. New York: Columbia University Press, 1941.

Aquinas, Thomas. *Summa Theologicae.* Ed. Petri Caramello. Rome: Marietti, 1950.

Augustine, Bishop of Hippo. *The Advantage of Believing.* Trans. Luanne Meagher. In *The Writings of Augustine,* vol. 2 of *The Fathers of the Church, A New Translation.* New York: CIMA Publishing Co., 1947.

——. *Confessionum.* PL 32.659–868.

——. *Contra Faustum manichaeum.* PL 42.207–518.

——. *De civitate Dei: Concerning the City of God Against the Pagans.* Trans. Henry Bettenson. New York: Penguin Books, 1972.

——. *De Genesi ad litteram.* PL 34.245–486.

——. *De ordine.* PL 32.977–2020.

——. *De Trinitate.* PL 42.819–1098.

——. *De utilitate credendi ad honoratum.* PL 42.65–92.

——. *In Joannis Evangelium.* PL 35.1379–1976.

——. *Lectures or Tractates on the Gospel According to St. John.* Trans. John Gibb. 2 vols. Edinburgh: T. and T. Clark, 1873.

——. *A Select Library of the Nicene and Post-Nicene Fathers of the Christian Church.* Ed. Phillip Schaff. Vol. 4, *St. Augustine, The Writings Against Manichæns and Against the Donatists.* Grand Rapids, Mich.: William B. Eerdmans, 1979.

——. *Sermones de scripturis.* PL 38.23–994.

Barron, W. R. J., ed. and trans. *Sir Gawain and the Green Knight.* Manchester: Manchester University Press, 1974.

Bernardis Silvestris. *De Mundi Universitate, libri duo; sive megacosmus et microcosmus.* Ed. Carl Sigmund Barach and Johan Wrobel. Frankfort: Minerva, 1964.

Caesarius of Heisterbach. *Dialogus Miraculorum.* Ed. Joseph Strange. Cologne: H. Lempertz, 1851.

Chaucer, Geoffrey. *The Riverside Chaucer.* Ed. Larry D. Benson. Boston: Houghton Mifflin Co., 1987.

Crossley-Holland, Kevin, ed. *Beowulf.* New York: Farrar, Straus & Giroux, 1968.

Gordon, E. V., ed. *Pearl.* Oxford: Clarendon Press, 1953.

Hillmann, Mary Vincent, ed. *The Pearl: Medieval Text with a Literal Translation and Interpretation.* 2d ed. Notre Dame: University of Notre Dame Press, 1967.

Hugh of Saint-Victor. *De arca Noe morale.* PL 176.617–80.
———. *De eruditione docta.* PL 176.739–812.
———. *De tribus diebus.* PL 176.814B.
Klaeber, Friedrich, ed. *Beowulf.* In *Beowulf and The Fight at Finnsburg,* 3d ed. Boston: D. C. Heath, 1950.
Menner, Robert J., ed. *Purity: A Middle English Poem.* Yale Studies in English, 61. New Haven: Yale University Press, 1920.
Peterson, Clifford, ed. *St. Erkenwald.* Haney Foundation Series, vol. 22. Philadelphia: University of Pennsylvania Press, 1977.
Quintilian. *The Institutio Oratoria of Quintilian with an English Translation.* Vol. 4. Trans. H. E. Butler. New York: G. Putnam's Sons, 1922.
Vantuono, William, ed. *The Pearl Poems: An Omnibus Edition.* Vol. 1, *Pearl and Cleanness.* Vol. 2, *Patience and Sir Gawain and the Green Knight.* New York: Garland, 1984.
———. *Sir Gawain and the Green Knight: A Dual-Language Version.* New York: Garland, 1991.
Woodbine, George E., ed. *Bracton: On the Laws and Customs of England.* Trans. Samuel E. Thorne. Cambridge, Mass.: Belknap Press of Harvard University Press, 1968.
Wyatt, Alfred J., ed. *An Anglo-Saxon Reader.* Cambridge: Cambridge University Press, 1965.

SECONDARY SOURCES

Ackerman, Robert W. " 'Pared out of Paper': *Gawain* 802 and *Purity* 1408." *Journal of English and Germanic Philology* 56 (1957): 410–17.
———. "The Pearl-Maiden and the Penny." *Romance Philology* 17 (1964): 615–23.
Alford, John A. "Literature and Law in Medieval England." *PMLA* 92 (1977): 941–51.
Alford, John A., and Dennis P. Seniff, eds. *Literature and Law in the Middle Ages: A Bibliography of Scholarship.* New York: Garland, 1984.
Allen, Judson Boyce, and Theresa Anne Moritz. *A Distinction of Stories: The Medieval Unity of Chaucer's Fair Chain of Narratives for Canterbury.* Columbus: Ohio State University Press, 1981.
Arthur, Ross G. "Gawain's Shield as *Signum.*" In *Text and Matter: New Critical Perspectives of the Pearl-Poet,* ed. Robert J. Blanch, Miriam Youngerman Miller, and Julian N. Wasserman, 221–27. Troy, N.Y.: Whitston, 1991.
———. "A Head for a Head: A Testamental Template for *Sir Gawain and the Green Knight* and *The Wife of Bath's Tale.*" *Florilegium* 6 (1984): 178–94.

———. *Medieval Sign Theory and Sir Gawain and the Green Knight.* Toronto: University of Toronto Press, 1987.

Ashley, Kathleen M. "Bonding and Signification in *Sir Gawain and the Green Knight.*" In *Text and Matter: New Critical Perspectives of the Pearl-Poet,* ed. Robert J. Blanch, Miriam Youngerman Miller, and Julian N. Wasserman, 213–19. Troy, N.Y.: Whitston, 1991.

———. "*Trawthe* and Temporality: The Violation of Contracts and Conventions in *Sir Gawain and the Green Knight.*" *Assays* 4 (1987): 3–24.

Astell, Ann W. "*Sir Gawain and the Green Knight:* A Study in the Rhetoric of Romance." *Journal of English and Germanic Philology* 84 (1985): 188–202.

Attreed, Lorraine C. "Medieval Children and Mortality: From *Pearl* Maiden to Princes in the Tower." *The Ricardian* 5.74 (1981): 390–94.

Bachman, W. Bryant, Jr. "*Sir Gawain and the Green Knight:* The Green and the Gold Once More." *Texas Studies in Literature and Language* 23 (1981): 495–516.

Bakhtin, M. M. *Rabelais and His World.* Trans. Hélène Iswolsky with an introduction by Krystyna Pomorska. Bloomington: Indiana University Press, 1984.

Baldwin, Anna P. "Sacramental Perfection in *Pearl, Patience,* and *Cleanness.*" In *Genres, Themes and Images in English Literature from the Fourteenth to the Fifteenth Century: The J.A.W. Bennett Memorial Lectures,* ed. Piero Boitani and Anna Torti, 125–40. Tubingen: Gunter Narr, 1988.

———. "The Tripartite Reformation of the Soul in *The Scale of Perfection, Pearl,* and *Piers Plowman.*" In *The Medieval Mystical Tradition in England: Papers Read at Dartington Hall, July 1984,* ed. Marion Glasscoe, 136–49. Cambridge: Brewer, 1984.

Barron, W. R. J. "The Ambivalence of Adventure: Verbal Ambiguity in *Sir Gawain and the Green Knight,* Fitt. I." In *The Legend of Arthur in the Middle Ages,* ed. P. B. Grout, et al., 28–40. Cambridge: Brewer, 1983.

———. "Chrétien and the *Gawain*-Poet: Master and Pupil or Twin Temperaments?" In *The Legacy of Chrétien de Troyes,* vol. 2, ed. Norris J. Lacy, Douglas Kelly, and Keith Busby, 255–84. Amsterdam: Rodopi, 1988.

———. "*Trawthe*' and Treason: The Sin of Gawain Reconsidered: A Thematic Study of Sir Gawain and the Green Knight.* Manchester: Manchester University Press, 1980.

Baswell, Christopher, and William Sharpe, eds. *The Passing of Arthur: New Essays in Arthurian Tradition.* New York: Garland, 1988.

Benson, C. David. "The Impatient Reader of *Patience.*" In *Text and Matter: New Critical Perspectives of the Pearl-Poet,* ed. Robert J. Blanch, Miriam Youngerman Miller, and Julian N. Wasserman, 147–61. Troy, N.Y.: Whitston, 1991.

Benson, Larry D. *Art and Tradition in Sir Gawain and the Green Knight.* New Brunswick, N.J.: Rutgers University Press, 1965.

———. "The Authorship of *St. Erkenwald.*" *Journal of English and Germanic Philology* 64 (1965): 393–405.

Benzon, William. "*Sir Gawain and the Green Knight* and the Semiotics of Ontology." *Semiotica* 21 (1977): 267–93.

Bergner, Heinz. "Two Courts: Two Modes of Existence in *Sir Gawain and the Green Knight.*" *English Studies* 67 (1986): 401–16.

Berington, J., and J. Kirk. *The Faith of the Catholics, Confirmed by Scripture and Attested to by the Fathers of the First Five Centuries of the Church.* Ed. J. Waterworth. 5th ed., revised. New York: Frederick Pusfet & Co., 1910.

Besserman, Lawrence. "Gawain's Green Girdle." *Annuale Mediaevale* 22 (1982): 84–101.

———. "The Idea of the Green Knight." *ELH* 53 (1986): 219–39.

Bishop, Ian. *Pearl in its Setting: A Critical Study of the Structure and Meaning of the Middle English Poem.* Oxford: Blackwell, 1968.

———. "Time and Tempo in *Sir Gawain and the Green Knight.*" *Neophilologus* 69 (1985): 611–19.

Blackstone, William. *Commentaries on the Laws of England.* Ed. Thomas M. Cooley. 2d ed., revised. Chicago: Callaghan and Company, 1876.

Blamires, Alcuin. "The Turning of the Year in *Sir Gawain.*" *Trivium* 17 (1982): 21–37.

Blanch, Robert J. " 'Al was this land fulfild of fayerye': The Thematic Employment of Force, Willfulness, and Legal Conventions in Chaucer's *Wife of Bath's Tale.*" *Studia Neophilologica* 57 (1985): 41–51.

———. "Color Symbolism and Mystical Contemplation in *Pearl.*" *Nottingham Mediaeval Studies* 17 (1973): 58–77.

———. "Games Poets Play: The Ambiguous Use of Color Symbolism in *Sir Gawain and the Green Knight.*" *Nottingham Mediaeval Studies* 20 (1976): 64–85.

———. "Imagery of Binding in Fits One and Two of *Sir Gawain and the Green Knight.*" *Studia Neophilologica* 54 (1982): 53–60.

———. "The Name and Fame of Gawain in *Sir Gawain and the Green Knight.*" *Studia Neophilologica* 64 (1992): 141–47.

———. "Religion and Law in *Sir Gawain and the Green Knight.*" In *Approaches to Teaching Sir Gawain and the Green Knight,* ed. Miriam Youngerman Miller and Jane Chance, 93–101. New York: MLA, 1986.

———. "Supplement to the *Gawain*-Poet: An Annotated Bibliography, 1978–85." *Chaucer Review* 25 (1991): 363–86.

———, ed. *Sir Gawain and Pearl: Critical Essays.* Bloomington: Indiana University Press, 1966.

Blanch, Robert J., Miriam Youngerman Miller, and Julian N. Wasserman. *Text and Matter: New Critical Perspectives of the Pearl-Poet.* Troy, N.Y.: Whitston, 1991.

Blanch, Robert J., and Julian N. Wasserman. "The Current State of *Sir Gawain and the Green Knight* Criticism." *Chaucer Review* 27 (1993): 401–12.

———. "Medieval Contracts and Covenants: The Legal Coloring of *Sir Gawain and the Green Knight.*" *Neophilologus* 68 (1984): 598–610.

———. "The Medieval Court and the *Gawain* Manuscript." In *The Medieval Court in Europe,* ed. Edward R. Haymes, 176–88. Munich: Fink, 1986.

———. "To 'Ouertake Your Wylle': Volition and Obligation in *Sir Gawain and the Green Knight.*" *Neophilologus* 70 (1986): 119–29.

Blenkner, Louis. "The Pattern of Traditional Images in *Pearl.*" *Studies in Philology* 68 (1971): 26–49.

———. "Sin, Psychology, and the Structure of *Sir Gawain and the Green Knight.*" *Studies in Philology* 74 (1977): 354–87.

———. "The Theological Structure of *Pearl.*" *Traditio* 24 (1968): 43–75.

———. "The Three Hunts and Sir Gawain's Triple Faults." *American Benedictine Review* 29 (1978): 227–46.

Bogdanos, Theodore. *Pearl, Image of the Ineffable: A Study in Medieval Poetic Symbolism.* University Park: Pennsylvania State University Press, 1983.

Boitani, Piero. "The World of Romance." In *English Medieval Narrative in the Thirteenth and Fourteenth Centuries,* trans. Joan Krakover Hall, 60–70. Cambridge: Cambridge University Press, 1982.

Boitani, Piero, and Anna Torti, eds. *Genres, Themes, and Images in English Literature from the Fourteenth to the Fifteenth Century: The J. A. W. Bennett Memorial Lectures.* Tubingen: Gunter Narr, 1988.

Borroff, Marie. "*Pearl*'s 'Maynful Mone': Crux, Simile, and Structure." In *Acts and Interpretation: The Text in Its Contexts, 700–1600: Essays on Medieval and Renaissance Literature in Honor of E. Talbot Donaldson,* ed. Mary J. Carruthers and Elizabeth D. Kirk, 159–72. Norman: Pilgrim Books, 1982.

———. "*Sir Gawain and the Green Knight:* The Passing of Judgment." In *The Passing of Arthur: New Essays in Arthurian Tradition,* ed. Christopher Baswell and William Sharpe, 105–28. New York: Garland, 1988.

Bowers, John M. "*Patience* and the Ideal of the Mixed Life." *Texas Studies in Literature and Language* 28 (1986): 1–23.

Bowers, R. H. *The Legend of Jonah.* The Hague: Nijhoff, 1971.

Braeger, Peter C. "Interpretation in Poetry and Homily: Two Middle English Versions of the Parable of the Vineyard." *Proceedings of the Medieval Association of the Midwest* 1 (1991): 97–116.

Bragg, Lois. "*Sir Gawain and the Green Knight* and the Elusion of Clarity." *Neuphilologische Mitteilungen* 86 (1985): 482–88.

Braswell, Mary Flowers. *The Medieval Sinner: Characterization and Confession in the Literature of the English Middle Ages.* Rutherford: Fairleigh Dickinson University Press, 1983.

Brewer, Derek S. "The *Gawain*-Poet: A General Appreciation of Four Poems." *Essays in Criticism* 17 (1967): 130–42.

Bridges, Margaret. "The Sense of an Ending: The Case of the Dream-Vision." *Dutch Quarterly Review* 14 (1984): 81–96.

Brundage, James A. *Medieval Canon Law and the Crusader.* Madison: University of Wisconsin Press, 1969.

Bruten, Avril. "Gawain's Green Girdle as a 'Sign.' " *Notes & Queries* 211 (1966): 452–54.

Brzezinski, Monica. "Conscience and Covenant: The Sermon Structure of *Cleanness.*" *Journal of English and Germanic Philology* 89 (1990): 166–80.

Burrow, J. A. *The Ages of Man: A Study in Medieval Writing and Thought.* Oxford: Clarendon, 1986.

———. *A Reading of Sir Gawain and the Green Knight.* London: Routledge, 1965.

———. *Ricardian Poetry: Chaucer, Gower, Langland and the Gawain Poet.* London: Routledge and Kegan Paul, 1971.

———. "The Two Confession Scenes in *Sir Gawain and the Green Knight.*" *Modern Philology* 57 (1959): 73–79.

Butturff, Douglas R. "Laughter and Discovered Aggression in *Sir Gawain and the Green Knight.*" *Literature and Psychology* 22 (1972): 139–49.

Calkins, Robert G. *Illuminated Books of the Middle Ages.* Ithaca: Cornell University Press, 1983.

Campbell, Alphonsus M. "The Character of King Arthur in the Middle English Alliterative Poems." *Revue de l'Université d'Ottawa* 45 (1975): 26–41.

Canfield, J. Douglas. *Word as Bond in English Literature from the Middle Ages to the Restoration.* Philadelphia: University of Pennsylvania Press, 1989.

Cantor, Norman F. *The Meaning of the Middle Ages: A Sociological and Cultural History.* Boston: Allyn and Bacon, 1973.

Caplan, Harry. "Classical Rhetoric and the Medieval Theory of Preaching." *Classical Philology* 27 (1933): 73–96.

———. "Rhetorical Invention in Some Medieval Tractates on Preaching." *Speculum* 2 (1927): 284–95.

Chance, Jane. "Allegory and Structure in *Pearl:* The Four Senses of the *Ars Praedicandi* and Fourteenth-Century Homiletic Poetry." In *Text and*

Matter: New Critical Perspectives of the Pearl-Poet, ed. Robert J. Blanch, Miriam Youngerman Miller, and Julian N. Wasserman, 31–59. Troy, N.Y.: Whitston, 1991.

Chapman, Coolidge Otis. "Ticius to Tuskan, *Gawain and the Green Knight*, line 11." *Modern Language Notes* 63 (1948): 59–60.

Chenu, M. D. *Nature, Man, and Society in the Twelfth Century: Essays on New Theological Perspectives in the Latin West*. Trans. Jerome Taylor and Lester K. Little. Chicago: University of Chicago Press, 1968.

Cherniss, Michael D. *Boethian Apocalypse: Studies in Middle English Vision Poetry*. Norman, Okla.: Pilgrim Books, 1987.

Christmas, Peter. "A Reading of *Sir Gawain and the Green Knight*." *Neophilologus* 58 (1974): 238–47.

Clark, J. W. "Paraphrases for 'God' in the Poems Attributed to the 'Gawain-Poet.' " *Modern Language Notes* 65 (1950): 232–36.

Clark, S. L., and Julian N. Wasserman. "Jews, Gentiles, and Prophets: The Sense of Community in *Patience*." *American Benedictine Review* 37 (1986): 230–55.

——. "Jonah and the Whale: Narrative Perspective in *Patience*." *Orbis Litterarum* 35 (1980): 1–19.

——. "The Passing of the Seasons and the Apocalyptic in *Sir Gawain and the Green Knight*." *South Central Review* 3.1 (1986): 5–22.

——. "The *Pearl*-Poet's City Imagery," *The Southern Quarterly* 16 (1978): 297–309.

——. "*Purity*: The Cities of the Dove and the Raven." *American Benedictine Review* 29 (1978): 284–306.

——. "*Purity* and *Das Neunfelsenbuch*: The Presentation of God's Judgment in Two Fourteenth-Century Works." *Arcadia* 18.2 (1983): 179–84.

——. "The Significance of Thresholds in the *Pearl*-Poet's *Purity*." *Interpretations* 12 (1980): 114–27.

——. "The Spatial Argument of *Pearl*: Perspectives on a Venerable Bead." *Interpretations* 11 (1979): 1–12.

Coldstream, Nicola. *Masons and Sculptors*. Medieval Craftsmen Series. Toronto: University of Toronto Press, 1991.

Cole, Carolyn Barry. "The Purpose and Practice of Troth in Medieval English Society and Literature." *DAI* 46.5 (1985): 1274A.

Colish, Marcia L. *The Mirror of Language: A Study in the Medieval Theory of Knowledge*. Rev. ed. Lincoln: University of Nebraska Press, 1983.

Conley, John, ed. *The Middle English Pearl: Critical Essays*. Notre Dame: University of Notre Dame Press, 1970.

Cooper, R. A., and D. A. Pearsall. "The *Gawain* Poems: A Statistical Approach to the Question of Common Authorship." *Review of English Studies* 39 (1988): 365–85.

Copleston, Frederick J. *A History of Philosophy*. Vol. 2. Westminster, Md.: Newman Press, 1950.

Cramer, Patricia. "Lordship, Bondage, and the Erotic: The Psychological Bases of Chaucer's *Clerk's Tale*." *Journal of English and Germanic Philology* 89 (1990): 491–511.

Crane, John Kenny. "The Four Levels of Time in *Sir Gawain and the Green Knight*." *Annuale Mediaevale* 10 (1969): 65–80.

Crawford, Donna. "The Structure of *Cleanness*." *Studies in Philology* 90 (1993): 29–45.

Curley, Michael J. "A Note on Bertilak's Beard." *Modern Philology* 73 (1975): 69–73.

Curtius, Ernst Robert. *European Literature and the Latin Middle Ages*. Trans. Willard R. Trask. Princeton: Princeton University Press, 1953.

Davenport, W. A. *The Art of the Gawain Poet*. London: Athlone, 1978.

Davidoff, Judith M. *Beginning Well: Framing Fictions in Late Middle English Poetry*. Rutherford: Fairleigh Dickinson University Press, 1988.

Dean, Christopher. *Arthur of England*. Toronto: University of Toronto Press, 1987.

Derolez, R. "Authorship and Statistics: The Case of the *Pearl*-Poet and the *Gawain*-Poet." *Occasional Papers in Linguistics and Language Learning* 8 (1981): 41–51.

Derrida, Jacques. *The Post Card: From Socrates and Freud and Beyond*. Trans. Alan Bass. Chicago: University of Chicago Press, 1987.

Didron, Adolphe Napoleon. *Christian Iconography, The History of Christian Art in the Middle Ages*. Vol. 1. Trans. E. J. Millington. New York: Frederick Ungar, 1965.

Dinzelbacher, Peter. "The Way to the Other World in Medieval Literature and Art." *Folklore* 97 (1986): 70–87.

Doob, Penelope B. R. *Nebuchadnezzar's Children: Conventions of Madness in Middle English Literature*. New Haven: Yale University Press, 1974.

Dove, Mary. *The Perfect Age of Man's Life*. Cambridge: Cambridge University Press, 1986.

Doyle, A. I. "The Manuscripts." In *Middle English Alliterative Poetry and Its Literary Background*." Ed. David Lawton. Cambridge: Brewer, 1982.

Ebbs, John Dale. "Stylistic Mannerisms of the *Gawain*-Poet." *Journal of English and Germanic Philology* 57 (1958): 522–25.

Eldredge, Laurence. "Late Medieval Discussions of the Continuum and the Point of the Middle English *Patience*." *Vivarium* 17 (1979): 90–115.

Engelhardt, George J. "The Predicament of Gawain." *Modern Language Quarterly* 16 (1955): 218–25.

Evans, W. O. "The Case for Sir Gawain Re-opened." *Modern Language Review* 68 (1973): 721–33.

Evans, William W. "Dramatic Use of the Second-Person Singular Pronoun in *Sir Gawain and the Green Knight.*" *Studia Neophilologica* 39 (1967): 38–45.

Ferguson, George. *Signs and Symbols in Christian Art.* New York: Oxford University Press, 1959.

Ferster, Judith. "Writing on the Ground, Interpretation in the Chester Play XII." In *Sign, Sentence, Discourse: Essays on the Theme of Language in Medieval Thought and Literature,* ed. Julian N. Wasserman and Lois Y. Roney, 179–93. Syracuse: Syracuse University Press, 1989.

Finlayson, John. "*Pearl:* Landscape and Vision." *Studies in Philology* 71 (1974): 314–43.

Finucane, Ronald C. *Miracles and Pilgrims, Popular Beliefs in Medieval England.* London: J. M. Dent and Sons, 1977.

Fisher, John H. "Wyclif, Langland, Gower, and the *Pearl* Poet on the Subject of Aristocracy." In *Studies in Medieval Literature in Honor of Professor Albert Croll Baugh,* ed. MacEdward Leach, 139–57. Philadelphia: University of Pennsylvania Press, 1961.

Fisher, Sheila. "Leaving Morgan Aside: Women, History and Revisionism in *Sir Gawain and the Green Knight.*" In *The Passing of Arthur: New Essays in Arthurian Tradition,* ed. Christopher Baswell and William Sharpe, 129–51. New York: Garland, 1988.

Fleming, John V. "The Centuple Structure of the *Pearl.*" In *The Alliterative Tradition in the Fourteenth Century.* Ed. Bernard S. Levy and Paul E. Szarmach, 81–98. Kent, Ohio: Kent State University Press, 1981.

Fletcher, J. B. "The Allegory of *The Pearl.*" *Journal of English and Germanic Philology* 20 (1921): 1–21.

Flint, Michael. "*Sir Gawain and the Green Knight:* Modality in Description." *Studia Neophilologica* 61 (1989): 157–60.

Foley, Michael. "The *Gawain*-Poet: An Annotated Bibliography, 1978–85." *Chaucer Review* 23 (1989): 251–82.

Fowler, D. C. "On the Meaning of *Pearl,* 139–40." *Modern Language Quarterly* 21 (1960): 27–29.

Freed, E. R. " 'Whoso shal telle a tale': Narrative Voices and Personae in Chaucer's *Canterbury Tales* and *Sir Gawain and the Green Knight.*" *Unisa Medieval Studies* 2 (1985): 80–93.

Gallagher, Joseph E. "*Trawþe* and *Luf-talkyng* in *Sir Gawain and the Green Knight.*" *Neuphilologische Mitteilungen* 78 (1977): 362–76.

Ganim, John M. "Disorientation, Style, and Consciousness in *Sir Gawain and the Green Knight.*" *PMLA* 91 (1976): 376–84.

———. *Style and Consciousness in Middle English Narrative.* Princeton: Princeton University Press, 1983.

Garner, Carl. "Gawain and the Green Goom." *Interlanguage* 1.1 (1982): 34–41.

Garrett, R. M. *The Pearl: An Interpretation.* Seattle: University of Washington Press, 1918.

Gertz, SunHee Kim. "The Green Knight Teaches Gawain How to Read." In *Proceedings of the Ninth Annual Meeting of the Semiotic Society of America,* ed. John Deely, 73–83. Lanham, Md.: University Press of America, 1985.

———. "*Translatio studii et imperii:* Sir Gawain as Literary Critic." *Semiotica* 63 (1987): 185–203.

Gilligan, Janet. "Numerical Composition in the Middle English *Patience.*" *Studia Neophilologica* 61 (1989): 7–11.

Gimpel, Jean. *The Cathedral Builders.* Trans. Teresa Waugh. New York: Grove Press, 1983.

Ginsberg, Warren. *The Cast of Character: The Representation of Personality in Ancient and Medieval Literature.* Toronto: University of Toronto Press, 1983.

Glenn, Jonathan A. "Dislocation of *Kynde* in the Middle English *Cleanness.*" *Chaucer Review* 18 (1983): 77–91.

Goltra, Robert. "The Confession in the Green Chapel: Gawain's True Absolution." *Emporia State Research Studies* 32.4 (1984): 5–14.

Goodlad, Lauren M. "The *Gamnes* of *Sir Gawain and the Green Knight.*" *Comitatus* 18 (1987): 45–58.

Gradon, Pamela. *Form and Style in Early English Literature.* London: Methuen, 1971.

Grant, Robert M. *Miracle and Natural Law in Graeco-Roman and Early Christian Thought.* Amsterdam: North Holland Publishing, 1952.

Greg, W. W. Review of Gollancz's EETS Facsimile (OS 162). *Modern Language Review* 19 (1924): 223–28.

Green, D. H. *Irony in the Medieval Romance.* Cambridge: Cambridge University Press, 1979.

Green, Richard Firth. "Gawain's Five Fingers." *English Language Notes* 27.1 (1989): 14–18.

Gross, Laila. "Telescoping in Time in *Sir Gawain and the Green Knight.*" *Orbis Litterarum* 24 (1969): 130–37.

Haines, Victor Yelverton. *The Fortunate Fall of Sir Gawain: The Typology of Sir Gawain and the Green Knight.* Lanham, Md.: University Press of America, 1982.

Hamilton, Ruth E. "Chivalry as Sin in *Sir Gawain and the Green Knight.*" *University of Dayton Review* 18 (1987): 113–17.

———. "Repeating Narrative and Anachrony in *Cleanness.*" *Style* 20 (1986): 182–88.

Hanna, Ralph. "Unlocking What's Locked: Gawain's Green Girdle." *Viator* 14 (1983): 289–302.

Hanning, Robert W. "Poetic Emblems in Medieval Narrative Texts." *Studies in Medieval Culture* 16 (1984): 1–32.

———. "Sir Gawain and the Red Herring: The Perils of Interpretation." In *Acts of Interpretation: The Text in Its Contexts, 700–1600: Essays on Medieval and Renaissance Literature in Honor of E. Talbot Donaldson.* Ed. Mary J. Carruthers and Elizabeth D. Kirk, 5–23. Norman, Okla.: Pilgrim Books, 1982.

Harwood, Britton J. "*Gawain* and the Gift." *PMLA* 106 (1991): 483–99.

———. "*Pearl* as Diptych." In *Text and Matter: New Critical Perspectives of the Pearl-Poet,* ed. Robert J. Blanch, Miriam Youngerman Miller, and Julian N. Wasserman, 61–78. Troy, N.Y.: Whitston, 1991.

Haymes, Edward R., ed. *The Medieval Court in Europe.* Munich: Fink, 1986.

Hendrix, Howard V. "Reasonable Failure: *Pearl* Considered as a Self-Consuming Artifact of 'Gostly Porpose.' " *Neuphilologische Mitteilungen* 86 (1985): 458–66.

Heng, Geraldine. "Feminine Knots and the Other *Sir Gawain and the Green Knight.*" *PMLA* 106 (1991): 500–514.

Henry, Robert L. *Contracts in the Local Courts of Medieval England.* New York: Longmans, Green and Company, 1926.

Hieatt, A. Kent. "Symbolic and Narrative Patterns in *Pearl, Cleanness, Patience,* and *Gawain.*" *English Studies in Canada* 2 (1976): 125–43.

Hieatt, Constance. "*Pearl* and the Dream-Vision Tradition." *Studia Neophilologica* 37 (1965): 139–45.

Higgs, Elton. "The Progress of the Dreamer in *Pearl.*" *Studies in Medieval Culture* 4 (1974): 388–400.

Hill, Ordelle G. "The Audience of *Patience.*" *Modern Philology* 66 (1968): 103–9.

———. "Sir Gawain's Holidays." *Kentucky Philological Association Bulletin* (1980): 17–26.

Hill, Thomas D. "Gawain's Jesting Lie: Towards an Interpretation of the Confessional Scene in *Sir Gawain and the Green Knight.*" *Studia Neophilologica* 52 (1980): 279–86.

Hoffman, Elizabeth A. "A Re-Hearing of *Sir Gawain and the Green Knight.*" *Proceedings of the Illinois Medieval Association* 2 (1985): 66–85.

Horgan, A. D. "Gawain's *Pure Pentaungel* and the Virtue of Faith." *Medium Ævum* 56 (1987): 310–16.

Hornsby, J. A. *Chaucer and the Law.* Norman, Okla.: Pilgrim Books, 1988.

Horrall, Sarah M. "Notes on British Library, MS Cotton Nero A.x." *Manuscripta* 30 (1986): 191–98.

Hunt, Tony. "Irony and Ambiguity in *Sir Gawain and the Green Knight.*" *Forum for Modern Language Studies* 12 (1976): 1–16.

Huntsman, Jeffrey F. "The Celtic Heritage of *Sir Gawain and the Green Knight.*" In *Approaches to Teaching Sir Gawain and the Green Knight,* ed. Miriam Youngerman Miller and Jane Chance, 177–81. New York: MLA, 1986.

Hussey, S. S. "*Sir Gawain* and Romance Writing." *Studia Neophilologica* 40 (1968): 161–74.

Irwin, John T., and T. D. Kelly. "The Way and the End Are One: *Patience* as a Parable of the Contemplative Life." *American Benedictine Review* 25 (1974): 33–55.

Johnson, Lynn Staley. "The *Pearl* Dreamer and the Eleventh Hour." In *Text and Matter: New Critical Perspectives of the Pearl-Poet,* ed. Robert J. Blanch, Miriam Youngerman Miller, and Julian N. Wasserman, 3–15. Troy, N.Y.: Whitston, 1991.

———. *The Voice of The Gawain-Poet.* Madison: University of Wisconsin Press, 1984.

Johnson, Wendell Stacy. "The Imagery and Diction of *The Pearl:* Toward an Interpretation." *ELH* 20 (1953): 161–80.

Johnston, Everett C. "The Significance of the Pronoun of Address in *Sir Gawain and the Green Knight.*" *Language Quarterly* 5.3–4 (1967): 34–36.

Kean, P. M. "Christmas Games: Verbal Ironies and Ambiguities in *Sir Gawain and the Green Knight.*" *Poetica* 11 (1979): 9–27.

———. *The Pearl: An Interpretation.* New York: Barnes and Noble, 1967.

Keenan, Joan. "Feasts and Fasts in *Sir Gawain and the Green Knight.*" *American Notes and Queries* 17 (1978): 34–35.

Kellogg, Alfred L. "*Pearl* and the Augustinian Doctrine of Creation." *Traditio* 12 (1956): 406–7. Reprinted in John Conley, ed., *The Middle English Pearl: Critical Essays,* 335–37. (Notre Dame: University of Notre Dame Press, 1970.)

Kelly, T. D., and John T. Irwin. "The Meaning of *Cleanness:* Parable as Effective Sign." *Mediaeval Studies* 35 (1973): 232–60.

Kiteley, J. F. "The *De Arte Honeste Amandi* of Andreas Capellanus and the Concept of Courtesy in *Sir Gawain and the Green Knight.*" *Anglia* 79 (1961): 7–16.

Kittendorf, Doris E. "*Cleanness* and the Fourteenth-Century *Artes Praedicandi.*" *Michigan Academician* 11 (1979): 319–30.

Kjellmer, Göran. *Did the "Pearl Poet" Write Pearl?* Gothenburg Studies in English, 30. Göteburg: University of Göteburg, 1975.

Knight, Stephen T. *Rhyming Craftily: Meaning in Chaucer's Poetry.* Sidney: Angus and Robertson, 1973.

Kooper, Erik. "The Case of the Encoded Author: John Massey in *Sir Gawain and the Green Knight.*" *Neuphilologische Mitteilungen* 83 (1982): 158–68.

Landesman, Charles, ed. *The Problem of Universals*. New York: Basic Books, 1971.

Lawton, David. "Middle English Alliterative Poetry: An Introduction." In *Middle English Alliterative Poetry and Its Literary Background*, ed. David Lawton, 1–19. Cambridge: Brewer, 1982.

Lee, Jennifer A. "The Illuminating Critic: The Illustrator of Cotton Nero A.x." *Studies in Iconography* 3 (1977): 17–46.

Lenz, Joseph M. *The Promised End: Romance Closure in the Gawain-Poet, Malory, Spenser, and Shakespeare*. New York: Peter Lang, 1986.

Lepow, Lauren. "The Contrasted Courts in *Sir Gawain and the Green Knight*." In *The Medieval Court in Europe*, ed. Edward R. Haymes, 200–208. Munich: Fink, 1986.

Levine, Robert. "Aspects of Grotesque Realism in *Sir Gawain and the Green Knight*." *Chaucer Review* 17 (1982): 65–75.

Levy, Bernard S. "Gawain's Spiritual Journey: *Imitatio Christi* in *Sir Gawain and the Green Knight*." *Annuale Mediaevale* 6 (1965): 65–106.

Liuzza, Roy. "Names, Reputation, and History in *Sir Gawain and the Green Knight*." *Essays in Medieval Studies: Proceedings of the Illinois Mediaeval Association* 6 (1989): 41–56.

Lock, Richard. *Aspects of Time in Medieval Literature*. New York: Garland, 1985.

Longsworth, Robert. "Interpretive Laughter in *Sir Gawain and the Green Knight*." *Philological Quarterly* 70 (1991): 141–47.

Lopez, Robert S. "Proxy in Medieval Trade." In *Order and Innovation in the Middle Ages: Essays in Honor of Joseph R. Strayer*, ed. William C. Jordan, Bruce McNab, and Teofilo F. Ruiz, 187–94. Princeton, N.J.: Princeton University Press, 1976.

Lowden, John. *Illuminated Prophet Books: A Study of Byzantine Manuscripts of the Major and Minor Prophets*. University Park: Pennsylvania State University Press, 1988.

Lowrie, Walter. *Art in the Early Church*. New York: Pantheon Books, 1947.

Luttrell, Claude. "The Folk-Tale Element in *Sir Gawain and the Green Knight*." *Studies in Philology* 77 (1980): 105–27. Reprinted, with some changes, in Derek Brewer, ed., *Studies in Medieval English Romances: Some New Approaches*, 92–112. (Cambridge: D. S. Brewer, 1988.)

———. "The Introduction to the Dream in *Pearl*." *Medium Aevum* 47 (1978): 274–91.

Lynch, Kathryn L. "Despoiling Griselda: Chaucer's Walter and the Problem of Knowledge in *The Clerk's Tale*." *Studies in the Age of Chaucer* 10 (1988): 41–70.

———. *The High Medieval Dream Vision: Poetry, Philosophy, and Literary Form*. Stanford: Stanford University Press, 1988.

McClure, Peter. "Gawain's *Mesure* and the Significance of the Three Hunts in *Sir Gawain and the Green Knight.*" *Neophilologus* 57 (1973): 375–87.

McColly, William, and Dennis Weier. "Literary Attribution and Likelihood-Ratio Tests: The Case of the Middle English *Pearl*-Poems." *Computers and the Humanities* 17 (1983): 65–75.

McGalliard, John C. "Links, Language, and Style in *The Pearl.*" In *Studies in Language, Literature, and Culture of the Middle Ages and Later: Studies in Honor of Rudolph Willard*, ed. E. Bagby Atwood and Archibald A. Hill, 279–99. Austin: University of Texas Press, 1969.

Machann, Clinton. "A Structural Study of the English Gawain Romances." *Neophilologus* 66 (1982): 629–37.

Macrae-Gibson, O. Duncan. "*Pearl:* The Link-Words and the Thematic Structure." *Neophilologus* 52 (1968): 54–64.

Madeleva, Mary. *Pearl: A Study in Spiritual Dryness*. New York: Phaeton Press, 1968.

Mâle, Émile. *The Gothic Image: Religious Art in France of the Thirteenth Century*. Trans. Dora Nussey. New York: Harper, 1958.

Mann, Jill. "Price and Value in *Sir Gawain and the Green Knight.*" *Essays in Criticism* 36 (1986): 294–318.

———. "Satisfaction and Payment in Middle English Literature." *Studies in the Age of Chaucer* 5 (1983): 17–48.

Marti, Kevin. *Body, Heart, and Text in the Pearl-Poet*. Lewiston: Edwin Mellen, 1991.

Matsuda, Takami. "The Linear View of the World in *Sir Gawain and the Green Knight.*" *Colloquia* 2 (1981): 1–23.

Matsumoto, Hiroyuki. "The Structure of *Cleanness.*" *Poetica* 13 (1980): 75–90.

Matthews, John. *Gawain: Knight of the Goddess—Restoring an Archetype*. Wellingborough: Aquarian Press, 1990.

Maxwell, Madeline M. "Ritual and Aggression in *Gawain and the Green Knight.*" *USF Language Quarterly* 23.3–4 (1985): 33–35.

Means, Michael H. "The Homiletic Structure of *Cleanness.*" *Studies in Medieval Culture* 5 (1975): 165–72.

Metcalf, Allan A. "*Sir Gawain* and You." *Chaucer Review* 5 (1971): 165–78.

Miller, Miriam Youngerman, and Jane Chance, eds. *Approaches to Teaching Sir Gawain and the Green Knight*. New York: MLA, 1986.

Milroy, James. "*Pearl:* The Verbal Texture and the Linguistic Theme." *Neophilologus* 55 (1971): 195–208.

Monden, Louis. *Signs and Wonders: A Study of the Miraculous Element in Religion*. New York: Desclee, 1966.

Moody, Patricia A. "The *Childgered* Arthur of *Sir Gawain and the Green Knight.*" *Studies in Medieval Culture* 8–9 (1976): 173–80.

Moorman, Charles. "The Role of the Narrator in *Pearl*." *Modern Philology* 53 (1955): 73–81.

Morgan, Gerald. "The Action of the Hunting and Bedroom Scenes in *Sir Gawain and the Green Knight*." *Medium Ævum* 56 (1987): 200–216.

———. *Sir Gawain and the Green Knight and the Idea of Righteousness*. Dublin: Irish Academic Press, 1991.

———. "The Validity of Gawain's Confession in *Sir Gawain and the Green Knight*." *Review of English Studies* 36 (1985): 1–18.

Morse, Charlotte C. *The Pattern of Judgment in the Queste and Cleanness*. Columbia: University of Missouri Press, 1978.

Neaman, Judith S. "Sir Gawain's Covenant: Troth and *Timor Mortis*." *Philological Quarterly* 55 (1976): 30–42.

Nelson, Cary. *The Incarnate Word: Literature as Verbal Space*. Urbana: University of Illinois Press, 1973.

Neuner, Josef, and Heinrich Roos. *The Teaching of the Catholic Church*. Ed. Karl Rahner. Staten Island, N.Y.: Alba House, 1967.

Newman, Barbara Florence. "Sin, Judgment, and Grace in the Works of the *Gawain*-Poet." *DAI* 46.10 (1986): 3027–28A.

Nicholls, Jonathan W. *The Matter of Courtesy: Medieval Courtesy Books and the Gawain-Poet*. Woodbridge: Brewer, 1985.

Nickel, Helmut. "Why Was the Green Knight Green?" *Arthurian Interpretations* 2.2 (1988): 58–64.

Niemann, Thomas C. "*Pearl* and the Christian Other World." *Genre* 7 (1974): 213–32.

Nims, Margaret F. "*Translatio*: 'Difficult Statement' in Medieval Poetic Theory." *University of Toronto Quarterly* 48 (1979): 215–30.

Nolan, Barbara, and David Farley-Hills. "The Authorship of *Pearl*: Two Notes." *Review of English Studies* 22 (1971): 295–302.

O'Bryan, Daniel W. "Sodom and Gomorrah: The Use of the Vulgate in *Cleanness*." *Journal of Narrative Technique* 12 (1982): 15–23.

Ong, Walter J. "The Green Knight's Harts and Bucks." *Modern Language Notes* 65 (1950): 536–39.

Pace, George B. "Gawain and Michaelmas." *Traditio* 25 (1969): 404–11.

Pächt, Otto, and J. J. G. Alexander. *Illuminated Manuscripts in the Bodleian Library*. Vol. 1–5. Oxford: Clarendon Press, 1973.

Passon, Richard H. " 'Entente' in Chaucer's *Friar's Tale*." *Chaucer Review* 2 (1968): 166–71.

Patch, H. R. *The Other World, According to Descriptions in Medieval Literature*. Cambridge: Harvard University Press, 1950.

Patrick, Marietta Stafford. "A Reading of *Sir Gawain and the Green Knight*." *Ball State University Forum* 24.4 (1983): 27–33.

Pattison, Robert. *The Child Figure in English Literature*. Athens: University of Georgia Press, 1978.

Peterson, Clifford J. "The *Pearl*-Poet and John Massey of Cotton, Cheshire." *Review of English Studies* 25 (1974): 257–66.

Petroff, Elizabeth. "Landscape in *Pearl:* The Transformation of Nature." *Chaucer Review* 16 (1981): 181–93.

Phillips, Heather. "The Eucharistic Allusions of *Pearl.*" *Mediaeval Studies* 47 (1985): 474–86.

Piehler, Paul. *The Visionary Landscape: A Study in Medieval Allegory*. London: Arnold, 1971.

Plummer, John. "Signifying the Self: Language and Identity in *Sir Gawain and the Green Knight.*" In *Text and Matter: New Critical Perspectives of the Pearl-Poet*, ed. Robert J. Blanch, Miriam Youngerman Miller, and Julian N. Wasserman, 195–212. Troy, N.Y.: Whitston, 1991.

Pollard, William F., Jr. "Images of the Apocalypse in *Gawain and the Green Knight.*" *Proceedings of the Patristic, Medieval, and Renaissance Conference* 3 (1978): 85–93.

Pollock, Frederick, and Frederic William Maitland. *The History of English Law Before the Time of Edward I*. 2nd ed. Cambridge: Cambridge University Press, 1952.

Prior, Sandra Pierson. " *Patience*—Beyond Apocalypse." *Modern Philology* 83 (1986): 337–48.

Puhvel, Martin. "Art and the Supernatural in *Sir Gawain and the Green Knight.*" *Arthurian Literature* 5 (1985): 1–69.

Purdon, Liam O. "Sodom and Gomorrah: The Use of Mandeville's *Travels* in *Cleanness.*" *Journal of the Rocky Mountain Medieval and Renaissance Association* 9 (1988): 64–69.

Randall, Dale B. J. "Was the Green Knight a Fiend?" *Studies in Philology* 57 (1960): 479–91.

Reed, Thomas L., Jr. " 'Boþe blysse and blunder': *Sir Gawain and the Green Knight* and the Debate Tradition." *Chaucer Review* 23 (1988): 140–61.

Reeves, Marjorie, and Stephen Medcalf. "The Ideal, the Real and the Quest for Perfection." In *The Later Middle Ages*, ed. Stephen Medcalf, 76–90. New York: Holmes and Meier, 1981.

Reichardt, Paul F. "Paginal Eyes: Faces Among the Ornamented Capitals of MS Cotton Nero A.X, Art. 3." *Manuscripta* 36 (1992): 22–36.

Reisner, Thomas Andrew. "The *Cortaysye* Sequence in *Pearl:* A Legal Interpretation." *Modern Philology* 72 (1975): 400–403.

Renoir, Alain. "Descriptive Technique in *Sir Gawain and the Green Knight.*" *Orbis Litterarum* 13 (1958): 126–32.

———. "An Echo to the Sense: The Patterns of Sound in *Sir Gawain and the Green Knight.*" *English Miscellany* 13 (1962): 9–23. Reprinted in Donald R. Howard and Christian Zacher, eds., *Critical Studies of Sir Gawain and the Green Knight,* 144–58. (Notre Dame: University of Notre Dame Press, 1968.)

Rhodes, James. "Vision and History in *Patience.*" *Journal of Medieval and Renaissance Studies* 19 (1989): 1–13.

Riehle, Wolfgang. *The Middle English Mystics.* London: Routledge and Kegan Paul, 1981.

Robertson, D. W., Jr. "The Heresy of *The Pearl.*" *Modern Language Notes* 65 (1950): 152–55. Reprinted in John Conley, ed., *The Middle English Pearl: Critical Essays,* 291–96. (Notre Dame: University of Notre Dame Press, 1970.)

———. "The Pearl as a Symbol." *Modern Language Notes* 65 (1950): 155–61.

———. *A Preface to Chaucer, Studies in Medieval Perspectives.* Princeton: Princeton University Press, 1962.

Roney, L. Y. "*Sir Gawain and the Green Knight.*" *Explicator* 37.1 (1978): 33–34.

Russell, J. Stephen. *The English Dream Vision: Anatomy of a Form.* Columbus: Ohio State University Press, 1987.

———. "Meaningless Dreams and Meaningful Poems: The Form of the Medieval Dream Vision." *Massachusetts Studies in English* 7.1 (1978): 20–32.

———. "*Pearl's* Courtesy: A Critique of Eschatology." *Renascence* 35 (1983): 183–95.

Sanderlin, George. "Point of View in *Patience.*" *Language Quarterly* 18 (1980): 31–32.

Savage, Henry L. "The Feast of Fools in *Sir Gawain and the Green Knight.*" *Journal of English and Germanic Philology* 51 (1952): 537–44.

———. "Hunting Terms in Middle English." *Modern Language Notes* 66 (1951): 216.

———. "Notes on *Sir Gawain and the Green Knight.*" *PMLA* 46 (1931): 169–76.

———. "The Significance of the Hunting Scenes in *Sir Gawain and the Green Knight.*" *Journal of English and Germanic Philology* 27 (1928): 1–15.

Schiller, Gertrude. *Iconography of Christian Art,* trans. Janet Seligman. Vol. 1, *The Passion of Jesus Christ.* London: Lund Humphries, 1972.

Schless, Howard H. "*Pearl's* 'Princes Paye' and the Law." *Chaucer Review* 24 (1989): 183–85.

Schleusener, Jay. "History and Action in *Patience.*" *PMLA* 86 (1971): 959–65.

Schmidt, A. V. C. "*Kinde Craft* and the *Play of Paramorez:* Natural and Unnatural Love in *Purity.*" In *Genres, Themes and Images in English Liter-*

ature from the Fourteenth to the Fifteenth Century: The J.A.W. Bennett Memorial Lectures, ed. Piero Boitani and Anna Torti, 105–24. Tübingen: Gunter Narr, 1988.

———. " 'Latent Content' and 'The Testimony in the Text': Symbolic Meaning in Sir Gawain and the Green Knight." Review of English Studies 38 (1987), 145–68.

Schnyder, Hans. "Aspects of Kingship in Sir Gawain and the Green Knight." English Studies 40 (1959): 289–94.

Schofield, W. H. "Symbolism, Allegory, and Autobiography in The Pearl." PMLA 24 (1909): 585–675.

Schotter, Anne Howland. "Vernacular Style and the Word of God: The Incarnational Art of Pearl." In Ineffability: Naming the Unnamable from Dante to Beckett, ed. Peter S. Hawkins and Anne Howland Schotter, 23–34. New York: AMS Press, 1984.

Sharon-Zisser, Shirley. "The Endless Knot: Aspects of Self-Reflexivity in Sir Gawain and the Green Knight." Yearbook of Research in English and American Literature (1988–89): 67–99.

Shedd, Gordon M. "Knight in Tarnished Armour: The Meaning of Sir Gawain and the Green Knight." Modern Language Review. 62 (1967): 3–13.

Shichtman, Martin B. "Sir Gawain and the Green Knight: A Lesson in the Terror of History." Papers on Language and Literature 22 (1986): 3–15.

Shoaf, R. A. The Poem as Green Girdle: Commercium in Sir Gawain and the Green Knight. Gainesville: University Press of Florida, 1984.

———. "The 'Syngne of Surfet' and the Surfeit of Signs in Sir Gawain and the Green Knight." In The Passing of Arthur: New Essays in Arthurian Tradition, ed. Christopher Baswell and William Sharpe, 152–69. New York: Garland, 1988.

Simpson, A. W. B. A History of the Common Law of Contract: The Rise of the Action of Assumpsit. Oxford: Clarendon Press, 1975.

Sims, James H. "Gawayne's Fortunate Fall in Sir Gawayne and the Grene Knight." Orbis Litterarum 30 (1975): 28–39.

Sklute, Larry. "Expectation and Fulfillment in Pearl." Philological Quarterly 52 (1973): 663–79.

Solomon, Jan. "The Lesson of Sir Gawain." Papers of the Michigan Academy of Science, Arts, and Letters 48 (1963): 599–608.

Southern, R. W. The Making of the Middle Ages. London: Hutchinson's University Library, 1953.

Spearing, A. C. The Gawain-Poet: A Critical Study. New York: Cambridge University Press, 1970.

———. Medieval Dream-Poetry. Cambridge: Cambridge University Press, 1976.

———. "Medieval Narrative Style." Poetica 17 (1984): 1–21.

———. *Readings in Medieval Poetry.* Cambridge: Cambridge University Press, 1987.

———. "Symbolic and Dramatic Development in *Pearl.*" *Modern Philology* 60 (1962): 1–12.

Stainsby, Meg. *Sir Gawain and the Green Knight: An Annotated Bibliography, 1978–89.* New York: Garland, 1992.

Stanbury, Sarah. "In God's Sight: Vision and Sacred History in *Purity.*" In *Text and Matter: New Critical Perspectives of the Pearl-Poet,* ed. Robert J. Blanch, Miriam Youngerman Miller, and Julian N. Wasserman, 105–16. Troy, N.Y.: Whitston, 1991.

———. "*Pearl* and the Idea of Jerusalem." *Medievalia et Humanistica: Studies in Medieval and Renaissance Culture* 16 (1988): 117–31.

———. *Seeing the Gawain-Poet: Description and the Act of Perception.* Philadelphia: University of Pennsylvania Press, 1991.

———. "Space and Visual Hermeneutics in the *Gawain*-Poet." *Chaucer Review* 21 (1987): 476–89.

———. "Visions of Space: Acts of Perception in *Pearl* and in Some Late Medieval Illustrated Apocalypses." *Mediaevalia* 10 (1988): 133–58.

Steinmetz, David C. "Late Medieval Nominalism and the *Clerk's Tale.*" *Chaucer Review* 12 (1977): 38–54.

Stephen, Henry John. *New Commentaries on the Laws of England.* 5th ed. London: Butterworths, 1863.

Stevens, Martin. "Laughter and Game in *Sir Gawain and the Green Knight.*" *Speculum* 47 (1972): 65–78.

Stiller, Nikki. "The Transformation of the Physical in the Middle English *Pearl.*" *English Studies* 63 (1982): 402–9.

Stock, Lorraine Kochanske. "The 'Poynt' of *Patience.*" In *Text and Matter: New Critical Perspectives of the Pearl-Poet,* ed. Robert J. Blanch, Miriam Youngerman Miller, and Julian N. Wasserman, 163–75. Troy, N.Y.: Whitston, 1991.

Tajima, Matsuji. "Additional Syntactical Evidence Against the Common Authorship of MS Cotton Nero A.X." *English Studies* 59 (1978): 193–98.

Tambling, Jeremy. "A More Powerful Life: *Sir Gawain and the Green Knight.*" *Haltwhistle Quarterly* 9 (1981): 1–23.

Taylor, P. B. "Commerce and Comedy in *Sir Gawain and the Green Knight.*" *Philological Quarterly* 50 (1971): 1–15.

———. "Gawain's Garland of Girdle and Name." *English Studies* 55 (1974): 6–14.

Tristram, Philippa. *Figures of Life and Death in Medieval English Literature.* New York: New York University Press, 1976.

Troyan, Scott D. "Rhetoric without Genre: Orality, Textuality and the Shifting Scene of the Rhetorical Situation in the Middle Ages." *Romanic Review* 81.4 (1990): 377–95.

Turville-Petre, Thorlac. *The Alliterative Revival.* Cambridge: D. S. Brewer, 1977.

Twomey, Michael W. "The Anatomy of Sin: Violations of *Kynde* and *Trawþe* in *Cleanness.*" *DAI* 40.9 (1979): 5046A, Cornell.

———. "*Cleanness,* Peter Comestor, and the *Revelationes Sancti Methodii.*" *Mediaevalia* 11 (1989 for 1985): 203–17.

———. "The Sin of *Untrawþe* in *Cleanness.*" In *Text and Matter: New Critical Perspectives of the Pearl-Poet,* ed. Robert J. Blanch, Miriam Youngerman Miller, and Julian N. Wasserman, 117–45. Troy, N.Y.: Whitston, 1991.

Underhill, Evelyn. *Mysticism: A Study in the Nature and Development of Man's Spiritual Consciousness.* 11th ed. New York: E. P. Dutton, 1926.

Van, Thomas A. "Walter at the Stake: A Reading of Chaucer's *Clerk's Tale.*" *Chaucer Review* 22 (1988): 214–24.

Vantuono, William. "John de Mascy of Sale and the *Pearl* Poems." *Manuscripta* 25 (1981): 77–88.

———. "*Patience, Cleanness, Pearl,* and *Gawain:* The Case for Common Authorship." *Annuale Mediaevale* 12 (1971): 37–69.

———. "The Structure and Sources of *Patience.*" *Mediaeval Studies* 34 (1972): 401–21.

Wallace, David. "*Cleanness* and the Terms of Terror." In *Text and Matter: New Critical Perspectives of the Pearl-Poet,* ed. Robert J. Blanch, Miriam Youngerman Miller, and Julian N. Wasserman, 93–104. Troy, N.Y.: Whitston, 1991.

Ward, Benedicta. *Miracles and the Medieval Mind: Theory, Record, and Event, 1000–1215.* Philadelphia: University of Pennsylvania Press, 1982.

Ward, Margaret Charlotte. "French Ovidian Beasts in *Sir Gawain and the Green Knight.*" *Neuphilologische Mitteilungen* 79 (1978): 152–61.

Wasserman, Julian N. "Language and Destiny in Chaucer's *Knight's Tale* and *Troilus and Criseyde.*" In *Sign, Sentence, and Discourse: Essays on the Theme of Language in Medieval Thought and Literature,* ed. Julian N. Wasserman and Lois Y. Roney, 179–224. Syracuse: Syracuse University Press, 1989.

———. "Weavers and Wordsmiths, Tapestries and Translations." In *Approaches to Teaching Sir Gawain and the Green Knight,* ed. Miriam Youngerman Miller and Jane Chance, 109–18. New York: MLA, 1986.

Wasserman, Julian N., and Lois Y. Roney, eds. *Sign, Sentence, Discourse: Essays on the Theme of Language in Medieval Thought and Literature.* Syracuse: Syracuse University Press, 1989.

Watts, Ann Chalmers. "*Pearl,* Inexpressibility, and Poems of Human Loss." *PMLA* 99 (1984): 26–40.

Weiss, Victoria L. "Gawain's First Failure: The Beheading Scene in *Sir Gawain and the Green Knight." Chaucer Review* 10 (1976): 361–66.

———. "The *Laykyng* of *Enterludez* at King Arthur's Court: The Beheading Scene in *Sir Gawain and the Green Knight."* In *The Medieval Court in Europe,* ed. Edward R. Haymes, 189–99. Munich: Fink, 1986.

———. "*Sir Gawain and the Green Knight* and the Fourteenth-Century Interlude." In *Text and Matter: New Critical Perspectives of the Pearl-Poet,* ed. Robert J. Blanch, Miriam Youngerman Miller, and Julian N. Wasserman, 229–41. Troy, N.Y.: Whitston, 1991.

Weitzmann, Kurt. *The Miniatures of the Sacra Parallela (Parisinus Graecus 923).* Studies in Manuscript Illumination, no. 8. Princeton: Princeton University Press, 1979.

Wellek, René. "The *Pearl:* An Interpretation of the Middle English Poem." In *Studies in English by Members of the English Seminar of Charles University* 4 (1933): 5–33. Reprinted in Robert J. Blanch, ed., *Sir Gawain and Pearl: Critical Essays,* 3–36. Bloomington: Indiana University Press, 1966.

Williams, David. "From Grammar's Pan to Logic's Fire: Intentionality in Chaucer's *Friar's Tale."* In *Literature and Ethics,* ed. Gary Wihl and David Williams, 77–95. Kingston: McGill-Queen's University Press, 1988.

———. "The Point of *Patience." Modern Philology* 68 (1970): 127–36.

Wilson, Edward. *The Gawain-Poet.* Leiden: E. J. Brill, 1976.

———. "Word Play and the Interpretation of *Pearl." Medium Ævum* 40 (1971): 116–34.

Wood, Ann Douglas. "The *Pearl*-Dreamer and the *Hyne* in the Vineyard Parable." *Philological Quarterly* 52 (1973): 9–19.

Wright, Thomas L. "*Luf-Talkyng* in *Sir Gawain and the Green Knight."* In *Approaches to Teaching Sir Gawain and the Green Knight,* ed. Miriam Youngerman Miller and Jane Chance, 79–86. New York: MLA, 1986.

INDEX

Abraham, 30, 58, 71, 74, 114, 131, 140
Ackerman, Robert W., 159, 164
Adam, 9, 58, 68, 71, 72, 101, 143
Alanus de Insulis, 3, 8, 20, 151
Aldhelm, 80, 83, 87, 101
Alexander, J. G., 169
Alford, John A., 160
Allen, Judson Boyce, 150–51
Ambiguity, 17, 53, 61–62, 64, 104, 113–14, 119, 121, 122, 125, 134–36, 138–39, 146, 155, 161, 171
Andreas Capellanus, 155–56
Apocalypse, 5, 7, 8, 13, 14, 16, 25, 53, 101, 153, 154, 164, 168
Aquinas, Saint Thomas, 46–47, 49, 50, 162, 163
Aristotelianism, 150, 165
Aristotle, 49, 56, 57, 165
Arma Christi, 87, 91, 103, 109, 168
Ars Praedicandi, 6, 115, 152, 171
Art/artistry, 49, 54, 67, 121
Arthur, King of England, 8, 18–22, 24, 28, 35, 36, 47, 53, 63, 105, 106, 143, 152, 159
Arthur, Ross G., 154, 156, 157
Ashley, Kathleen, 154, 156, 160, 171, 174
Astell, Ann W., 170, 171, 172, 174
Attreed, Lorraine C., 152
Audience/reader, 17, 25, 61, 81, 88, 112–15, 119–22, 124–25, 128–34, 136, 138–39
Augustine, Bishop of Hippo, 14, 21, 28, 46–47, 52–53, 136, 162; *Confessiones*, 7, 10, 25, 49, 55, 153; *Contra Faustum manichaeum*, 49–50, 51, 56, 57, 163–64, 165;

De civitate Dei, 162, 163–64; *De Genesi ad litteram*, 51, 151, 153, 162, 164; *De Ordine*, 155; *De Trinitate*, 151, 162; *De utilitate credendi*, 46–48, 52, 162, 163, 164; *In Joannis evangelium*, 162; *Sermonum mai*, 153
Awe. *See* Wonder
Ax, 19, 66, 103–6, 107, 169

Babylon, 13, 66, 107
Bachman, W. Bryant, Jr., 164, 165
Bakhtin, M. M., 17–18, 22, 24, 155
Baldwin, Anna P., 161, 163
Bargaining, 64, 71, 104, 115
Barking nuns, 83
Barron, W. R. J., 160, 161, 169, 170, 174
Beatitudes, 131–32, 134–36, 140, 44
Belshazzar, 8, 10, 16–18, 20, 53–54, 90–92, 101, 103, 107, 111, 121–24, 130, 132, 149, 152, 154, 159, 169, 174
Benson, C. David, 165
Benson, Larry, 164, 165, 166
Benzon, William, 149
Beowulf, 6, 159
Bercilak, 14, 18, 28, 35–39, 137, 138
Bergner, Heinz, 159, 169, 173
Berington, J., 160
Bernard Sylvestris, 68, 167
Besserman, Lawrence, 164
Biblia Pauperum, 3
Binding, 38, 45, 121, 154, 160
Bishop, Ian, 151, 153, 163, 164, 175
Blackstone, William, 157, 158
Blake, William, 6
Blamires, Alcuin, 151
Blanch, Robert J., 149, 154, 155, 156, 159, 160, 163, 164, 169